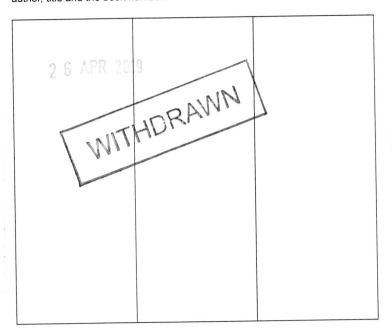

SOLDIERS
OF A
DIFFERENT
GOD

SOLDIERS
OF A
DIFFERENT
GOD

HOW THE COUNTER-JIHAD MOVEMENT
CREATED MURDER, MAYHEM AND
THE TRUMP PRESIDENCY

CHRISTOPHER OTHEN

AMBERLEY

First published 2018

Amberley Publishing
The Hill, Stroud
Gloucestershire, GL5 4EP

www.amberley-books.com

Copyright © Christopher Othen, 2018

The right of Christopher Othen to be identified
as the Author of this work has been asserted in
accordance with the Copyrights, Designs and
Patents Act 1988.

ISBN 978 1 4456 7799 6 (hardback)
ISBN 978 1 4456 7800 9 (ebook)

British Library Cataloguing in Publication Data.
A catalogue record for this book is available
from the British Library.

Typesetting and Origination by Amberley
Publishing.
Printed in the UK.

CONTENTS

INTRODUCTION

A CLASH OF CIVILISATIONS IN NEW YORK

They looked up from their desks and saw the airplane coming for the office windows and nothing they could do. Those white-collar workers with sharp suits and pensions and families back home had a few moments to realise their lives were finished and then the passenger jet hit somewhere between floors ninety-three and ninety-nine of the World Trade Center's north tower.

The Boeing 767 impacted at 08:46 on the sunny morning of 11 September 2001. A second plane was already on its way. At the controls were suicidal hijackers who thought flying into buildings gave them a shortcut to heaven. They came in low over the skyscraper canyons of Manhattan and fireballed through the Center's south tower seventeen minutes after the first attack.

A third plane hit the Pentagon in Virginia at 09:37. A fourth heading for Washington crashed upside down into a field when passengers understood they were dead anyway and charged the cockpit.

The burning towers of the World Trade Center stood for ninety minutes then collapsed. The falling debris brought down a third building. By the end of the day almost 3,000 people had died.

Islamic extremists had been plotting to fly planes into national landmarks for years. Back on Christmas Eve 1994 some Algerian jihadists hijacked an Air France passenger plane out of Algiers and aimed it at the Eiffel Tower. An intervention by French commandos during a refuelling stop in Marseille ended that dream.

A few weeks later a Manila apartment complex in the Philippines caught fire and a hairy-faced Kuwaiti using the name Ramzi Yousef went on the run. Documents left behind alerted local police to an Islamist terror plot scheduled for the end of January. Yousef wanted to murder Pope John Paul II, bomb eleven airplanes heading for America, and fly a plane into the CIA headquarters at Langley.

The Algerians belonged to the Groupe Islamique Armé (Armed Islamic Group) and only cared about taking over their own country. Ramzi Yousef had more global aims, and funding from an extremist Islamist organisation born in the quagmire of Afghanistan.

In the late 1970s this land of mountains and poppy fields was a Soviet puppet state. Russian troops propped up a wobbly government against mujahideen tribesmen who preferred Islam to socialism. America supplied the mujahideen with money and weapons; the Muslim world provided manpower. Both actions would backfire. The most radical elements of the mujahideen mutated into the Taliban and took control of the country after the Soviets finally withdrew. The foreign volunteers went through their own mutation, worldviews bubbling together into a stew of fundamentalist Sunni Islam, contempt for corrupt Arab governments, hate for Israel, and lust for a new Caliphate. A hardcore stayed on after the Russian withdrawal and formed al-Qaeda (the Base), an international machine for jihad headed by an ascetic millionaire from Saudi Arabia called Osama Bin Laden. Taliban leaders looked the other way while al-Qaeda initiated a wave of terror attacks across the Muslim world and beyond, culminating in Ramzi Yousef plotting war on America.

Yousef got arrested in an Islamabad guesthouse before anything could happen, surrounded by flight schedules and bomb parts. A few years later his uncle, thirty-two-year-old Saudi citizen Khalid Sheikh Mohammed, approached Bin Laden with a new take on the plan. Mohammed still liked a plane strike on America but had a different set of targets. Bin Laden put up funds and picked the hijackers. In September 2001 al-Qaeda militants pulled knives on the flight crews of four airplanes and brought down the Twin Towers in the name of radical Islam.

The 9/11 attacks scrambled the brains of the Western world and set off the search for a coping metanarrative. Italy's prime minister Silvio Berlusconi seemed to have the answer when he pinned the Muslim world as the latest of democracy's natural predators.

'We must consider the superiority of our civilization,' he said, 'a system that has guaranteed well-being, respect for human rights and – in contrast with Islamic countries – respect for religious and political rights. The West is superior. It has at its core – as its greatest value – freedom, which is not the heritage of Islamic culture.'

Berlusconi was one of those loudmouthed millionaire politicians who liked bikini models and controversy and said what he thought. Sharper minds with a better view of the geopolitical battlefield hustled him out of the spotlight. The narrative changed. American government spokespeople assured everyone that only radicals and extremists posed a threat; political commentators called al-Qaeda a disgrace to the peaceful religion of Islam; a few daring journalists hinted that US intervention in the oil-rich Middle East had stirred up a lot of resentment over the years. No one wanted to antagonise an entire religion with talk about civilisational superiority.

Flag-waving patriots and urban liberals got the message. Al-Qaeda was bad; your average Muslim was good. Four months after 9/11, a survey by the ABC news channel found only 14 per cent of Americans believed mainstream Islam encouraged violence.

Not everyone bought it. Readers who got through all 368 dense pages of Samuel P. Huntington's *The Clash of Civilizations: And the Remaking of World Order* saw things very differently.

*

Sam Huntington was a smiling skull on a stick who had spent his life bouncing between academia and the White House. He entered the world back in 1927 to a New York family which made its money from hotel trade journals. By the time he got to university everyone could see Huntington had an IQ that knocked professors off their chairs.

He spent most of his career teaching political science at Harvard's Department of Government. A sabbatical advising the White House during the Vietnam War gave a slap in the face to anyone who hoped Huntington was a humanitarian. His big plan was deforesting rural South Vietnam to drive peasants out of the arms of Viet Cong propagandists and into areas controlled by Americans. The generals sprayed Agent Orange over the jungle; the trees withered, everyone got cancer, and the communists won the war.

Huntington shrugged off the blame and went back to Harvard where he wrote books about military relations with civil society, and the democratisation of Third World nations. His work valued results over conventional morality. It got him a permanent ban from the National Academy of Sciences by shocked academics, and generous review space in those parts of the media that admired men with computers for brains and ice chips for hearts. Huntington went on to found the heavyweight *Foreign Affairs* magazine and make good money advising white South Africans how to defend their apartheid state.

In 1993 he published an article about the future causes of world conflict. That compact slice of geopolitics became widely influential when Huntington expanded it into a full-length book three years later. *The Clash of Civilizations* appeared at a time when the collapse of communism had left the US with no real enemies, no competitors, no existential threats. Liberal democracy had officially triumphed. Huntington's book came along and stuck a knife into all that optimism.

'It is my hypothesis that the fundamental source of conflict in this new world will not be primarily ideological or primarily economic,' he said. 'The great divisions among humankind and the dominating source conflict will be cultural. Nation states will remain the most powerful actors in world affairs, but the principal conflicts of global politics will occur between nations and groups of different civilizations.'

Ideology was dead in Huntington's world. No one would ever go to war again for artificial political systems like communism or fascism or welfare-state socialism. The warrior blocs of tomorrow were cultures bottled up in distinct civilisations: the West, Central and South America, the Muslim world, Russia and the Orthodox world, the East of Japan and China, Sub-Saharan Africa. Future clashes would come from incompatible world views grinding against each other. The triggers would be economic shortages, religion, protectionism interpreted as prejudice, and different cultures pushed into proximity by modernity and globalisation.

Huntington identified three areas where clashes could occur: between neighbouring states of different civilisations; in 'cleft' states where different civilisations occupied the same space, such as Ukraine with its Western and Orthodox populations; and in global conflicts between entire civilisations. The West's dominant position would drag it into every major battle. No diplomacy or negotiation could prevent the fighting.

'A conflict between liberal democracy and Marxism-Leninism was between ideologies which, despite their major differences, ostensibly shared ultimate goals of freedom, equality and prosperity,' Huntington said. 'A traditional, authoritarian, nationalist Russia could have quite different goals. A Western democrat could carry on an intellectual debate with a Soviet Marxist. It would be virtually impossible for him to do that with a Russian traditionalist.'

The biggest danger Huntington could see was a clash between the Muslim world and the West. Islam and Christianity had been at each other's throats since the Umayyad Caliphate invaded Europe in the eighth century. Since then there had been Crusades, imperialism, betrayals, and jihad.

Huntington was not the first person to look into a crystal ball and see a struggle with Islam. In 1990 British Orientalist Bernard Lewis had also used the term 'clash of civilisations' to describe a comparable conflict; Indian Muslim journalist and politician Mobashar Jawed Akbar made similar claims. Others had made arguments in the same direction as early as the 1920s. Huntington was the first to do it in a bestselling book.

He had some facts to back up the thesis. Readers remembered the 1989 fatwa issued by Iran's Ayatollah Ruhollah Khomeini against British author Salman Rushdie for blasphemy. The resulting chaos sent Rushdie into hiding, his novel *The Satanic Verses* on to global bestseller lists, and sixty people to the morgue. The book's Japanese translator got stabbed to death in the hallway outside his University of Tsukuba office. A few years later an early al-Qaeda bomb attack on the World Trade Center killed six people but failed to collapse the towers. Other plots swam half-remembered through the international section of broadsheet newspapers.

Sales were strong when *The Clash of Civilizations* came out but some reviewers accused Huntington of racism and unsupportable generalisations. The truly cynical saw academic fearmongering by a professional political scientist looking to scare up some work. They had a few years to feel superior before religious extremists flew planes into buildings to accelerate a new Caliphate. Huntington's clash of civilisations suddenly looked a lot more real.

*

Donald John Trump was a tall, hulking godfather type with a wispy haircut that was either a bad combover or unfortunate genes. He made his billions in real estate and his reputation in the gossip columns.

The night before 9/11 he'd been at a Marc Jacobs fashion show in the Manhattan meatpacking district, posing for the paparazzi and hanging with celebrities like Sarah Jessica Parker and Hillary Swank. He spent the next morning in his penthouse apartment at the fifty-eight-storey Trump Tower skyscraper on Fifth Avenue watching a TV interview with retired General Electric chairman Jack Welch.

A chaotic collage of news flashes broke into the regular programming. Trump's apartment had a window view of the World Trade Center. He turned from television images of smoke rising from cityscape to see the real thing happening four miles away.

Trump was better known as a celebrity than a businessman, always ready to give the media a quote somewhere between straight talk and tone-deaf tactlessness. New Jersey-based WWOR television channel got through to Trump's office that morning and ran a live interview. They asked what he'd do if he were President.

'I'd be taking a very, very tough line,' Trump said. 'I mean, you know, most people feel they know at least approximately the group of people that did this and where they are. But boy would you have to take a hard line on this. This just can't be tolerated.'

He couldn't stop himself boasting one of his buildings was now tallest in the skyline. The interview finished with talk about rebuilding the city and putting the heart back in New York. Other public figures were fielding similar calls across the nation. Someone rang Senator Hillary Clinton. The veteran Democrat had a lifetime of political engagement and carefully coiffured hair that moved as often a glacier. Players in the Democrat Party had already begun to see her as a potential president and worthy successor to husband Bill. She had some tough 9/11 rhetoric for the world.

'Every nation has to be either with us, or against us,' she said. 'Those who harbour terrorists, or who finance them, are going to pay a price.'

The man with the real power in America wasn't taking calls. Republican President George W. Bush was in a bunker somewhere trying to cope with the worst loss of life from enemy action on American soil since Pearl Harbor. His generals advised war.

The Global War on Terror was a multi-pronged attack on the fundamentalist Taliban government in Afghanistan who harboured al-Qaeda, Islamic groups in the Horn of Africa, the extremist Abu Sayyaf group in the Philippines, al-Qaeda forces in Somalia, and Saddam Hussein's government in Iraq. Islamic radicalism was to be replaced by democracy. 'I think our motto should be, post-9/11,' said Ann Coulter, leggy blonde journalist darling of the right, 'raghead talks tough, raghead faces consequences.'

Troops went in and bullets started flying. The American public supported the war until coffins wrapped in the Stars and Stripes started rolling off military airplanes. The Muslim world had proved less enthusiastic about democracy than expected. Afghanistan bogged down into a bloody slog of base sieges and roadside bombs. The toppling of Hussein in Iraq brought anarchy. It didn't help that Bin Laden and the al-Qaeda leadership had escaped. Republicans continued to back President Bush; Democrats talked about wars for oil; leftists around the world started experimenting with a worldview in which Muslims became the new oppressed proletariat.

For all its unpopularity, the War on Terror had some unusual supporters. Dishevelled British journalist and New York resident Christopher Hitchens was a one-time Trotskyite turned cynical observer of Islam after the fatwa on his friend Salman Rushdie. The 9/11 attacks pushed him into the pro-war camp. The chain-smoking iconoclast lost a lot of friends when he gloatingly rubbed the left's nose in the homophobia, misogyny and reactionary politics of the Muslim world. Enemies accused him of hating Islam. Hitchens played the atheist card. He hated all religions. 'Faith is the surrender of the mind,' he said, 'it's the surrender of reason, it's the surrender of the only thing that makes us different from other mammals.'

For all his militant materialism, Hitchens was careful to agree with the War on Terror narrative. Radical Islamists were the enemy, not ordinary Muslims. In a town house on the Upper East Side a long-time friend of his took a very different line.

*

Seventy-two-year-old Oriana Fallaci had interviewed statesmen, dictators, and revolutionaries all round the world since breaking into journalism as a teen in Florence. In recent years she had slowed down to nurse what looked to be a final novel through a diagnosis of terminal cancer, although this didn't stop her smoking, drinking and talking politics until the early hours with friends like Hitchens. Then the airplanes hit the World Trade Center. Advisors may have been able to keep Silvio Berlusconi quiet, but no one could stop Fallaci pouring out her fury like molten lava. No one dared.

She ditched her novel to write a violent Italian polemic about Islam. The thesis of *La Rabbia e l'Orgoglio* was aggressively simple: moderate Muslims did not exist, and immigration into the West would destroy democracy. The book got translated into a fistful of languages and good sales figures. Reviews were surprisingly polite, with fewer accusations of racism than expected. Journalists were prepared to give a pass to a dying woman known for her passionate engagement with leftist causes. They would be less chivalrous with those who came after her.

Fallaci devoted her last years to raging against the narrative that al-Qaeda radicals did not represent the Muslim world. A small but growing number of Westerners agreed. What would come to be called the counter-jihad was stirring in a primordial soup of internet newsgroups, newspaper opinion pieces, and the new online blog format. Soon sites like Gates of Vienna, Jihadwatch, Little Green Footballs and Atlas Shrugged were warning the world that Islam posed an absolute threat to democracy and freedom. ACT! for America fought against sharia law on the home front. Over in Britain, journalist Melanie Phillips told her readers that Muslim immigration was creating Londonistan. The 2007 Counter-Jihad Conference in Brussels brought activists face-to-face with mentors like controversial Jewish Egyptian academic Bat Ye'or. Two years later British conference attendees hooked up with an Evangelical Christian millionaire and football hooligans from the English Defence League.

The establishment's first instinct was to blast the movement as a Trojan horse for the far-right. Reality was more complicated. Counter-jihadism had created an unlikely coalition: homosexuals opposed to Islamic prejudice, conservative Jews who saw genocide in Muslim hatred of Israel, feminists unable to reconcile their freedoms with Islam, populist politicians looking for an easy road to power, and working-class patriots happy to beat foreigners back into the sea. Fellow travellers like French novelist Michel Houellebecq and German thriller writer Akif Pirinçci shot like comets over the skyline, their personal obsessions matching orbits with counter-jihad beliefs. The movement had no formal structure and no central command, although many prominent figures knew each other. All believed the West was cutting its own throat and using Islam as the blade.

The core of counter-jihad thought was simple. Islam could never be compatible with Western values. The faith had too much homophobia, misogyny and anti-Semitism; too little separation of church and state. It was a clash of civilisations amplified by globalisation and population drift. Birth rates and immigration would soon make Islam dominant in Europe and possibly America, a cultural takeover enabled by corrupt governments and applauded by privileged liberals blind with political correctness.

Some counter-jihadists spiced up their message with Oswald Spengler's ideas of civilisational decline, projecting images of Rome falling to the barbarians on to the decadence of the modern West. Others gave the villain's role to capitalism, a vampire squid sucking up low-wage workers from the Third World to spray over Europe. Most blamed weak-willed liberals with too much money and the naive belief Muslims liked voting for them in elections. No one could agree on a cure. Solutions included ending Islamic immigration, forced deportation, calls for a new patriarchy, public displays of sexuality, educational programmes, better security vetting and a fresh crusade to retake Constantinople.

The success of the English Defence League turned this movement of bloggers and authors into an army of street activists. By 2010 journalists were reporting on 10,000-strong marches. Similar anti-Islamic movements blossomed across the West: the Norwegian Defence League, Hooligans gegen Salafisten, Stop Islamisation of Europe, the European Freedom Initiative. Then a murder spree by unbalanced Norwegian supporter Anders Breivik brought down a media storm and disillusioned many.

The movement resurrected itself when the Arab Spring gave birth to the Syrian Civil War. The Islamic State movement carved out a Caliphate that found supporters around the world. A wave of terror attacks hit Europe and America: the *Charlie Hebdo* murders in Paris, the Nice truck attack, the Fort Hood shooting, the Pulse nightclub massacre. The migrant crisis turned up the heat when millions rushed the borders of Hungary and Greece. France's Front National and Germany's Alternative für Deutschland became the best-known political parties at home and abroad by adopting counter-jihad policies.

Prominent American counter-jihad bloggers got jobs writing for Breitbart News, a right-wing news outlet that liberal critics thought too close to the transgressors of the alt-right. Senior people at Breitbart had the ear of a New York billionaire considering a run in the 2016 presidential election. The grassroots movement of ACT! for America offered support if their policies became law. Donald Trump would face off against Hillary Clinton with a campaign promise to stop Muslim immigration that had the counter-jihad cheering.

Trump was the latest in a long line to weaponise the burning Twin Towers of 9/11 New York. The first seed had been sown only months after the attacks when a Dutch academic and media personality became head of a small political party called Leefbaar Nederland. He was gay and fiercely opposed to Islam. Someone shot him five months later.

GAY, LIBERTARIAN, AND POPULIST IN HILVERSUM

The Murder of Pim Fortuyn, 2002

Media Park was a sprawl of broadcast studios near the railway station in Hilversum, a North Holland town known for its radio and television presence but not much else. In the early evening of 6 May 2002 exterior speakers crackled 3FM's interview with Pim Fortuyn into a deserted car park. The general election was nine days away and everyone expected the controversial politician to come out on top.

A man crouched in bushes nearby. He had thin blond hair and a face square as a tombstone. He had spent two hours waiting for Fortuyn to leave the studio. The politician would be easy to recognise; the fifty-four-year-old's bald head was on billboards all over the country, leaning in over a blue and yellow colour scheme with an awkward smile. 'At your service!' ran the campaign slogan, in English.

The Dutch political scene had been dominated for the last decade by a coalition government of left and right that left little room for anyone not part of the machine. The May elections looked to be more of the same. Then Fortuyn turned up as leader of Leefbaar Nederland (Liveable Netherlands), a small centrist party that had been picking up protest votes in recent years. He wasn't afraid to smash taboos.

The country's 850,000 Muslims made up around 5 per cent of the population but were considered off-limits as a campaign topic by coalition politicians. Fortuyn ignored all that and went straight for the throat in an interview with *de Volkskrant* newspaper.

'I don't hate Islam,' he said. 'I consider it a backward [*achterlijk*] culture.'

Achterlijk can also mean mentally disabled. A retarded culture. Fortuyn was an out-and-proud homosexual. He saw the growing numbers of Muslims as a threat to his lifestyle and the Netherlands' famous tolerance. In the volatile space between 9/11 and the election his comments went over like a spark in a gas tank. Leefbaar Nederland kicked him out, everyone ignored his more moderate plan to legalise existing illegal immigrants, and the media compared him to any fascist demagogue they could spell.

'Dangerous.'

'A polder [i.e. Dutch] Mussolini.'

'Right-wing extremist.'

'Ego-tripper.'

'A political wild man.'

'Racist.'

'Narcissist.'

Fortuyn held on to the leadership of rebellious local branch Leefbaar Rotterdam and started up his own Lijst Pim Fortuyn (Pim Fortuyn List). He vowed to continue his election run.

Journalists digging into Fortuyn's background for dirt found only a car crash of abandoned beliefs: a short stretch as a communist, a longer run supporting the centre-left Partij van de Arbeid (Labour Party), a bit of libertarianism. Some time inside the establishment tent, some outside. All filtered through a hedonistic lifestyle, a Catholic heart, and a sharply analytical mind that had turned out thirteen books on politics and cultural issues.

The coalition government condemned his *de Volkskrant* interview; the Dutch left sent him hundreds of death threats; journalists and politicians queued up to spit out condemnation. Leftist politician Thom de Graaf quoted *The Diary of Anne Frank* at him. At a book launch in March activists shoved a pie laced with urine and something worse in his face. Fortuyn hired a bodyguard and lashed out at the people in power.

'If anything were to happen to me,' he said in a television appearance, 'they are responsible. Maybe they didn't pull the trigger, but they fostered the climate. This has to stop. This demonisation has to stop.'

Fortuyn emerged from the radio station at Media Park just after 6.00 p.m. with his driver for that day, a meaty businessman and ice hockey enthusiast called Hans Smolders. A 3FM employee trotted alongside. The man waiting in the bushes wore latex gloves and a hat and sunglasses. A 9mm Star Firestar M43 automatic pistol with seven in the magazine lay buried nearby, wrapped in plastic under a few inches of dirt.

*

The Netherlands first met Islam in the Dutch East Indies, a sunlit inkblot spray of 13,000 islands where the Pacific washed into the Indian Ocean. The men from Amsterdam arrived in the sixteenth century looking for spices and tea. Soon they owned the place.

White settlers built plantations in Sumatra, laid out coffee fields in Java and drilled for oil in the Celebes. Local aristocrats collaborated. Everyone else lived their lives, cursed the foreign infidels, and got as much European schooling and medicine as their new overlords allowed. Independence movements powered by native Islam were big news from the nineteenth century onwards. Dutch readers scanning newspaper stories like 'The Unrests in Bantam' (1888), 'The Unrests in Sukabumi' (1902), 'Unrest in Kota Waringin' (1907) and 'Unrests in Makassarand' (1910) learned that *'prang sabil'* was local for jihad. A combination of faith and nationalism chased the European colonialists out after the Second World War.

The Dutch reconnected with Islam a few decades later when an international recruitment drive opened the doors to Turks and Moroccans willing to do lousy jobs for good money. Refugees and migrants from Bosnia to Afghanistan joined them. Soon most big towns had their own 'satellite cities', districts named for the rash of grey dishes picking up foreign channels.

Tolerance and colonial guilt made everyone get along for a while. Towards the end of the twentieth century the mask began to slip. Cultures rubbed against each other like sandpaper, groups refused to integrate, values went to war. In 1997 Fortuyn made his first stab at populism by writing *Tegen de islamisering van onze cultuur: Nederlandse identiteit als fundament* (Against the Islamisation of Our Culture: The Centrality of Dutch Identity). The book claimed Islam was incompatible with Judeo-Christian humanist culture and attacked Muslim homophobia, inequality between men and women, opposition to the separation of church and state, and domination of children by their parents. Fortuyn wanted secular integration. Ending Muslim migration was a priority.

'When you need to mop up the spilt water,' he said, 'you have to turn off the tap first.'

He was still a man of the left back then. He had been associate professor of Marxist sociology at the University of Groningen and spent time behind a civil servant's desk running the department for student travel cards. No one saw any contradiction between his leftist views and his home life as a cigar-smoking elitist with a huge house, Armani suits, a sleek butler, and two pampered, floppy-eared dogs. *Tegen de islamisering van onze cultuur* got media coverage and Fortuyn started getting wheeled on to chat shows as the obligatory controversial guest. His views slid towards the right.

Then came 9/11 and Leefbaar Nederland. New York provided the first nudge towards political action, but the real shove came from a wave of homophobic attacks by young Muslims in Fortuyn's home town of Rotterdam. Moroccan-born imam El Mounmi spat petrol on the flames in a television interview where he called homosexuality a contagious disease and Europeans lower than dogs and pigs. A court action for discrimination got torpedoed by a religious freedom defence. A leading gay website surveyed its readers, with results showing that 91 per cent supported the statement 'New Dutchmen have to tolerate our tolerance or they don't belong here'.

The issue of integration spread beyond the gay community and became a talking point across the political spectrum. The author of *Tegen de islamisering van onze cultuur* found himself the figurehead of a broad movement looking to shake up the establishment's complacent approach to multiculturalism. The media pressured Fortuyn for a manifesto. He reached for his most recent book.

'As you may know, the press is too lazy to read anyway,' said Fortuyn. 'So I have summarized my thirteen books in *De puinhopen van acht jaar Paars* [The Wreckage of Eight Purple Years].'

De puinhopen was an acidic attack on the socialist (red) and conservative/liberal (blue) coalition governments (purple) of the last eight years. Smugness, corruption, elitism. Fortuyn's solutions were an eclectic selection close to the libertarian end of Dutch centralist politics: gay marriage, civil liberties, reduced government, Euroscepticism, secularism, local government, women's rights, freedom of speech, the free market. The capitalist aspects of Fortuyn's worldview appealed to rightists and other policies had enough leftism to please old friends from the communist days. A Marxist publisher had been in the picture during the book's early stages until things got too controversial.

Then came the *de Volkskrant* interview. Many thought Fortuyn had destroyed his own campaign, but proof of his popular appeal came in the March local elections when Leefbaar Rotterdam got 36 per cent of the votes and became largest party on the council. It looked like criticising Islam could open the doors to political power in the Netherlands.

After the results, police in central Holland intercepted a phone call in which anonymous environmentalist activists told each other Fortuyn had to die. The police decided the threat wasn't serious and failed to pass it to the security services.

*

The man at Media Park watched Fortuyn stroll towards his car. He dug the pistol out the earth with gloved hands and put it in his jacket pocket and walked into the car park. On the outside speakers, 3FM had returned to its regular mix of chart music and occasional throb of heavy rock.

Fortuyn was chatting to his companions when the man walked past. The politician barely registered his presence. The man went a few paces and turned around. His pale Germanic face and blond hair and giraffe-like neck made him look like he should have been piloting a panzer over the Polish frontier; instead they'd somehow found themselves attached to a burningly sincere green activist in the Netherlands. Volkert Van der Graaf pulled out the pistol and opened fire.

Van der Graaf was a thirty-two-year-old who found it easier to relate to animals than people. As a child he agonised over pinning worms to fishing hooks. As a teenager he wiped the oil off birds rescued from a Zeeland slick and begged his parents to stop serving meat. The adult Volkert was a haughty perfectionist, emotionally distant from those around him and intolerant of opposing views.

By the time he hit college to study Environmental Health at the University of Wageningen, Van der Graaf had become a vegan animal rights activist. He was conscientious and forgettable. No lecturer could remember him when he left the room. After graduation Van der Graaf turned his politics into a career by founding Vereniging Milieu Offensief (Environmental Offensive Association – VMO), a government-subsidised activist group which pushed legal challenges against livestock farms looking to expand.

Van der Graaf had a girlfriend and young daughter and a fulfilling career when Fortuyn announced his run for government. He abandoned it all after discussions with fellow greens convinced him Pim Fortuyn was a fascist who deserved death. The VMO leader paid no attention to Fortuyn's leftist past or the Lijst Pim Fortuyn's non-white members.

'In my eyes this was a highly vindictive man who used feelings in society to boost his personal stature,' said Van der Graaf. 'I could see no other option than to do what I did.'

The amateur assassin planned the hit by printing off Fortuyn's schedule from the internet and downloading maps of Media Park. The gun was bought illegally in a café, the ammunition somewhere else. He tried to disguise his appearance with a cap and dark glasses. An attempt to shave off a wispy beard on the way to Hilversum failed when the razor wouldn't work. The escape plan consisted of running to his car. Van der Graaf thought he could kill the highest-profile politician in the country and drive home without being caught. He was half right.

Five shots hit Fortuyn in the back and skull. One went wide into the bag of the 3FM employee. Fortuyn went down and the gunman took off running. Smolders and two Media Park employees chased him across a nearby road, shouting for the police and punching numbers into their phones. Armed police cornered Van der Graaf at a petrol station on the other side of the road. He dropped the gun, still wrapped in plastic, and surrendered.

Back in the car park Pim Fortuyn lay on the tarmac bleeding out. Someone called an ambulance. He died face up on the car park tarmac with his shirt ripped open and a white bandage on his head and paramedics pumping his chest.

The Netherlands had last seen a political assassination back in the Second World War when the victims had been wearing jackboots and no one cried at their funerals. Fortuyn's death broke some kind of emotional dam. There were riots across the country; a crowd attacked the parliamentary buildings in The Hague; politicians were moved to safe houses and those known as enemies of Fortuyn got pistols for protection; tens of thousands of Dutch people attended Fortuyn's funeral; millions more watched on television.

Fortuyn went to the polls as a posthumous candidate. The Dutch embraced a dead man. Lijst Pim Fortuyn received 1.6 million votes in the 15 May 2002 elections, giving them 17 per cent of the vote, second only to the Christen-Democratisch Appèl (Christian Democratic Appeal). The Lijst joined a three-party coalition government and immediately proved correct the critics who claimed Pim Fortuyn's charisma had been the only thing holding the party together. By October 2002 the Lijst's internal squabbles had torn it apart, wrecked the coalition, and set the party on a rapid drop into insignificance. It officially dissolved six years later, but everyone knew it had been a walking corpse within five months of Fortuyn's death.

Some Lijst Pim Fortuyn loyalists refused to believe Van der Graaf acted alone. Conspiracy theories bounced around the Netherlands blaming the murder on leftist gangs, the CIA, the government. A chain-smoking thriller writer wove them into a bestselling novel. A dishevelled blond slob of a filmmaker called Theo van Gogh turned the novel into a film.

Van Gogh had made his name with well-shot quality cinema of the subversive tone middle-class audiences associated with art. His first film, *Luger*, a 1982 thriller about a fascist gunman and his hostage, became notorious for a scene where a cat gets shoved in a tumble drier. Van Gogh played the gunman. Recently he'd shocked audiences further with outrageous comments and some low-budget films that slapped the face of liberalism. Everyone was curious to see how his Pim Fortuyn movie would turn out.

By the time *06/05* hit cinemas in December 2004, Van Gogh was dead in an Amsterdam bicycle lane at the corner of Linnaeusstraat and Tweede Oosterparkstraat with eight bullets and a knife in him.

2

AM I BEATING MY WIFE HARD ENOUGH?

The Controversial Lives of Theo van Gogh and
Ayaan Hirsi Ali, 2003–04

The most popular thriller writer in the Netherlands had a nasty cigarette habit. Smoking too much for too many years had given Tomas Ross yellow fingers and a face with more creases than a fifty-nine-year-old deserved. More intellectual critics on the Dutch literary scene made bitchy comments about him writing too much as well.

Ross had churned out over thirty novels in twenty-three years. His debut hit bookshops back when he was still Willem Pieter Hogendoorn, a serious journalist for *Het Vaderland* who thought a pseudonym would protect his professional reputation. Then the first royalty cheque came in and Hogendoorn's commitment to journalism went out the window. He quit the newspaper business and set his typewriter to mass production. Fans loved his blend of deep research, conspiracy theories and fictional characters bumping against real individuals. In 2003 Hogendoorn published a controversial take on a real-life event. *De zesde mei* (The Sixth of May) retold the murder of Pim Fortuyn.

A year after his murder, the Lijst leader remained a hero to many. The murderer had recently got eighteen years in prison, the maximum under Dutch law. Volkert Van der Graaf appealed and got slapped down, but would be out on parole in twelve years anyway. Few Fortuyn supporters liked that. Millions watched as Fortuyn's coffin was disinterred live on television when his family belatedly remembered he'd asked to be buried near his Italian holiday home.

Establishment efforts to guide the narrative had failed. Sociologist Wim Lunsing pushed a theory that the assassin had been provoked by the fur coats Fortuyn sometimes wore. That got little traction. Others saw the murder as a logical consequence of anti-Islamic rhetoric, arguing that Muslims and their allies couldn't listen passively while hate was being spread around. The theory went over fine with sympathetic dinner party guests but no one dared broadcast it too widely. Blaming Fortuyn for his own assassination could still cause a riot in the wrong bar.

The dead man's partisans kept mourning. They wallowed in conspiracy theories that gave deeper meaning to the assassination: Dutch intelligence services eavesdropping on Fortuyn; police failure to pass on the death threat phone conversation; rhetoric against Fortuyn by the government and media creating a climate for assassination; a cabal of animal rights activists helping Van der Graaf; America ordering the hit to prevent Fortuyn becoming Dutch leader after he opposed buying the Joint Strike Fighter plane supported by Washington.

No proof ever appeared for the wilder accusations. Government ministers agreed the police could have pursued the death threat with more pep but blamed errors in the system. Law enforcement tried to regain public trust with a crackdown on the rougher end of green activism. Conspiracy theories continued to spread.

Ross cashed in with *De zesde mei*. The novel starts with fictional VMO activist Anke released from prison after a laboratory break-in to rescue research animals escalated into murder. She wants to leave politics behind but Dutch intelligence services pressure her to rejoin VMO as an informer. Anke unwillingly agrees and has to juggle a new relationship, a nosey photographer, and suspicious colleagues. She babysits for Volkert van der Graaf and discovers his plan to kill Fortuyn, assisted by other activists. The book ties the conspirators to a real-life unsolved murder of an environmental official. Anke tells her intelligence contacts but Fortuyn still gets shot. The contacts admit they wanted him dead because of his interference in the Joint Strike Fighter deal.

De zesde mei was no one's idea of great literature and even Ross fans complained that Fortuyn and Van der Graaf spent most of the book off-page. It still managed to sell a respectable 60,000 copies. The author generated some publicity by supporting conspiracy theories about Fortuyn's assassination. 'I know not everyone believes in it,' Ross said. 'But hey, there are also still people who believe Lee Harvey Oswald killed Kennedy.'

Theo van Gogh bought the movie rights. The Dutch knew Van Gogh as a successful director and familiar face on television, usually saying something outrageous. He hosted shows, guested on others, did a radio programme, wrote articles and think pieces for the media. He specialised in causing offence. A gay critic was 'a slobbering chocolate knight', women 'slits' and 'boxes'; he wished a brain tumour on a leftist politician.

'If anyone deserves cancer,' he said, 'it is Paul Rosenmöller [a Green politician], scoutmaster of politically correct Holland. May the cells in his head shape into a jubilant tumour. Let us piss on his grave.'

Van Gogh called Muslims *geitenneukers* (goatfuckers) but was equal-opportunity enough to accuse Jews of exploiting the Holocaust. His books, usually compilations of newspaper columns, had goading titles like *Sla ik mijn vrouw wel hard genoeg?* (Am I Beating My Wife Hard Enough?) and *Allah weet het beter* (Allah Knows Best). He was one of those trying-too-hard characters, straining to be tasteless, which more conformist societies throw up in place of genuine eccentrics.

Despite the public persona, Van Gogh was serious about *De zesde mei* and believed Pim Fortuyn had been the victim of a conspiracy. He saw proof in Van der Graaf having only a single bullet left in his gun when arrested. 'That is a habit only professional killers are acquainted with,' he said. 'No matter how paranoid it may sound, I predict that this is not the work of a lone nutcase, but a conspiracy.'

Hogendoorn started writing the screenplay. The equally prolific Van Gogh worked on a handful of other projects while he waited. One would make a member of Amsterdam's Muslim community angry enough to kill.

*

On 29 August 2004 Dutch television viewers who enjoyed high culture settled down to watch three hours of *Zomergasten*, a magazine show themed around discussions between guest and presenter. This evening the guest in the armchair was a willowy Somali-born Dutch politician and outspoken critic of Islam called Ayaan Hirsi Ali. She had brought along a short film.

Submission: Part 1 was ten minutes of Arabic actresses in a mosque-like setting. They talk to Allah in English, with Dutch subtitles, about the abuse men have inflicted on them and justified using the Quran. Rape, abuse, marital violence. The women wear burqas transparent below the neck that show their bodies but hide their faces. The camera swoops around and cuts to women with Quranic verses painted on their bodies.

Hirsi Ali helped script the film and narrated. Theo van Gogh directed. They had first met at a party in February the previous year when Van Gogh charged up to the elegant Somali and gave her a bear hug.

'I'm Theo van Gogh,' he said. 'I voted for you.'

The thirty-four-year-old Hirsi Ali had only stood in the election because she needed protection from death threats. In 2002 she hit the headlines when a Muslim group tried to prosecute her for calling the Prophet Muhammad a paedophile. The Dutch prosecutor decided she had not broken any laws. Muslims who disagreed with the decision threatened rape and decapitation.

At the time Hirsi Ali had been an up-and-coming public figure, famous for a past as an asylum seeker who had escaped chaos in Somalia and an arranged marriage to a relative. She'd reached the Netherlands in the early 1990s and found her worldview challenged by life in a liberal, multicultural society where church and state had no claims on each other. There was a Dutch boyfriend, horror stories shared with other Muslim women about their treatment back home, some reading of Freud, a master's in political science. Religion took a distant second place to feminism. She got a job with a leftist think tank called the Wiardi Beckman Stichting (Wiardi Beckman Foundation). Her first project was researching links between Muslim integration and problems in the welfare system.

Hirsi Ali had only been at work eight days when she found herself crowding round a television with colleagues to watch the Twin Towers burn in New York. Later there were images of Muslim kids celebrating the attacks and Bin Laden citing the Quran in justification.

'I picked up the Quran and the Hadith,' she said, 'and started looking through them, to check. I hated to do it, because I knew that I would find Bin Laden's quotations in there.'

Hirsi Ali's deep dive into Islamic theology convinced her that al-Qaeda were not heretics warping the Prophet's message but faithful followers obeying his teachings. The revelation took a sledgehammer to her already reduced faith. Whatever was left standing crumbled to dust after reading *Atheïstisch manifest: drie wijsgerige opstellen over godsdienst en moraal* (Atheist Manifesto: Three Philosophical Essays on Religion and Morality) by Dutch philosopher Herman Philipse. She became a born-again unbeliever and launched a one-woman media assault on Islam.

'The true doctrine of pure Islam,' she wrote in *Trouw* newspaper, 'as laid down in the Quran and the traditions of the Prophet Muhammad, calls believers to initiate violent actions against unbelievers, apostates and homosexuals, for example, while an oppressive stance on women is pointed out as standard.'

The next year brought the Muhammad-as-paedophile prosecution and flood of death threats. She was involved with the left-wing Partij van de Arbeid at the time and asked for protection. Party leaders seemed reluctant. Hirsi Ali was evolving into something leftists did not want in their ranks. Cisca Dresselhuys, editor of feminist magazine *Opzij* (Out of the Way!), suggested that a run for parliament with the centre-right Volkspartij voor Vrijheid en Democratie (People's Party for Freedom and Democracy) might be an easier route to a round-the-clock police bodyguard.

A left-wing feminist atheist like Hirsi Ali seemed an odd fit for a party whose main interest was preserving the free market. She persuaded the VVD gatekeepers with an appeal to individual liberty.

'The oppression of women in Holland,' she said, 'is against the philosophy of your party.'

The party opened its doors and on 30 January 2003 she won a seat in the Tweede Kamer (House of Representatives). The victory gave her the security to ramp up a media offensive against Islam. She appeared on talk shows and news programmes to tell the Netherlands that multiculturalism was bad because it allowed Islamic misogyny to flourish in ghettoes; that Muhammad liked little girls; that mainstream Islam was a danger to Western values.

Van Gogh thought she was great. A year after meeting at the party he got in touch and suggested they make *Submission: Part 1* to spread the message. Hirsi Ali accepted, although she had plenty of reservations about her new collaborator's larger-than-life personality.

*

Friends wanted to believe Theo van Gogh's outrageousness was just an act. They told each other he didn't really hate homosexuals, women and Muslims. Pim Fortuyn had been a friend; his closest collaborators were female; he made the sympathetic 2002 television series *Najib en Julia* (Najib and Julia) about an interracial teen love affair. Every time they got close to convincing themselves, van Gogh would offend everyone by saying something even worse.

He was born in 1957 to middle-class parents in the respectable backwater of Wassenaar. Van Gogh had quality pedigree: a great-grand-uncle was troubled painter Vincent and a more recent uncle got executed by the Nazis for resistance activities. Celebrities hanging in a family tree cast shade on lower branches. Theo spent his life trying to be his own man and never quite succeeded. Where the public saw a controversial director, the family saw a man-child who regularly came home for mother to do his laundry.

Van Gogh tried a straight career with law school but dropped out to pursue his dream of making movies. The Nederlandse Filmacademie (Dutch Film Academy) wouldn't give him a chance but the theatre world offered experience in stage management and a bit of acting. In 1982 van Gogh started his independent film career by writing, directing, and starring in *Luger*.

He did a good line in gloomy, anti-establishment arthouse cinema. Middle-class types who leaned to the left and wore black polo necks appreciated his work. Van Gogh seemed set for a career at the respectable but challenging end of Dutch cinema when something flipped a switch deep in his creative machinery. He turned his back on the film establishment to go rogue, shooting fast and cheap with a work ethic Tomas Ross would envy. Four films in 1994, two in 1996.

Slashed budgets and a guerrilla approach energised van Gogh's work. *Interview* took three days to shoot on video and impressed reviewers. Follow up *06*, a raw look at the phone sex industry, earned a submission to the foreign film section of the Academy Awards. Subsequent movies jeered the wealthy artistic types who liked his earlier work and threw a few spears at Islam. The new van Gogh approach was unexpectedly popular. A more mainstream audience discovered the joy of being shocked by the pudgy enfant terrible.

Hirsi Ali did all the talking when *Submission: Part 1* premiered on *Zomergasten*. The film needed an articulate female voice to promote it, not a man who lived to cause offence. She talked with the interviewer about issues from her new book, *De zoontjesfabriek: Over vrouwen, islam en integratie* (The Son Factory: About Women, Islam and Integration).

'A Muslim woman has more status if they have more children,' said Hirsi Ali, 'so when my grandmother was asked how many children she had, she said: "one". She had nine daughters and one son. She said that about our family. That we had only one child. "And what will we do?" asked my sister and me. "You're going to produce sons," she replied. I was desperate. What should I bear in my life on earth? Sons! A factory to make sons. I was nine years old.'

Submission: Part 1 got a lot of interest and focused public attention on Islamic attitudes to women. Feminists, conservatives, Muslims and liberals found themselves forced into unlikely alliances. The filmmakers received praise, abuse and more death threats. Van Gogh loved the controversy and suggested *Part 2* deal with Islam and homosexuality. A man called Mohammed Bouyeri got to him first.

3

NO SYMPATHY FOR UNBELIEVERS

The Death of Theo van Gogh, 2004

He lay in the road, begging for his life. A man with a scrubby beard and shaved head and Moroccan robes stood over him with a pistol.

'Have mercy, have mercy,' said Theo van Gogh. 'Don't do it, don't do it.'

Friends had been warning him about the danger ever since al-Qaeda started blowing things up in Europe nine months ago. On 11 March 2004 one of its cells detonated bombs on four Madrid trains during the morning rush hour. CCTV cameras caught the grey blurs of commuters moving up and down stairs and along platforms, then white flashes and panic and dead screens. The attack killed 192 people. In early April members of the cell blew themselves and most of their apartment out the second storey window of a block in Leganés when police raided the place. Survivors went on the run.

'We will defeat them,' said Prime Minister José María Aznar. 'We will succeed in finishing off the terrorist band, with the strength of the rule of law and with the unity of all Spain.'

There wasn't much unity in Spain that spring. The attacks occurred a few days before a tight election and the government initially blamed Basque terrorists, a line aimed at discrediting left-wing opponents and avoiding controversy over Spain's role in the War on Terror. The truth came out before voters went to the polls. Aznar's Partido Popular (People's Party) lost to the socialists.

No Pim Fortuyn figure emerged from the attacks. Spaniards saw the bombings as a political statement against soldiers in Iraq, unconnected to any religious theme. The new socialist government pulled out of the American-led coalition and announced the danger was over. Conservatives around the world expressed their disgust.

'All those umbrellas in the rain at those demonstrations of defiance proved to be pretty pictures for the cameras, nothing more,' said Canadian journalist Mark Steyn. 'The rain in Spain falls mainly on the slain. In the three days between the slaughter and the vote, it was widely reported that the atrocity had been designed to influence the election. In allowing it to do so, the Spanish knowingly made polling day a victory for appeasement and dishonoured their own dead.'

Over in Amsterdam, van Gogh refused to believe he was in any danger. Hirsi Ali felt less secure. Her second book, *De maagdenkooi* (The Virgin's Cage), called for a feminist Enlightenment to bring Islam into line with Western values. Dutch Muslim men were not happy. She defeated a court case about religious discrimination with a free speech defence, then found out members of the Arab-Dutch rap group Den Haag Connection had released a track called 'Hirsi Ali diss' ('We're preparing a liquidation, a bomb attack, against Hirsi Ali/That's my reaction to what she said on TV about integration') that threw in a shout out to Volkert van der Graaf and some anti-African racism that got overlooked in the controversy. The police made arrests and the free speech issue got complicated.

Fellow VVD members began to turn against Hirsi Ali, seeing an obsessive pushing for her own martyrdom. Only a blond forty-year-old with a toothy smile and a long history in the party took her side.

Geert Wilders was a Catholic from Venlo with some Indonesian in his blood via a biracial mother. He quit a career in health insurance to join the VVD and climbed the ladder from speech writer to elected representative. Along the way he picked up a Hungarian diplomat wife, a love of peroxide, and the experience of seeing his once middle-class Utrecht constituency turn into a satellite city. It sharpened a long-standing scepticism toward Islam born from youthful travels through the Middle East and nurtured by his political mentor Frits Bolkestein, EU commissioner for Internal Market and Service.

'I don't hate Muslims,' Wilders said. 'I hate Islam.'

Wilders supported Hirsi Ali when critics shot holes in her story of oppression and asylum. Reports accused her of growing up in Kenya with a middle-class family rather than enduring poverty and violence in Somalia; of being devout enough as a teenager to attend a Muslim Brotherhood school, where she objected to anything resembling a Western liberal curriculum; of marrying the relative from Canada despite her mother's opposition before taking her husband's money for a ticket to Canada and instead heading for asylum in the Netherlands.

Hirsi Ali denied most of the allegations but accepted she had lied on her asylum application. She continued the fight. Weekly magazine *Elsevier* made her person of the year in 2004. She gave a tough speech at the awards ceremony.

'It has been shown with tiresome emphasis that there is no such thing as one Islam,' she said. 'There are as many Islams as there are Muslims. [...] But what all Muslims share is the conviction that the basic principles of Islam should not be criticised, revised or contradicted. It is against this background that I would ask if we have to fear Islam or not. What concerns me are the basic principles. The origin of Islam lies in the Quran and the Prophet's way of life (Sunnah), and it is the duty of all Muslims to copy this lifestyle in their moral and daily life.'

On 10 November 2004 Dutch police raided a house in The Hague and dragged out two Muslim men with plans to attack the Tweede Kamer. The would-be jihadists belonged to a group known to authorities as the Hofstad Network. Hirsi Ali and Wilders were on their hit list. The arrests came too late to save Theo van Gogh.

*

Mohammed Bouyeri was a twenty-six-year-old Dutchman with Moroccan parents. He grew up moderate and law-abiding in Amsterdam's Overtoomse Veld district. Locals spent the late 1990s rioting; Bouyeri stayed home and studied hard to get into university. He was an integration success story.

The first cracks appeared at college, where he struggled with and dropped five separate degree subjects. Accountancy, business administration and others came and went. Bouyeri left without a degree and turned to his Sunni faith for comfort. He began lecturing fellow Muslims on the evils of alcohol, drugs and premarital sex. Anger replaced moderation. He tried to shut down a student bar in 2000 with a gang of locals and someone broke his ankle in the struggle. The next year Bouyeri pulled a knife on a local boy dating his sister and got twelve weeks in prison. He used the time to study the Quran.

His mother died not long after his release. His father and sister relocated to Morocco. Bouyeri stayed in Amsterdam but lost his job at a youth centre for refusing to serve alcohol and objecting to men and women socialising. His temper began burning out of control. Fare-dodging and other minor offences escalated into screaming confrontations with the police. He attended the El Tawheed Mosque, notorious as the meeting place for two of the 9/11 hijackers, and linked up with a group of like-minded radical Muslims in the Hofstad Network.

The authorities put the network under surveillance but considered Bouyeri a minor figure. He was not among the four members arrested for planning a bomb attack then released through lack of evidence. The authorities stopped watching him in late October 2004. In the early morning of 2 November he hid a HS2000 pistol underneath a long Moroccan robe called a *djellaba* and rode a bicycle east through the city. The man he was hunting took the same route to work every day.

Theo van Gogh was cycling past a council building on the corner of the Linnaeusstraat and Tweede Oosterparkstraat on the way to his production office when Bouyeri caught up with him. He shot van Gogh off his bike. Two pedestrians went down from stray bullets.

Van Gogh ran to the other side of the road and collapsed in the bicycle lane. Bouyeri stood over him, loaded a fresh clip and shot Van Gogh again. He cut the dying man's throat with a knife. He tried to saw off Van Gogh's head but the blade was blunt so Bouyeri stuck the knife into the dying man's chest and used a smaller knife to stab a note to the body. The note threatened Hirsi Ali, the West, and all Jews; it referenced Takfir wal-Hijra, an Egyptian jihadist group with a broad influence among radical Islamists and an al-Qaeda ally. Then Bouyeri ran off and left Van Gogh dead on the street with his electric-blue shirt riding up over a white belly and straining braces.

Police cornered Bouyeri near the murder scene and put a bullet in his leg. The assassin was carrying a poem titled *In bloed gedoopt* (Drenched in blood), a badly written piece of bloodlust and martyrdom.

> To the enemy I have something to say …
> You will surely die …

Wherever in the world you go ...
Death is waiting for you ...
Chased by the knights of DEATH ...
Who paint the streets with Red.

Bouyeri appeared in court with a Quran under his arm. He admitted everything and showed no remorse.

'I don't feel your pain,' he told van Gogh's mother. 'I don't have any sympathy for you. I can't feel for you because I think you're a non-believer.'

He got life in prison under a new terrorism law.

*

Van Gogh's death was the second political assassination in two years. Emotions boiled over again, hotter than before. Public spaces filled with stacks of cellophane-wrapped flowers, pools of flickering candles, angry shouting matches. Violent threats were made on the internet and racist slogans were sprayed on walls. Mosques and an Islamic school burned down; churches were counter-attacked. The streets saw marches against violence by Muslim migrants and Dutch liberals, bicycle rides against intolerance, a billboard campaign against racism with the slogan 'Stop de hetze!' (Stop the Smears!). Nearly 20,000 people in Amsterdam banged pots and pans to protest the murder, and Minister of Integration Rita Verdonk gave an emotional speech.

'He was outspoken,' she said. 'And at times on the edge. But in this country, that is allowed! And in this country, nobody can be murdered for expressing his opinion! We do not want that! We do not want that ...'

Even Van Gogh's worst critics came out to praise him. No one had any time for arguments floated by some on the left that freedom of speech had limits and that provocation could kill. 'He was an asshole,' said journalist Leon de Winter, 'but he was my asshole.'

The media in the rest of Europe and abroad preferred to paint van Gogh as a court jester who paid the price for racism, with his predecessor Pim Fortuyn as just another far-right opponent of immigration. Few people outside the Netherlands cared that the deaths intersected homophobia and misogyny, Islam and self-censorship, libertarianism and environmental leftism. It was hard to boil that mess down into a snappy headline.

Life went on among the flatlands and canals. Theo Van Gogh's film *06/05*, about Fortuyn's murder, was released at the end of the year. It turned out to be a competent thriller that won an award for one of its stars. Hirsi Ali went into hiding and would soon flee to America when the controversy over her asylum application escalated into criminal charges. Wilders quit the VVD to form his own Groep Wilders (Wilders Group), which mutated into the Partij voor de Vrijheid (Party for Freedom). He got more popular and his anti-Islam rhetoric grew more extreme. The Dutch media began to paint him as the new Pim Fortuyn.

Both Wilders and Hirsi Ali warned supporters that Theo van Gogh would not be the last victim of radical Islam, and predicted Europe would see more murders and terror attacks. They were right. London was the next target.

4

DHIMMITUDE IN LONDONISTAN

Bat Ye'or and Terror Bombings on the Tube, 2005

It was 1957 and she was pretty, petite, sun-kissed, and Jewish. The army officer with the whip stole her last £20 as she waited in line at Cairo airport.

Three millennia of Jewish life in Egypt was ending thanks to a strip of water that connected the Mediterranean with the Red Sea. The Suez Canal had been built by French engineers, funded by Ottoman money and turned into a valuable trade route by the British. Now it was a warzone.

A year earlier Egyptian president Gamal Abdel Nasser had torn up a long-standing agreement and nationalised the canal. The locals celebrated. Britain, France, and Israel sent in the troops. The British wanted their money-making business back; France saw Nasser as an Islamic madman who supported rebels in France's Algerian colony; Israel blamed Egypt for the Arab saboteurs who crept over borders to plant bombs. The offensive went badly wrong when America surprised everyone by supporting Nasser. The invading armies pulled out and left behind burnt-out tanks on the canal banks and sunken ships blocking the waterway.

The Jewish community in Egypt had outlived pharaohs, mamelukes and the Ottoman Empire. It couldn't survive the wave of government persecution that followed the West's defeat. Soldiers seized Cairo's Jewish hospital. Civil servants nationalised Jewish-owned department stores. Bank accounts were confiscated, professionals exiled from their jobs, prominent members of the community placed under house arrest. It seemed only a matter of time before something worse happened.

Many Jews fled the country. Twenty-four-year-old Gisèle Orebi and her family were among 25,000 who gave up property and citizenship in return for an airplane ticket and a passport stamped 'Exit Visa with No Return'. Then long waits on the tarmac at the airport with the sun blazing down and shadows cutting into the ground. An Egyptian officer cracked a whip as he stalked the queues, pausing to steal the last pound notes from Orebi's pockets. The KLM flight to Amsterdam and freedom.

A local Jewish charity got Orebi a grant to study at University College London's Institute of Archaeology. She went from the scorching sun of Egypt to ice-cold rented rooms, pawned belongings and museum tours every day just to keep warm. Half feral after her experiences, she spent her days writing novels in the college canteen and snarling at anyone who thought they could sympathise. A tall, jug-eared Jewish post-graduate student called David Littman won her heart with gentleness and biscuits and long talks about history. Marriage brought a British passport, followed by a move to Switzerland for further studies.

Littman and Orebi shared a support for Jewish causes passionate enough to attract attention in Tel Aviv. In 1961 Mossad agents enlisted them for Operation Mural. They moved into a Casablanca apartment with their new baby and smuggled 530 Jewish children out from under the hammer of a Moroccan government ban on emigration.

Back in Switzerland, Orebi put her activism on hold to write a historical novel about the Jews of Egypt. A lot of research went into the book. Too much, said the publishers who turned it down. Orebi junked the novel and stripped out the history as a standalone work of non-fiction. *Les Juifs en Egypte* was published in 1971 under the pen name Bat Ye'or (Hebrew for 'Daughter of the Nile') to respectful reviews and some occasional snark from academics who didn't like competition from gifted amateurs. Orebi had found her mission: recording the history of Jewish communities in Arab states. Her research was solid, her narrative biased. She blamed Islam for her exile and saw all Muslims as natural-born enemies.

Two main themes ran through *Les Juifs* and subsequent books: Dhimmitude and Eurabia. The first was rooted in historical fact. Jews, Christians and other unbelievers living in Islamic nations were historically known as *dhimmis*. Muslim rulers tolerated them in exchange for reduced legal rights, separate legal systems and the annual *jizya* tax.

'Dhimmitude is a complex historical evolution linked to Islam's relations with non-Muslims,' Orebi wrote. 'It is correlated to the jihad ideology and jurisdiction and integrated into the shariah. It is rooted into the Quran, the Sunnah and the biographies of the Prophet Muhammad. In other words it is within the very core of Islam.'

Her major work on the subject would come out a month after the 9/11 attacks. *Islam and Dhimmitude: Where Civilizations Collide* had a title that echoed Sam Huntington and a thesis which argued dhimmis were not the tolerated guests who appeared in the works of contemporary scholars. Orebi painted non-Muslim citizens as little more than slaves, forced to wear identifying stars on their clothing and under constant pressure to convert. Many academics disagreed with her conclusions and weren't happy with Orebi's claims that dhimmitude still existed in the modern world, with Islam demanding global submission from all non-Muslims, as individuals or nations. *Islam and Dhimmitude* ended with a call for Jews and Christians to form a united front.

Orebi's second theme emerged in a book that hit shelves in the spring of 2005 and would become a holy text to the counter-jihad movement. *Eurabia: The Euro-Arab Axis* pushed the idea that back in the 1970s the Arab world had agreed mutually favourable foreign policies with the European Economic Community, forerunner to the European Union. This resulted in special treatment for Muslims living in the West, privileged immigration quotas and a united front against Israel. Orebi argued that what began as co-operation had ended in dhimmitude, with submissive EU politicians allowing their continent to become Eurabia, an Islamised Europe.

Eurabia was dismissed as a conspiracy theory by mainstream reviewers ('scaremongering,' said *The Economist*) but lapped up by Jewish historians like Daniel Pipes, David Pryce-Jones and Martin Gilbert. They were still discussing it when al-Qaeda hit London a few months later.

*

Rush hour on the London Underground, about 8.40 a.m. on 7 July 2005. A chubby-faced, bearded Asian man called Mohammad Sidique

Khan squeezed on to the second carriage of a Circle Line train at King's Cross. The British capital had won its bid to host the 2012 Summer Olympics the previous day and newspaper headlines were full of sporty enthusiasm. Khan got a seat near the first set of double doors with a black rucksack on his lap.

By 8.59 the train was pulling out of Edgware Road. Khan looked down into his rucksack, reached inside, and blew the whole carriage apart with a fertiliser bomb.

'I just saw a quick movement,' said Daniel Biddle, on his way to work as projects manager for a construction firm, 'then there was just a big, white flash, the kind of noise that you get when you tune a radio in, that kind of white sound, and it just felt like the carriage I was standing in filled – just expanded at such a vast rate and contracted quickly and, with that, it blew me off my feet and through the carriage doors into the tunnel.'

Simultaneously, another man detonated a bomb on a Circle Line train between Liverpool Street and Aldgate. A third man blew a Piccadilly Line train off the tracks between King's Cross and Russell Square. An hour later a fourth suicide bomber blew up a number 30 bus in Tavistock Square. He had planned to die on the underground with the others but train cancellations and a defective detonator messed up his martyrdom.

The attacks in London killed fifty-two people and injured over 700, some seriously. Daniel Biddle lost both legs and an eye.

Britain went into shock. Television schedules jammed up for days with debates about race and tolerance. Someone petrol-bombed an Aylesbury house belonging to one of the terrorists. You couldn't visit a pub without getting into an argument about Islam and immigration. Prime Minister Tony Blair condemned anyone who blamed the bombings on ordinary Muslims but didn't seem in any hurry to reassess official policy towards extremist Islamist groups in Britain. Gisèle Orebi saw it all as dhimmitude.

'Mental dhimmitude has been implemented in Europe over the course of thirty years by politicians, intellectuals, the Churches, and the media, all of whom sided with the jihadist Palestinian terrorists against Israel's wars of liberation from dhimmitude,' she wrote in her Bat Ye'or persona. 'Tony Blair's posturing in the wake of the London bombings is the cover-up of this cowardly policy that seeks protection from the terrorists by offering them Britain as a safe haven, from where they have sent killers in Israel, America, Bali, and other places.'

Britain had barely recovered when a fresh group of bombers appeared two weeks later. On 21 July five African Muslims living in Britain set off for the capital carrying rucksacks stuffed with a homemade explosive mix of chapatti flour and liquid hydrogen peroxide. They got the recipe wrong. The bombs failed and police rounded up the gang within a week. Media talking heads restarted the conversation about racism, imperialism and religious fanaticism.

A year later, Mohammad Sidique Khan came back from the dead with his own explanation for the bombings. Bad-quality footage of him somewhere in Pakistan that liked pinning carpets to walls was all over the British media. Al-Qaeda had released his martyrdom video. Khan claimed the terror attack was revenge for Western violence against the Muslim world.

'Until we feel security, you will be our targets,' he said. 'Until you stop the bombing, gassing, imprisonment and torture of my people we will not stop this fight. We are at war and I am a soldier. Now you too will taste the reality of this situation.'

Khan was thirty years old when he died, a second-generation British citizen whose parents came from Pakistan. He came from the Beeston part of Leeds, a poor northern suburb with boarded-up houses and industrial estates and a salad of immigrants from Asia, Africa and Eastern Europe. Local Muslim life revolved around the mosque, the Islamic bookshop, the community centre, and cricket in the park during summer.

Khan was smart enough to get himself into Leeds Metropolitan University to read Business Studies, then work in a local benefits office and a primary school with a side line helping troubled teenagers. He radicalised early. The jihadist sermons of Jamaican-born imam Abdullah el-Faisal, known to his parents as Trevor William Forrest, had woken something inside Khan while still a student. El-Faisal was jailed in 2003 for soliciting murder and inciting racial hatred but by then Khan had already made internet contact with other extremists. He visited training camps in Afghanistan and Pakistan, and had possible involvement in the 2002 Indonesia bombings that killed hundreds of people, as well as the following year's suicide bombings in Tel Aviv.

Back in Britain, Khan connected with a nineteen-year-old Jamaican follower of El-Faisal called Germaine Lindsay, who embraced radical Islam when he wasn't working as a carpet fitter. Two other bombers came on board through the paintball and white-water rafting events Khan organised for young Asian men in Beeston. In 2005 they all took a train to London for explosive dismemberment and martyrdom. Khan and Lindsay left wives and young daughters.

Gisèle Orebi didn't believe Islamic terror attacks or martyrdom videos would wake Britain and Europe to the threat posed by Eurabia. The establishment was too deep in cognitive dissonance. The only hope was a populist fightback against dhimmitude. She enthusiastically supported a Danish newspaper which ran some blasphemous drawings of the Prophet Muhammad two months after the London terror attack to make a point about freedom of speech.

'A revolt,' Orebi said, 'to assert Western values of freedom of opinion, speech, and religion.'

The Muslim world saw things differently. Two hundred people died.

5

SELF-CENSORSHIP DURING THE CARTOON WAR

Denmark, Melanie Phillips and Freedom of Expression,
2005–06

The Saudis knew the desert city as Makkah. The rest of the world called it Mecca, birthplace of the Prophet Muhammad and holiest site in Islam. Each year millions of Muslims made a hajj here to walk counter-clockwise round the black block of the Kaaba, run between the hills of Safa and Marwah, perform vigils, and throw stones at three grey pillars symbolising the devil. Extras included head shaving, animal sacrifice and complaining about the Saudis knocking down thousand-year-old mosques to build more hotels.

Over 2.5 million pilgrims attended the January 2005 hajj. Saudi Arabia declared it a success. No fires, bombs, airplane crashes or hotel collapses, and only a small stampede that killed three people, alḥamdulillāh.

Mecca was quiet for the rest of the year until December hit and representatives of fifty Muslim nations came together in a gilded conference room dripping with chandeliers. The Third Extraordinary Session of the Islamic Summit Conference had assembled to discuss economic reform and women's rights and other challenges. Two days of meetings led to the frank admission that 'The Islamic Nation was in Crisis' and a ten-year modernisation plan.

The plan went nowhere, although it excited a few Western observers. The real story from the conference was delegates' reactions to a dossier from Denmark being circulated unofficially by a group calling itself the European Committee for Prophet

Honouring. The dossier contained forty-three pages of photocopied images. It would lead to diplomatic breaches, dead bodies and an unexpected rise in the share price of Lego.

The trouble started back in September when a bland-faced Danish writer called Kåre Bluitgen naively told journalists he couldn't find anyone willing to illustrate his new children's book *Quranen og profeten Muhammeds liv* (The Quran and the Life of Muhammad). The book was respectful, Denmark's artists scared. They blamed the London bomb attacks, the murder of Theo van Gogh, and a 2004 incident when a University of Copenhagen lecturer was smacked around in the street for reading the Quran to non-Muslims in class.

Centre-right Danish broadsheet *Morgenavisen Jyllands-Posten* ran a story enjoying Bluitgen's leftist discomfort. The culture editor, a crop-haired fortysomething with the unlikely name of Flemming Rose, asked forty-two cartoonists to make a point by drawing the Prophet Muhammad. Twelve agreed and the paper ran their submissions next to an opinion piece about the dangers of self-censorship. A few were straight portraits, one showed a hunched cartoonist hiding his drawing, one had a cheerful schoolchild named Muhammad writing 'the editors of *Jyllands-Posten* are a bunch of provocateurs' in Persian on a blackboard, another by veteran cartoonist Kurt Westergaard showed the Prophet with a fizzing bomb in his turban.

'Modern, secular society is rejected by some Muslims,' said Rose. 'They demand a special position, insisting on special consideration of their own religious feelings. It is incompatible with contemporary democracy and freedom of speech, where one must be ready to put up with insults, mockery and ridicule.'

Most Danes dismissed the cartoons as a publicity stunt but the Islamisk Trossamfund (Muslim Society in Denmark) saw blasphemy and organised marches and press conferences. The society represented Denmark's 200,000 Muslims, around 4 per cent of the population and growing rapidly. The government weighed up the lost votes and nudged police into investigating *Jyllands-Posten*. The Danish prime minister felt especially vulnerable; he had once awarded Ayaan Hirsi Ali a free speech medal at a party function.

The investigation kept everyone quiet until police announced their findings. No crime had been committed. Opponents of censorship celebrated, but combative members of the Islamisk Trossamfund formed a group called the European Committee for

Prophet Honouring. The main men behind it were the pouchy-faced Lebanese immigrant Ahmed Akkari and a fifty-nine-year-old Palestinian called Imam Ahmad Abu Laban who had lived in Denmark for twenty years. The two men put together a dossier on the cartoons and booked plane tickets to Makkah.

The dossier brought together the *Jyllands-Posten* cartoons, protest letters from Danish Muslims and some unrelated images sent to Islamisk Trossamfund by trolling right-wing types, including a shot of a French farmer wearing a pig mask at some backwoods festival. Akkari and Laban claimed the cartoons were printed in colour and everything else in black and white to distinguish them. Not everyone at the conference realised the significance. An accompanying fact sheet wrongly claimed Islam was not recognised as a religion in Denmark, and that the Danish prime minister owned *Jyllands-Posten*.

A lot of people back home, including many Muslims, regarded Akkari and Laban as troublemakers looking to stir things up. The men behind the European Committee for Prophet Honouring declared innocent motives. 'We have been addressing the issue with a cool head,' said Laban. 'We were trying to seek academic and religious help from the Middle East. We are not professional enough to know what would be the response of media, nor the interest of politicians there.'

The dossier caused outrage and horror in Mecca. The Organisation of the Islamic Conference condemned the cartoons and several countries broke diplomatic relations with Denmark. Muslim protests erupted worldwide. Mobs burned down Danish embassies in Syria, Lebanon and Iran. Others attacked the Norwegian and Austrian embassies in Damascus. There was more arson at EU offices in Gaza and the Italian consulate in Libya. Violent riots shook Afghanistan, Nigeria and Pakistan. At least 200 people died. Cynics saw geopolitics in the burning buildings.

'What is happening in the Middle East is primarily political manipulation,' said French Islamism scholar Oliver Roy. 'Syria taking revenge for its expulsion from Lebanon, Hamas striking back at the European Union for its rebuff on financial aid, Afghans anticipating the replacement of US troops by European ones, and Iranians lashing back at the EU for its stance on the nuclear issues.'

Italy's *La Stampa* and France's *France Soir* were among newspapers that republished the cartoons in sympathy. Middle East nations boycotted Danish products and cost dairy manufacturers somewhere north of 134 million euros. Free speech supporters promised to buy Danish. Sales of Lego and bacon went up.

The protests spread to London.

*

One of the demonstrators outside the Danish embassy in Knightsbridge was wearing a suicide bomb vest. The rest of the all-male crowd had placards and anger.

'Europe You Will Pay. Your 9/11 Is On Its Way'.

'Freedom Go To Hell'.

'Behead Those Who Insult Islam'.

Chants went up praising the London tube bombers. It was a chilly day in early February 2006 and a thin line of police in fluorescent yellow jackets were doing their best to keep the peace between Danish diplomacy and 450 demonstrators from al Ghurabaa and the Saviour Sect. Both protest groups had originated in al-Muhajiroun, a radical movement that had made headlines for calling the 9/11 hijackers 'The Magnificent Nineteen' and getting shut down by the government.

Police ignored the chants, preferring public tranquillity over wading in with truncheons. The demonstration continued in the cold. The crowd eventually dispersed and the suicide bomb vest turned out to be fake. Its wearer, a twenty-two-year-old convicted crack dealer from Bedford called Omar Khayam, claimed he was exercising his freedom of speech, just like the *Jyllands-Posten*. He got grabbed on violation of parole and went back to prison.

The media ran some aggressive headlines, but when tempers cooled most people agreed the police handled the whole thing well. The government praised itself for showing tolerance. Not everyone agreed. One well-known journalist thought it was all just dhimmitude.

'Self-censorship over Islam has been the order of the day ever since the Rushdie affair,' said Melanie Phillips, 'and it was instructive to see that yet more "moderate" British Muslims have been saying that the cartoons would never have been published had Rushdie been killed. That's the kind of comment that these days doesn't even merit any comment in dhimmi Britain.'

Melanie Phillips had glasses, cropped grey hair, and the face of a schoolteacher too strict to be likeable. She grew up in London to a Jewish immigrant family from Eastern Europe. Her father sold dresses, her mother ran a children's clothes shop. Both were solid left-wingers with enough political flexibility to send their daughter to a private school and Oxford University.

Phillips went into journalism and worked her way up to *The Guardian*, house journal for the British left and sympathetic to strikers, immigrants, revolutionaries and the Soviet Union. The new hire turned out to be no one's idea of an unquestioning foot soldier. Phillips got into trouble for claiming the black community's problems were self-inflicted and writing a play which poked around the touchy subject of Palestine and anti-Semitism. She lasted sixteen years at *The Guardian* until left-wing politics and support for Israel could no longer coexist. Phillips quit the paper to spend the 1990s sliding rightwards.

When 9/11 hit she was married with children and had a job at conservative tabloid the *Daily Mail*. She turned out stories about the destruction of Western liberal values, the problems of immigration, and moral degeneration. The al-Qaeda attacks focused her mind on the dangers of Islam in Europe. Reading Bat Ye'or's *Eurabia* changed her worldview.

'Bat Ye'or's scholarship is highly impressive, and her analysis is as persuasive as it is terrifying,' Phillips wrote in *The Jewish Chronicle*. 'There are, however, alarming signs of attempts in the West to shut down such discussions on spurious grounds of prejudice. This is, of course, itself a prime example of the condition of "dhimmitude" which Bat Ye'or so graphically describes.'

Phillips saw this dhimmitude concentrated on the left, which preferred cosying up to Islam rather than challenging its misogyny, homophobia and anti-Semitism. In 2004 veteran socialist George Galloway launched his Respect party, bringing together disenfranchised leftists and moderate Muslims. Phillips disapproved. She didn't believe Muhammad's followers could be moderate.

'They are fuelled by an ideology,' she said, 'that itself is non-negotiable and forms a continuum that links peaceful, law-abiding but nevertheless intensely ideological Muslims at one end and murderous jihadists at the other.'

She decided to write her own book about the localised version of Eurabian dhimmitude all around her. *Londonistan: How Britain is Creating a Terror State Within* came out in 2006 through conservative American publishing house Encounter Books. The title was borrowed from the dismissive term French intelligence used for Britain's policy of giving safe harbour to radical Islamic groups on the understanding their new home would be unaffected by terrorism.

Londonistan argued that politicians had turned the UK into a base for Islamic militancy by allowing Arab refugees with hard-line views to settle in the capital. Nothing had been done to stop the new arrivals radicalising the existing Muslim population. The Christian church was too weak and cowardly to oppose Islam; the establishment too committed to liberal multiculturalism; the average Briton worshipped too hard at the shrine of tolerance to do anything when bombs started exploding on tube trains. Anyone who objected to Islam got shouted down as a racist.

The book got positive reviews in right-wing papers ('a passionate rage in a book that could not be more timely,' said *The Daily Telegraph*) and less positive ones elsewhere. *The Independent* pointed out that Phillips' desire for a war between good and evil came uncomfortably close to the Manichean worldview of al-Qaeda. A few critics hinted at racism in the book, but Phillips' Jewish background stopped them going too far.

Londonistan sold well in the summer of 2006 and popularised Bat Ye'or's theories as seen through the lens of British conservatism. But its attack on Islam was a glow worm compared to the burning sun of a far more famous journalist dying of cancer in a New York brownstone. Oriana Fallaci's readership dwarfed Phillips and her rage against Islam burned more furiously.

Fallaci was one of those tough, chain-smoking reporters who could get shot in Mexico, pawed by Yasser Arafat and patronised by Henry Kissinger, then pound out award-winning copy on a portable typewriter in a departure lounge without losing her air of cool femininity. When 9/11 hit, the Italian journalist was in semi-retirement and working on a long novel about family. She put it aside to turn out *La Rabbia e l'Orgoglio* (The Rage and the Pride), a molten stream of anti-Islamic feeling.

Fallaci shrugged off the death threats and abuse when it came out. She had cancer and knew death was coming. Not even a lawsuit that involved a Muslim convert with a past as the follower of a notorious fascist cult leader could intimidate her.

6

MEDIEVAL RAGS AND CHRISTIAN ATHEISTS IN FLORENCE

The Dying of Oriana Fallaci, 2006

At the end she was a shrunken and emaciated old woman who shuffled around a tiny kitchen in a New York townhouse cooking greasy sausages for any guests who looked like they needed fattening up. Oriana Fallaci had twelve tumours in her lungs and no one at the hospital could understand how she was still alive.

Sheer force of will, she told them.

Doctors limited her to liquids; she drank champagne and spirits. They told her to keep calm; she swore like a sailor. Fallaci was dying of cancer and angry at the world. Anyone who disliked profanity was out of luck.

'*Brutto stronzo* [arsehole] ... *vaffanculo* [fuck you, or fuck off] ... *cretini* [cretins] ... .'

When the planes came in low over Manhattan in September 2001 Fallaci watched the whole thing on television – picture only, the sound was busted. The shaky camerawork, the orange and black explosions blooming through the towers, the stunned news anchors. Four days later a suave fortysomething Italian with a wing of dark hair falling over his brow turned up at her door. Ferruccio de Bortoli was a veteran journalist who had spent the last four years as editor of *Corriere della Sera*, one of Italy's oldest newspapers, which long ago had shed its liberal skin and matured into a best-selling centre-right broadsheet.

Bortoli asked Fallaci to step out of retirement and write a piece for his paper. He hoped she was strong enough to do it.

Oriana Fallaci had been fighting cancer for a decade. It came from years of smoking four packs a day, but she preferred to blame the burning oil wells set alight by Saddam Hussein's troops in retreat from Kuwait. It better fitted her self-image as a tough journalist travelling the world and talking truth to power. She had covered wars in Vietnam, India and the Middle East, and followed leftist guerrillas in South America and Greece. She got shot by Mexican soldiers while covering student protests before the 1968 Olympics and was dragged down a flight of stairs by her hair and left for dead in the local mortuary.

Back then Fallaci was pencil-slim with long black hair that centre-parted around an oval face. She had a sleek Italian sexiness to her (bare feet, black eyeliner) that teased straight answers to hard questions from the world's most powerful men. That mix of silk and steel made them say things they later regretted.

Fallaci persuaded Makarios III, Greek orthodox patriarch and President of Cyprus, to talk about his weakness for women. She told Ayatollah Khomeini that the chador was a medieval rag and threw it across the room. The Iranian leader stalked out of the interview but his son later said it was the only time he saw his father laugh. The Ayatollah granted her a second interview if she agreed to keep the chador on. Others emerged more bruised.

'The most disastrous conversation I ever had with any member of the press,' said Henry Kissinger, former American Secretary of State.

Fallaci had retired from journalism by the mid-1990s to fight cancer and jet between her hometown of Florence and a Manhattan townhouse on the Upper East Side. She was a private and solitary woman who kept her heart closed to the world.

'To speak of oneself means to lay bare one's own soul, expose it like a body to the sun,' she said. 'To lay bare one's own soul is not at all like taking off one's brassiere on a crowded beach!'

Fallaci spent the time working on *Un cappello pieno di ciliegie* (A Hatful of Cherries), a novel about her ancestors. Then came 11 September 2001 and Bortoli on her door step. The world had changed, irrevocably. She forgot her cancer, abandoned *Un cappello pieno di ciliegie*, and went back to the typewriter and overflowing ash tray with new purpose. Bortoli got his article at the end of September.

It was 12,000 words of pure hate. Anyone who disliked Islam was in for a treat.

*

Florence is a northern city of bridges, rivers and biscuit-coloured roofs. Fallaci grew up poor in a working-class neighbourhood, the eldest daughter of a liberal father who hated Mussolini.

She was ten years old when the war came. Her father ran an underground anti-fascist network that helped downed Allied pilots escape. Fallaci acted as lookout and messenger. She was fourteen when the government kicked out Mussolini and surrendered to the first person driving a tank who spoke English. In the post-war chaos she wanted to be a doctor but did some journalism to pay her way through university. Bad health killed the medical studies and turned her into a full-time reporter. It was no loss. Fallaci loved writing.

'I sat at the typewriter for the first time and fell in love with the words that emerged like drops, one by one, and remained on the white sheet of paper,' she said. 'Every drop became something that if spoken would have flown away, but on the sheets as words, became solidified, whether they were good or bad.'

She did time on the crime beat, became a feature writer, and was a foreign correspondent by the mid-1960s. There were articles for *Corriere della Sera, Le Nouvel Observateur, Der Stern, Life, Look, New York Times Magazine, Washington Post* and *The New Republic*. Fallaci was always a woman of the left. She supported student protests, anti-colonial movements, bearded revolutionaries. She covered the Vietnam War from both sides but only got deported from the south. Revolutionary movements in Brazil, Peru, Argentina and Bolivia loved her coverage.

By the 1970s she had leveraged her growing fame into a series of interviews with important people ('those bastards who decide our lives') for Italian magazine *L'Europeo*. Fallaci had no respect for rank or position and had bruising interviews with Golda Meir and the Shah of Iran. With others she could be calm and flirtatious, or cutting and enraged when subjects refused to cooperate.

'Has anyone ever told you that you resemble Stalin?' she asked Lech Wałęsa of Solidarność. 'I mean physically.'

Her interviews were translated for magazines around the world. She had a long and unsatisfying affair with a married Frenchman until an encounter that changed her life. In 1973 she interviewed Alexandros Panagoulis, a Greek poet whose politics wobbled between liberalism and anarchism. Fallaci met him when he got out of prison after serving five years for trying to assassinate the head of Greece's military junta. Panagoulis was darkly handsome, moustached, and ten years younger. Fallaci had met her soulmate.

They had a tempestuous three years together. The poet sneered at her feminism and Fallaci, the cynical globetrotter, was reduced to tearfully begging him to abandon a futile fight against the Greek government. She got pregnant. Panagoulis punched her in the stomach and killed the baby.

He died in a 1976 road accident back in Greece after the junta had lost power and democracy was back on the menu. Fallaci insisted it was an assassination. She wrote the novel *Un uomo* (A Man) based on his life and turned her miscarriage into *Lettera a un bambino mai nato* (Letter to a Child Never Born). There were more interviews but big names no longer trusted her and the enthusiasm she felt for left-wing icons was fading. She did some journalism in Lebanon and elsewhere and a final bit of reporting from Kuwait during the Gulf War, where she threatened to kill herself after being denied access to the front lines. Then the diagnosis of cancer and the retreat from public life.

Fallaci returned to journalism after 9/11 with the article about Islam and the West for *Corriere della Sera*. She showed no mercy.

'You ask me about the contrast between the two cultures?' she said. 'Well, to be honest, it annoys me even to talk about two cultures, to put them on the same plane. Let's be honest. Our cathedrals are more beautiful than the mosques and the synagogues.'

Opposing Islam had given her a reason to live a few years longer.

*

La Rabbia e l'Orgoglio was a lengthy stream of consciousness in essay form, addressed directly to Bortoli. It spewed rage and venom like an out-of-control firehose. After years of hiding her emotions, Fallaci dropped the castle walls and exposed her soul.

"And I'm very, very, very angry,' she wrote. 'I'm angry with a cool, lucid, rational anger, an anger that wipes out any detachment, any indulgence, that commands me to answer, and finally to spit on them. And I do spit on them."

She spat everywhere. The article laid waste to Yasser Arafat, unpatriotic Americans, unpatriotic Italians, the Quran, Islam, Muslims who urinated in public, women who accepted the burqa, anyone who allowed Muslims to study at American universities, and gutless cowards who complained about racism instead of fighting Islam. Praise was reserved for the American people, President George Bush, and New York mayor Rudy Giuliani. For Fallaci, the 9/11 attacks were a declaration of war on the West by an inferior alien culture.

'Because when the destiny of the West is at issue,' she said, 'the survival of our civilization, we are New York. We are America. We Italians, we French, we English, we Germans, Austrians, Hungarians, Slovaks, Poles, Scandinavians, Belgians, Spaniards, Greeks, Portuguese. If America falls, Europe falls, the West falls.'

Fallaci morphed her own leftist history into proto-counter-jihadism. Her preference for Soviet invaders over the Afghan mujahideen became a prescient judgment on the destructive power of Muslim culture. Her character-driven novel about Italian soldiers guarding against bombers in Lebanon was now a study in the clash of civilisations. Arguments with Yasser Arafat, Muammar Gaddafi and Ayatollah Khomeini were reworked into skirmishes with representatives of an existential enemy.

Half the population of Italy read *La Rabbia e l'Orgoglio* and the other half pretended it had. A publisher asked her to expand the essay into a book. It sold a million copies in Italy and 500,000 in Europe. Some reviewers loved it ('splendidly offensive and gloriously rude,' said Mark Steyn) but others didn't understand how a leftist could think this way. The sheer rage of the prose blasted flat most criticism but even friends worried about her obsession with Arab hygiene and the permeable line she drew between race and religion.

'Written in the hot flush that overtook her on September 11,' said Christopher Hitchens, 'and originally published as a screed in the Milan daily *Corriere della Sera*, this is a sort of primer in how not to write about Islam.'

Even the hard right was cautious. Irish journalist Derek Turner, writing in *The Occidental Quarterly*, a 'Journal of Western Perspectives on Man, Culture, and Politics', managed to sound moderate compared to Fallaci.

'While Westerners will never understand Muslims,' he said, 'and may even feel amused contempt for their belief system, attacking Islam so viciously and so publicly is unlikely to assist in that mutual accommodation that has become so urgently necessary.'

A Swiss Islamic group joined forces with an anti-racism organisation to bring a case for inciting racial hatred. Italy turned down an extradition request, citing freedom of speech, but Fallaci was advised to avoid flying through Zurich. French Muslims and leftists launched their own court case. She reacted by starting a new book.

*

La Forza della Ragione (The Force of Reason) came out in 2004 and took a hammer to Europeans who thought Islamophobia worse than Islamic fundamentalism. Fallaci's arguments were direct as ever: rationality and reason were in danger of being snuffed out by the combined forces of Islam and Western liberalism. Islam was on the march into Europe.

'From the Strait of Gibraltar to the fjords of Sørøy, from the cliffs of Dover to the beaches Lampedusa, from the steppes of Volgograd to the valleys of the Loire and the hills of Tuscany, the fire is spreading. In each one of our cities there is a second city.'

Those second cities were the districts populated by Europe's growing Muslim population, loyal to the Quran and homeland traditions, contemptuous of the new world. Pim Fortuyn had called them satellite cities. Fallaci saw the terraces of grey dishes as enemy trenches in the latest wave of a millennium-long invasion by migrants who could not assimilate even if they wanted. She despaired that Muslim children would never be able to understand Dante Alighieri or Alessandro Manzoni.

The rest of the book was unfocused rage at the traitors and cowards who had allowed the invasion in the name of social justice and political correctness; at the conservative right who welcomed Muslim migrants for their taxes; at European governments who prostrated themselves before the Arab world; at critics who attacked Fallaci for racism like medieval inquisitors, uninterested in truth or logic; at Yasser Arafat again; and at boxer Muhammad Ali, who once burped in Fallaci's face during an interview.

Europe is not doomed, the book concluded, but the clock is ticking for anyone who wants to save it.

'The sons of Allah,' she told a journalist, 'breed like rats.'

La Forza della Ragione was heartfelt, extreme and chaotic. Even admirers shook their heads at an anger that distorted arguments and warped facts. Fallaci ignored them and managed another book the same year. *Oriana Fallaci intervista Oriana Fallaci* (Oriana Fallaci

Interviews Oriana Fallaci) was a long self-interview that expanded on her anti-Islam argument.

There might have been other books to come from her emaciated body but in May 2005 she was pulled away from her typewriter by further legal action. A controversial Italian Muslim convert with jailbird friends and fascist ties had convinced a judge to try Fallaci on charges of 'defaming Islam'. She was looking at prison time.

7

RIDING THE ISLAMIC TIGER

Hitler, Mao, and Guénon United in Struggle, 2006

Anyone watching the talk show that day saw a heated debate about crucifixes and two guests smacked in the face. *Rosso e Nero* broadcast out of Verona and specialised in people talking over each other, a host trying to keep control, and the public ringing in to interrupt the rare occasions anyone got close to a coherent argument.

On 10 January 2003 Emilio Adel Smith was on camera explaining his campaign to get crucifixes removed from his children's school and replaced with Quran verses. A boxy forty-two-year-old with close-cropped hair and a beard, Smith didn't like the Christian cross and wanted to make sure viewers knew it. He wasn't keen on Dante Alighieri's *Divina Commedia* or the frescos in Bologna Cathedral either.

Smith had been campaigning for months on the issue, causing controversy and stirring up clouds of historical sediment. At least 96 per cent of Italians had been baptised Catholic and weren't keen on surrendering their religious symbols to please a Muslim. But the law that kept crucifixes on school walls dated from Mussolini's time, and judges remained reluctant to enforce the dictates of a long-dead fascist state. It made for a tricky legal argument, but good television.

Backing up Smith on *Rosso e Nero* was a rat-faced man of mystery called Massimo Zucchi, alleged to have been a far-left Brigate Rosse (Red Brigade) terrorist in a former life. Now he was a devout Muslim and general secretary of Smith's Partito Islamico Italiano (Italian Islamic Party). He was here to support his boss. The pair had met through Claudio Mutti, a well-known and controversial figure in Italy's Islamic community, which was 1 million strong and growing fast. Back in 1980 there had been only 50,000 Muslims in the country. The new arrivals came fleeing wars in Iran, Iraq, Afghanistan and Sub-Saharan Africa; escaping chaos in Albania; sailing from Morocco in search of a better life. Those with jobs worked for low pay in seasonal agriculture and the construction industry. The rest got by on welfare and spent their days worshipping at the three official mosques in Rome, Milano and Catania, or behind closed doors at the hundreds of Islamic Cultural Associations around the country that doubled as unofficial mosques.

Smith's anti-crucifix lawsuit wasn't helping the community's image problem. A recent poll among students at Rome's Sapienza University found half believed Muslims supported international terrorism and had 'cruel and barbaric laws'. The Lega Nord, a right-wing party pushing autonomy for Italy's northern states, called the cultural centres breeding grounds for al-Qaeda cells and wanted them shut down. Oriana Fallaci was a bestseller.

To confuse things further, Smith was a convert, born in Alexandria to an Italian architect with a job designing palaces for King Farouk. Smith senior got his young Egyptian mistress pregnant and married her but raised his son Catholic. The family moved to Italy when Adel was young. He worked as an Arabic–Italian translator but soured on his new homeland when an Egyptian friend abandoned Islam for the Jehovah's Witnesses. Seeing tradition so casually jettisoned awoke something in Smith. He reconnected with his mother's religion, picked up an obedient wife swaddled in headscarves, and moved to Albania in 1990s for a job as a printer. A few years later Smith returned and set up his own print business in the central Italian village of Ofena. Some of the work he did for political groups with strong opinions about Judaism was borderline illegal.

He moved into politics by founding a small organisation of expat Albanians called the Unione dei musulmani d'Italia (Union of Italian Muslims). He followed it with 2001's Partito Islamico Italiano. Neither group had much success until Smith became notorious for rowing with a nurse in his terminally ill mother's hospital room and throwing a crucifix out the window, calling it 'a small body on two wooden sticks'. The publicity helped him launched a lawsuit demanding the crucifixes be removed from his children's' primary school in Ofena.

The Italian face of Islam had a gift for inflammatory quotes and a bad temper. He'd recently punched a guest on another talk show when the debate got heated.

Rosso e Nero was in full flow when twenty young men pushed and shuffled their way on to the small soundstage. A lot of black hooded jackets, scarves over faces, short haircuts, a red flag with a Celtic cross on a white circle, some chanting. Fascists from the recently formed party Forza Nuova had gatecrashed the show.

Massimo Zucchi looked worried. Smith moved a chair between himself and the protesters. It didn't help. The Forza Nuova boys surrounded the two Muslims and a camera was pushed away to stare at a blank wall while Smith and Zucchi got slapped around and knocked to the floor. *Rosso e Nero*'s hosts tried ineffectually to stop the attacks. The fascists left with blood on their knuckles.

The incident made the papers and the attackers got a few months in jail. The media attention didn't help Smith, whose crucifix court case got dismissed soon after, but he found another cause. In 2005 he wrote the pamphlet *L'Islam punisce Oriana Fallaci* (Islam Punishes Oriana Fallaci) and used the Unione dei musulmani d'Italia to launch a lawsuit against her for defaming Islam. Zucchi filed the paperwork and Smith went back on the talk shows. Their target was dying of cancer in New York.

'When I heard, I laughed,' said Fallaci. 'Bitterly, of course, but I laughed. No fun, no surprise, because the process is only a demonstration that everything I have written is true.'

Fallaci increasingly conflated Islam with the fascism her father had fought in the war. Others shared the worldview. Her friend Christopher Hitchens popularised the term 'Islamofascism' to describe fundamentalist Muslim ideology. George Bush used it to describe al-Qaeda. Oriana Fallaci thought Islamofascism and mainstream Islam were one and the same.

She would not have been surprised to know that the man who introduced Zucchi to Smith was a full-blooded Nazi.

*

Glasses, a moustache, a combover. Claudio Mutti looked like less like a dangerous far-righter and more like the professor he had once been.

Born in a working-class district of Parma back in 1946, Mutti worked his way up to lecturer in Romanian and Hungarian at the University of Bologna by his thirties.

The 1970s were the *Anni di piombo*, the years of lead, when terrorists both right- and left-wing tore Italy apart in a battle for opposing utopias. The Brigate Rosse robbed banks, killed policemen, and kidnapped and murdered Prime Minister Aldo Moro. Fascists planted bombs, assassinated enemies and tried a failed coup. Things got complicated when groups framed the other side for bomb attacks and the security services manipulated everyone like puppets.

Mutti was always on the right. As a young academic he followed the Belgian Jean Thiriart, a former Nazi collaborator with big ideas about pan-European unity and support for Arab nations against Israel. When Thiriart dropped out of politics to concentrate on his optometry business Mutti switched allegiance to Franco Freda, a prematurely white-haired far-right intellectual connected to groups like the Ordine Nuovo (New Order) and Movimento Sociale Italiano (Italian Social Movement).

Freda's short 1969 book *La disintegrazione del sistema* (The Disintegration of the System) laid out a battle plan for esoteric revolutionaries of right and left to come together and overthrow the bourgeois liberal system. It was a dense text, full of references to big names like Karl Marx and Plato, and lesser-known men like the monocled Baron Julius Evola. The book advocated direct action and had no conscience.

'The fact remains that, for a political soldier,' wrote Freda, 'purity justifies any hardness, indifference any deceit, while the stamp of the impersonal stamped on the fight dissolves all moral worries.'

Freda and his followers began calling themselves Nazi-Maoists. Both left and right hated them. There were accusations of terrorism followed by decades of trials, reversals, escapes, more trials, more acquittals. In the end everyone was more confused over who did what than when it all began. Mutti spent time in prison, lost his job, and ended up back in his mother's Parma apartment. In 1979 he converted to Islam.

His path to Allah had begun with Baron Julius Evola, an aristocrat turned philosopher out of Rome with slicked-back hair, bad teeth and a mess of esoteric beliefs. Evola's thought smelted down Nietzsche, the Kali Yuga, elitism, Eastern religions, Oswald Spengler's civilisational pessimism, reaction, mountaineering and mysticism into a cannon ball and fired it at the modern world. Every neo-fascist terrorist had books like *Gli uomini e le rovine* (Men Among the Ruins) and *Cavalcare la tigre* (Ride the Tiger) on a bookshelf. Evola died in the early 1970s but remained a fascist prophet for some, a guide through the unstoppable decay of European civilisation to others. A handful of close readers like Mutti used the baron as a gateway drug to something deeper.

The biggest influence on Evola's thought was horse-faced Frenchman René Guénon. A writer and schoolteacher from the first half of the twentieth century, Guénon's failure to achieve a conventional academic career wobbled him into an eccentric orbit of his own. His writings reawoke the long-forgotten philosophy of perennialism, the idea that all existing religions are decaying fragments of the once unified, antediluvian true word of God. The Frenchman believed that the world in general, and Europe in particular, had been in steady spiritual decline since this religious big bang, a process accelerated by modernity. A revival was only possible through the mass adoption of a vigorous religion whose practices surround the faithful in everyday life. A youthful flirtation with the occult had soured him on unorthodox practices, Hinduism wasn't keen on converts, and Christianity in all its flavours had become weak and corrupt. Guénon chose Islam.

He converted in 1910 and moved to Egypt twenty years later. Guénon books like *La Crise du monde modern* (Crisis of the Modern World) never sold well but inspired readers on their own spiritual journeys that often ended in the mosque. His philosophy became known as Traditionalism and admirers included everyone from Evola to Mircea Eliade, Frithjof Schuon to Alexander Dugin. An American naval officer called Steve Bannon read Guénon in the late 1970s and it changed his life.

Guénon had no interest in the far-right but Mutti cheerfully combined Islam with his existing politics. Visitors to his mother's apartment found a room full of kitsch Islamic tat, with Quranic quotes on sparkly metallic paper and photographs of Mecca in cheap plastic frames, and a Nazi Reichskriegsflagge propped behind a filing cabinet. Mutti spent his time annotating texts, criticising Zionism, and teasing out an alternate history of Islam based around white converts in the Ottoman Empire and a disciple of Muhammad who might have been European.

Mutti had contacts across the continent with far-right groups and arranged printing for pamphlets illegal in their home countries. His printer was Emilio Adel Smith. The Italo-Egyptian had no problem with anti-Semitism and swastikas. Mutti introduced him to Massimo Zucchi, who saw more Maoist than Nazi in his fellow convert, and kept in touch. Then came the Oriana Fallaci lawsuit that threatened to drag in Mutti and anyone else with dubious politics who knew Smith.

A woman who believed Islam would destroy Europe, a dead French philosopher who thought it would save the continent, a Nazi-Maoist who believed Islam would rebirth a fascist empire, and two converts who thought it would save the world. It would have made an interesting courtroom showdown. Cancer got there first.

*

Fallaci became more pessimistic as the pain got worse. She could no longer see a future for Europe or herself and started referencing Bat Ye'or more frequently.

'Europe is no longer Europe,' she told a *Wall Street Times* journalist. 'It has become the "Eurabia", a colony of Islam, where the Islamic invasion does not proceed only in a physical sense but also penetrates into the minds and in the culture. The servility towards the invaders has poisoned democracy, with obvious consequences for the freedom of thought and the concept of freedom.'

This emaciated woman, wincing as she sipped cold champagne and smoked a cigarillo, reminded the journalist of philosopher Oswald Spengler and his obsession with Western decline. Fallaci could no longer see a way to save Europe or herself and talked of suicide. The only thing that cheered her up was a private audience with newly appointed Pope Benedict XVI.

'He is adorable! He agrees with me – but completely!'

She refused to talk about their meeting but started referring to herself as a Christian atheist. In private she had long phone conversations with Archbishop Rino Fisichella, rector of the Pontifical Lateran University.

In November 2005 an American conservative group called the David Horowitz Freedom Center gave her the Annie Taylor Award for Bravery, named after a woman who went over Niagara Falls in a barrel at the dawn of the twentieth century and nearly killed herself. The next month the Anti-Defamation League awarded Fallaci the Jan Karski Eagle Award; the city of Milan bestowed on her the Ambrogino d'oro, its highest honour; the President of the Italian Republic awarded the Benemerita della Cultura for her cultural contributions. The council of Tuscany presented a gold medal the following February, and a counter-jihad blog in America called Little Green Footballs started its own Fallaci awards for anyone who publicly opposed Islam.

The awards and recognition didn't stop Emilio Adel Smith's court case. Fallaci claimed the *L'Islam punisce Oriana Fallaci* pamphlet contained a death threat against her. Smith denied the charge. Expensive lawyers argued and press releases flew around. Another lawsuit against Fallaci began making its way through the Paris courts at this time, spurred by Muslims working with a collection of anti-racist groups in France including the Ligue des Droits de l'Homme (Human Rights League). Conviction in either case would put the seventy-six-year-old journalist in prison. The Italian trial was scheduled for June 2006 but got pushed back. Fallaci remained in Manhattan until her health deteriorated in September. She flew home to Florence, a mess of weeping sores and dying flesh, no longer caring about arrest and prison. She was barely conscious in hospital on 12 September when her new hero Pope Benedict XVI gave a lecture at the University of Regensburg in Germany that would kill two people.

The speech initially bored anyone outside the small overlap of hardcore Catholics and early church enthusiasts but got reported around the world thanks to the inclusion of an ancient quote from Manuel II Palaiologos, one of the last Byzantine emperors. Manuel II had watched as the Ottoman Empire encircled the last remnants of Roman civilisation in the East. The emperor saw no point sweetening his words.

'Show me just what Muhammad brought that was new,' he said, 'and there you will find things only evil and inhuman, such as his command to spread by the sword the faith he preached.'

Benedict quoted it as an example of religious extremism, but many Muslims understood the words to be the Pope's own. Those who knew the source thought Benedict should never have repeated it. There were marches and riots in Islamic countries, death threats, burnt churches, the murder of an Italian nun in a Mogadishu children's hospital, and a decapitated Assyrian Christian priest in Iraq. Fallaci died in hospital three days later, unconscious and unaware of the violence. She was buried in the Cimitero Evangelico degli Allori cemetery alongside family members and next to a monument to Panagoulis. The world saw widespread mourning at her death, some gloating, and many careful obituaries that praised the writing and discussed her transformation into an anti-Islamic warrior with carefully neutral words.

Friends thought it was probably best she didn't live long enough to see Benedict XVI express regret for his speech. The Pope's apology was close enough to grovelling to stop the violence but annoyed those who honoured Fallaci's memory. Christopher Hitchens wrote a sharp piece for *Slate* that pointed out Christianity also spread its message through violence, and threw in some barbed comments about Benedict's cowardice.

'And of course now we hear, as could have been predicted, the pathetic and unconvincing apologies issued by his spokesmen and finally Ratzinger himself,' Hitchens wrote. 'These will only serve to convince infuriated Muslims that by threatening reprisal, calling for the severing of diplomatic relations with the Vatican, and issuing a few more sanguinary fatwas, they can force yet another retreat.'

A year after Fallaci's death something happened that might have given her hope for the future. The world's biggest counter-jihad conference took place in the heart of the European Union. The views of Fallaci and Bat Ye'or and Melanie Phillips were going global.

8

THE WARBLOGGER WHO FELL FROM GRACE IN BRUSSELS

Organised Opposition to Islam Begins, 2007

Charles Foster Johnson broke a lot of hearts when he refused to go to Belgium. The world didn't normally get upset when a middle-aged man with a pony tail and love of mellow jazz-fusion stayed home. This was different. The father of modern counter-jihad activism had rejected his political offspring.

Johnson was a forty-seven-year-old computer guy running a blog called Little Green Footballs and posting about code when the 9/11 attacks changed his life. He spent the day before the planes came writing a piece about 'Placement of Web Page Elements'. It earned one comment. He woke up the next morning and turned on the television and saw the World Trade Center burning.

'I grew up in Hawaii,' he said. 'But I was born in New York. After I moved away at age 10, I would read the news stories about how the World Trade Center towers were getting closer to finishing. When they were attacked that day, that really hit home for me in a way that reached back into my childhood.'

Overnight, Little Green Footballs changed from a code blog into the first counter-jihad web presence. Johnson posted everything he could find about al-Qaeda, Islam, and the Middle East. He gave out annual awards. Anyone who made a name opposing Islam got the Fallaci. Those too sympathetic to Muslims got a Fiskie, named for left-wing journalist Robert Fisk who told the world he completely understood why a gang of Afghan refugees beat him up.

Little Green Footballs called itself a warblog and didn't take prisoners. Liberals were 'idiotarians' or 'LLL' (Loony Liberal Left); Islam was 'RoP' (Religion of Peace), used with heavy sarcasm after terror attacks; blog supporters were 'lizards', after an insult thrown their way in the comment section by a passing critic. The site became a rallying point for those online Americans who went against the prevailing narrative of blaming only Bin Laden and thought Islam itself was the real enemy.

Chuck Johnson was an unlikely political activist. He spent his twenties sliding along the fret board as a hired-gun guitarist for the inoffensive jazz of Al Jarreau and Stanley Clarke. Touring the world and living out of a suitcase soon got old. By the early 1980s Johnson had discovered a love of computers and spent his time between tours coding with a friend. When the pair's G+Plus programming language became an unexpected commercial success Johnson ditched the music industry and set up Codehead Software in Los Angeles. The money came rolling in. Life was sweet and mellow until the al-Qaeda attacks turned the world upside down and Johnson became a pro-Bush, pro-Israel, pro-War on Terror all-American hawk.

The early counter-jihad was a broad church. In 2004 the far-right Flemish separatist party Vlaams Blok (Flemish Block) was banned by the government in Brussels. Johnson blamed the move on the party's opposition to Islam, not its anti-immigration policies or talk of secession.

'A victory for European Islamic supremacist groups,' he said about the ban. Vlaams Blok dodged the bullet by dissolving the party, changing its stationery and reforming immediately as Vlaams Belang (Flemish Interest). The new party got close to a million votes in the Flemish parliamentary elections that year. Johnson saw that as a victory.

Rightists closer to home remained unconvinced by the counter-jihad. The polls may have showed 22 per cent of Americans didn't want a Muslim neighbour, but most Republicans still publicly clung to the government line that al-Qaeda, not Islam, was the enemy. Little Green Footballs stayed peripheral until some crudely forged documents about George W Bush's military service started circulating during the 2004 election. Johnson unexpectedly became a conservative hero after a neat animated gif he created to publicise their anachronistic typefaces went viral.

Little Green Footballs started getting half a million views a day from grateful mainstream Republicans who thought it had helped get Bush re-elected. New readers came for the conservatism and found they agreed with the anti-Islamic rhetoric. Johnson leveraged his growing readership into the founding of Pajamas Media, an online media hub that boasted a network of citizen journalists and some serious funding from venture capitalists.

By 2007 Little Green Footballs and its readers looked like a united happy family pushing anti-Islamic feeling towards the mainstream. But underneath, the cracks were starting to appear. Anyone who burrowed deep enough into the blog comments section could find complaints from previously loyal readers about Johnson's unwillingness to peel himself off the couch and get involved with activism away from the computer. Others thought he got undeserved credit for just saying what a lot of people already thought.

'Charles Johnson is one of those guys who jumps out in front of the parade,' said a critic, 'and thinks he's leading it.'

A hardcore of Little Green Footballs readers began to transmute into something tougher and more active. They had plans for taking counter-jihadism out into the real world and didn't care if Johnson got left behind.

*

Music critics drool over cult artists who only sell 100 records but inspire everyone who heard them to start their own band. Little Green Footballs was the blog version. Many of its earliest commenters went on to become prominent counter-jihad voices.

The first branch off the tree was Jihadwatch. In 2003 a dark, bearded Greek Catholic called Robert Spencer asked Johnson for help designing a blog. The programmer cheerfully obliged. Spencer was a loyal Little Green Footballs reader with a deep knowledge of Islam and some interesting friends.

Spencer grew up a Melkite Greek Catholic in New York. His grandparents had been driven out of what became Turkey in ethnic clashes following the First World War. Spencer's father worked for the Voice of America radio station and fought the Cold War against the Soviets one broadcast at a time. His son rebelled by working at a Maoist bookshop but turned to the right at the University of North Carolina, where he took a Masters in Early Christian Studies. There was some teaching, marriage and children, and then work with conservative think tanks. Spencer read a lot about Islam at a time when no one else did and made himself useful to right-wing types like David Horowitz who were interested in the Middle East.

He was thirty-nine years old when al-Qaeda attacked New York. Spencer had the ideal skillset to take on America's new enemy. Books poured out of him: *Islam Unveiled: Disturbing Questions about the World's Fastest Growing Faith* in 2002, *Onward Muslim Soldiers: How Jihad Still Threatens America and the West* and *Inside Islam: A Guide for Catholics – 100 Questions and Answers* in 2003, with many more to come over the years. He became a frequent commenter on the Little Green Footballs blog, pushing the message that Islam carried war in its very DNA. 'The Quran's commandments to Muslims to wage war in the name of Allah against non-Muslims are unmistakable,' he said. 'They are, furthermore, absolutely authoritative as they were revealed late in the Prophet's career and so cancel and replace earlier instructions to act peaceably. Without knowledge of the principle of abrogation, Westerners will continue to misread the Quran and misdiagnose Islam as a "religion of peace".'

He accused Muhammad of paedophilia, claimed Islam was taking over Europe and might one day do the same to America, and believed radical Muslims hugely outnumbered moderates. The Little Green Footballs crowd lapped it up, despite Spencer's habit of quoting only the most extreme Islamic material he could find. They flocked to the Jihadwatch site when it opened for business. Funding came from Horowitz, a former Marxist turned right-winger who ran the online *Frontpage* magazine and had made headlines with an award named for Oriana Fallaci. Visitors to Jihadwatch found a site that sold Spencer's books, parsed the Quran, and posted a blizzard of articles every time a Muslim did or said anything against the Western norm. Spencer had little hope that peace with Islam could be achieved.

'The jihadists will not be bought off by negotiations or concessions,' he said. 'This is the revival of a 1,400-year-old war, and we need to be prepared for the fact that it will not end anytime soon – and prepared to defend ourselves militarily and ideologically.'

Along with the writing, blogging and occasional appearances on Fox News, Spencer found time to act as mentor to another Little Green Footballs reader who was making a name for herself with anti-Islamic invective in the comments section. Pamela Geller began her own Atlas Shrugs blog in 2004. Her posts had all the tenderness of a kiss from a blowtorch but in person she was a flirty, purring pussycat.

'Her golden skin is still sun-kissed,' wrote an overwhelmed young *Village Voice* reporter, 'and her large light-brown eyes peer from behind impossible eyelashes that rest upon her sculpted cheekbones whenever she blinks or winks or bats her eyes ...'

Geller came from Long Island and grew up Jewish and middle class. She was a financial analyst before marrying rich and turning into a trophy wife who raised four kids in between flicking through fashion magazines. Then 9/11 happened. Geller saw it from the South Shore beach, the Twin Towers burning in the distance. The horror gave her a new purpose in life. She found Little Green Footballs and Robert Spencer's books before making the leap to her own blog.

Atlas Shrugged acted as a news aggregator of every media story about Islamic terror and outrage. Beheadings in Egypt, clerics condemning homosexuals, liberals caving in to outrageous demands, concerns that a Democrat politician called Barack Obama might be Muslim ('an Islamophiliac' was the most generous assessment Pamela Geller would give him). The posts were short and punchy. Geller reprinted the *Jyllands-Posten* Muhammad cartoons and did occasional videos beachside in a bikini.

Geller's anti-Islamic crusade had friends in strange places. Atlas Shrugged featured an interview with anti-Islamic British blogger Lionheart about his self-titled blog. Lionheart was really Paul Ray from Dunstable, a twentysomething with short hair, designer clothes and an interest in the far-right British National Party. Ray claimed the BNP wasn't anti-Semitic – which would have surprised the party's left-wing opponents and many of its own members – and plastered pro-Israel slogans over his blog. My enemy's enemy is my friend.

In the summer of 2007 Ray got an invitation to join an American counter-jihad group called the Center for Vigilant Freedom. It had been created by another Little Green Footballs commenter turned blogger who had a lot of friends in Denmark and Belgium. Baron Bodissey and his Gates of Vienna site were about to take counter-jihad off the internet and into the real world.

*

It was September 1683 and the Polish winged hussars looked like Roman legionnaires on horseback. The wooden frames of ostrich feathers at their backs fluttered in the wind as they charged down the hills towards the Ottoman lines.

Vienna had been under siege for two months. Holy Roman Emperor Leopold I's nerve had failed at first sight of the Islamic army under Grand Vizier Kara 'Black' Mustafa. He fled the capital and left his garrison behind. The emperor's soldiers sharpened their swords and dug in for siege. They refused Mustafa's demand to surrender.

'Let him come,' said city commander Count Ernst Rüdiger von Starhemberg. 'I'll fight to the last drop of blood.'

Mines toppled city walls. Corpses lay in streets running with sewage and smashed by artillery. Within weeks less than a third of Starhemberg's garrison was still on its feet, desperately holding on as Leopold I did the rounds of foreign capitals begging fellow Christians for help. In late autumn a relief force of 72,000 men arrived under John III Sobieski, obese and handlebar-moustached King of Poland. An infantry battle at Nussdorf weakened Ottoman forces, then the Polish cavalry charge sent them running. Germans and Austrians finished off the survivors.

'At the siege of Vienna in 1683 Islam seemed poised to overrun Christian Europe,' ran the slogan at the top of the Gates of Vienna blog, over 400 years later. 'We are in a new phase of a very old war.'

Baron Bodissey built his online city of pixels and code in 2004 after a few years lurking around the Little Green Footballs site. He took his pseudonym from an unappreciated elitist philosopher in Jack Vance's sci-fi novels who is eventually expelled from the human race by the council of egalitarians. The reference was only likely to be picked up by the kind of people who spent their downtime reading science fiction by the shelf load, all speculative hard sci-fi full of rational heroes who saw further than the sheep around them and were recognised as leaders by a grateful humanity.

Bodissey's real name was Edward S. May. He was a fiftysomething software engineer from Virginia with clipped moustache and brushed-back hair. His blog posted news reports on Islamic terror attacks and government reactions, held discussions on how to deal with Islam's encroachment of the West, and vented frustration at the blindness of the general public. It all began when his wife 'Dymphna' lost her daughter and May suggested blogging as a way to distract from the howling emotional pain. That worked until Dymphna's chronic fatigue syndrome limited her involvement and the Baron took the controls. The Gates of Vienna soon became a major node in the counter-jihad scene. Little Green Footballs and associates were glad to see a likeminded blog.

'The Baron and Dymphna are more than welcome in our family,' said Pajamas Media.

The Gates of Vienna hosted other anti-Islamic writers, including a Norwegian who used the pseudonym 'Fjordman' and a plump blonde hausfrau from Austria called Elisabeth Sabaditsch-Wolff. Paul Weston, a weathered-looking evangelist, acted as British correspondent. The comments section had an equally international flavour. Danes and Belgians were well represented. Everyone seemed to share the Baron's belief that homegrown leftism was as much to blame as Islam.

'We agree with Fjordman and many others that the Jihad is just a symptom, and that the enemy lies within,' May wrote. 'This war is a civil war within the West, between traditional Western culture and the forces of politically correct multicultural Marxism that have bedeviled it for the last hundred years. It is being fought in the back halls and cloisters of the culture, with untenured nobodies like me wielding a salad fork against the broadswords and maces of the fully-armored knights of the media and the academy.'

May was determined to take the fight against the Marxist knights on to a real-world battlefield. No one knew much about his past but occasional comments on the blog hinted at involvement in grassroots Republican activism under Reagan and Bush. Around 2006 May began to float a number of different ideas, which he called memes, to push the counter-jihad message: publishing a book of Fjordman's writing, soliciting donations to buy a controlling interest in a liberal media outlet (preferably *The Washington Post*), entryism into popular culture.

The comment section was enthusiastic. Someone suggested approaching right-wing Hollywood actors Ron Silver and Bo Derek for funding. Someone else suggested an Islamophobic awards ceremony. Anti-Muslim songs with catchy choruses ('Islam is Lame', 'Killer Krazies of the Quran Want You!'). Pro-Israel activities. Real-world protests. Reintroducing national service in Britain.

An email list sprang up and the 910 Group was born, named for the day before the al-Qaeda attacks on America. The group started with twenty-eight names and quickly metastasized. Membership remained secret but IT specialist Christine Brim, a severe-looking brunette fond of pearls, played a major role as did whatever academic psychologist ran the Awesternheart blog. The 910 Group's logo was a blue phoenix with 'Rebirth' and 'Resistance' over its wings, rising from the rubble of the World Trade Center.

By March 2007 the group had absorbed other, smaller groups including British activists from the Talk Veritas and Infidel Bloggers Alliance sites. The expanded 910ers transformed themselves into the non-profit Center for Vigilant Freedom. May found himself in charge of a decentralised network of websites and activists. Some of the loudest voices in the CVF were Danes radicalised by the cartoon crisis, and Belgians watching their demographics change. They wanted real-world conferences to discuss tactics, philosophy and networking.

It was going to be a busy year for Baron Bodissey.

9

A GATHERING OF CRUSADERS

Networking the Counter-Jihad, 2007–08

It began with some Danes who liked marching and flags. Anders Gravers Pedersen was a crop-haired butcher from a small North Jutland town, with a stomach the size of a zeppelin. The fortysomething loved beer and pork and unsuccessfully running for parliament with the anti-immigration Den Danske Forening (Danish Association).

The Forening was one of those respectable right-wing outfits that didn't like foreigners but tried to be reasonable about it, preferring policy papers and calm debate to anything more dramatic. Attempts to smear the group as far-right usually failed; the founders were resistance veterans from the war with enough cash to sue anyone who called them Nazis. Pedersen thought Den Danske Forening's obsession with respectability prevented it getting anything done. Not even the cartoon crisis could get members out on the streets.

'All they wanted was only to talk internally about the Islam problems,' Pedersen said, 'and publish a well-informed magazine four times a year.'

Pedersen and some of the rowdier types from Jutland quit in 2005 and started their own group. Stop Islamiseringen af Danmark (Stop the Islamification of Denmark) marched around opposing censorship and new mosques. It was rough going at the start. Leftists attacked rallies and called for boycotts; neo-Nazis punched Pedersen when he waved an Israeli flag. The public dripped lemon juice into the cut when the SIaD leader got only seventy-three votes in the 2007 parliamentary elections. Pedersen kept on going, pushing the implications of the cartoon crisis in a country that took freedom of speech for granted. His views began to receive a sympathetic hearing from Danes, even if no one wanted to vote for him.

Other Danish counter-jihad outfits appeared, including the Islamkritisk Netværk (Islam-Critical Network) website and the Trykkefrihedsselskabet (Free Speech Society). The Netværk didn't last long but the Trykkefrihedsselskabet had more staying power. It been started by sixty-two-year-old veteran journalist and former socialist activist Lars Hedegaard after some harsh criticism of Islam got him blackballed from International PEN, the longstanding group dedicated to literary freedom of expression. Hedegaard made his counter-jihad feelings clear by giving the first Trykkefrihedsselskabet press freedom awards to Flemming Rose, Mark Steyn and cartoonist Kurt Westergaard.

Stop Islamiseringen af Danmark remained the biggest name. Its marches and confrontations showed how the counter-jihad could get its message offline and out there into real-world spaces. Edward May's Danish friends wanted the Center for Vigilant Freedom to light a torch from the same fire.

'During an online meeting of the directors of CVF back in February,' wrote Dymphna, 'someone raised the topic of dissatisfaction among the members of the Danish chapter of Vigilant Freedom. The Danes were fed up with all the talk; they wanted some *action*.'

Edward May made some calls. Only contacts in Britain seemed to have the ability to take practical steps. In March, an expatriate known as 'Exile' made introductions and got Pedersen chatting with his British counterparts, notably Stephen Gash, prominent member of a small group active in the north of England called No Sharia Here. Gash was a bald fiftysomething doctor who spent most of his free time writing letters to newspapers about the superiority of northern England, and losing elections for right-wing parties. He got 0.6 per cent of the vote in a Sedgefield by-election for the anti-immigration English Democrats.

Danes and Britons got on well enough to organise a UK/Scandinavia counter-jihad summit in Copenhagen for April. Pedersen's SIaD provided security. CVF members from Denmark and Britain attended, as did some Swedes, the blogger Fjordman, and a few other counter-jihadists. Edward May left Dymphna running the blog and flew in from America.

The summit was a success. Pedersen gave a speech, calling the CVF brothers in the fight against Islam. He formed Anti-Jihad Danmark to link up with other local organisations. Gash and Pedersen liked each other enough in person to create Stop Islamisation of Europe (SIOE), an umbrella group of national cells modelled on the Danish original. May took the microphone to praise Denmark as birthplace of the real counter-jihad, call for alternatives to the mainstream media, and invoke the legendary Danish warrior Holger Danske, who will wake from his sleep beneath the mountain when his nation is threatened. May had a light, businesslike voice in person, but his thinking was apocalyptic as ever.

'We really are at a cultural version of the Gates of Vienna,' he said. 'The enemy has driven the traditional culture back inside its fortifications, and is busy digging tunnels to undermine the walls. Many of our people have been captured or converted, and the remnant is just barely holding out, drinking rainwater from the rooftop cisterns and eating dogs just to stay alive. Only this time there will be no King of Poland to ride down the hill in a glorious charge. This time there will be no Jan III Sobieski to save our sorry fundament. We're going to have to do this one ourselves.'

The success of the summit encouraged the CVF to plan a pan-European conference later in the year. May reached out to members for help. A man in Belgium had some useful contacts.

*

The standard debate chamber at the European Parliament had gleaming wood desks littered with microphones and bottled water rolling back in concentric semi-circles up a carpeted floor. Normally places like this hosted diplomats arguing about milk quotas and border controls. On 18 October 2007 one chamber had been commandeered by men and women planning the defeat of Islam.

The counter-jihad owed its perch in the heart of Europe to a forty-eight-year-old Flemish journalist with mutton chops, a handlebar moustache and a taste for controversy. Paul Beliën liked to stir things up. In 1990 the *Gazet van Antwerpen* sacked him for leaking a story about King Baudouin's stance on abortion to *The Wall Street Journal*. A few years later Beliën contributed to the enthusiastically pro-European Union book *Visions of Europe* alongside Margaret

Thatcher, then changed his mind and wrote another book damning the EU to hell.

These days the world knew Beliën as the man behind *The Brussels Journal*, a conservative online magazine that pushed counter-jihad ideas. The magazine started in 2005 and got into trouble inside a year with an angry article called 'Geef ons Wapens!' (Give us Weapons!). A Belgian teen had been murdered by a pair of Polish Roma. Beliën mistakenly thought the killers were Muslim immigrants and made a lot of noise about immigration, crime and ethnic backgrounds. His article brought down a media storm, and government agencies started investigating allegations Beliën's children had been improperly homeschooled. Beliën and his wife, Dr Alexandra Colen, a Vlaams Belang politician, hired expensive lawyers who eventually got the allegations dismissed. *The Brussels Journal* editor carried on with his fight against Islam.

He tried to speak in Copenhagen but an airport strike kept him home. The CVF missed him enough to ask Beliën's help organising its October 2007 conference. The Belgian suggested Vlaams Belang act as host. The new incarnation of the far-right Vlaams Blok had toned down the nationalist rhetoric, upped support for Israel and focused its attention on Islam. Party members had proved their dedication to the counter-jihad when the mayor of Brussels banned the first rally by Stop Islamisation of Europe, held outside the EU parliament on 11 September. Over 200 marchers came anyway to find a wall of police and prominent Vlaams Belang members like Filip Dewinter and Frank Vanhecke being dragged away in handcuffs.

'It is not our demonstration,' said Vanhecke, 'but we sympathise with the aims.'

Beliën's Vlaams Belang contacts were happy to use their party privileges and booked a room in the European parliament for 18 October, with the action shifting to the Flemish parliament the next day. Invitations went out and big names accepted. Counterjihad 2007 Brussels saw at least seventy organisations and individuals take part in two days of speeches, policy papers, working lunches, tables lined with coffee cups, socialising over drinks, and networking opportunities. Others attended remotely through WebEx conferencing.

Dr Andrew G. Bostom gave a lecture on Islamic anti-Semitism; David Littman talked about creeping dhimmitude at the United Nations; Robert Spencer lectured on *Islam – Is it the real problem?*;

Lars Hedegaard gave a speech; Dr Arieh Eldad from the hard right of the Israeli Knesset talked about his country's fight with terrorism; representatives of thirteen nations supplied local reports on Islam. Pamela Geller flew in to look well-groomed in the audience, while Paul Beliën helped things along on the podium. Edward May was behind the scenes making sure everything ran smoothly. Guyanese former Muslim Patrick Sookhdeo attended; Elisabeth Sabaditsch-Wolff of Gates of Vienna was there; well-heeled British property developer Ann Marchini made the trip. A contingent of Evangelical Christians from Britain turned up, including Gates of Vienna writer Paul Weston and barrister Andrea Minichiello Williams. In breaks from discussing Islam the evangelicals chatted about the coming Rapture when true believers would shed their mortal shells and fly to heaven.

Bat Ye'or gave the keynote speech. She called it *Eurabia: How Far Has It Gone?*.

'The EC correlated a massive Muslim immigration to a strategy of peace and stability in the Mediterranean,' she said, 'hoping that the Euro-Arab symbiosis through economic development, soft diplomacy and multiculturalism would guarantee peace, markets, and oil. In the Euro-Arab policy, Muslim immigration is welcomed as an element of a Mediterranean geo-strategy conducted as a partnership with the Arab-Muslim world on the base of pacifism and continual funding and services provided to the Arab world, similar to the subsidies given to the economically underdeveloped EU member-states.'

The speech was a rehash of what Bat Ye'or had been saying for years. So were most people's speeches. The conference's importance lay in bringing together dedicated counter-jihadists at the heart of European power and showing them that they amounted to a movement. Edward May hoped everyone would go home with plans for combating Islam in their home countries.

The most important counter-jihad blogger was missing. Charles Johnson had refused to attend.

*

The world saw the founder of Little Green Footballs as an online Republican stormtrooper who couldn't sleep for hating Islam. The reality was a laidback Hawaiian surfer dude who played jazz fusion guitar in a proudly middle-of-the-road band called Catzeye. Johnson was never as right-wing as his followers liked to believe. For all his Republicanism, anyone who dived into Johnson's blog posts found support for abortion, contempt for creationism, and visceral dislike of the religious right.

The Brussels conference changed something. He turned down an invitation from Edward May to attend and could barely bother to be very polite about it. In the weeks after, that obvious lack of enthusiasm curdled into open dislike for the event and its organisers. Johnson denounced Vlaams Belang as neo-Nazi holocaust deniers and condemned anyone who would attend anything connected with them. He banned commenters by the bucketload when they tried to debate the issue, and posted pictures of Vlaams Belang members modelling Celtic crosses, along with links to damning left-wing reports. Johnson seemed adamant Oriana Fallaci would never have attended the conference. Anyone who disagreed was a fascist.

Commenters at the Gates of Vienna retaliated. They pointed out that Brussels was an odd kind of fascism if attendees included Patrick Sookhdeo from Guyana and Jewish writers like Bat Ye'or. Some claimed Johnson had not known about the Vlaams Belang involvement until after he decided to stay home. They painted him as a keyboard warrior, happy to fight Islam from the internet but reluctant to make the move into real life politics. Quotes got dug up about his earlier support for the Flemish far-righters. Links were made between his computer skills and supposed authoritarian tendencies.

'He's a self-taught programmer who likes machine language best,' ran Johnson's bio in a 1986 edition of *Analog Computing*, 'because of the total control possible.'

It just got nastier. When the smoke cleared it became obvious most attendees had known little about Vlaams Belang before the controversy and didn't care much about its policies afterwards. Bat Ye'or and David Littman had nothing especially negative to say about their hosts. Pamela Geller wrote blog posts defending the party and highlighted its support for Israel. My enemy's enemy is my friend.

'One thing is clear,' said Pamela Geller. 'Vlaams Belang is the only party that has gone out of its way to support Israel. No political party in Belgium has supported Israel. Vlaams Belang has been the only party staunchly behind Israel for the past 10 years.'

The counter-jihad blogging movement splintered. Charles Johnson sold his share of Pajamas Media and set Little Green Footballs on course to a more liberal place. He seemed glad to leave behind the movement he had spawned, with its history book references to Sobieski at Vienna, the fall of Constantinople in 1453, crusader knights in the Holy Land, the sword and the cross. Blog traffic dropped but Johnson preferred his new, less extreme readership.

Everyone else regrouped around Gates of Vienna. The next Counterjihad Conference in 2008 symbolically took place in the Austrian capital, with a line-up of new and old faces. Debates focused on practical measures to roll back Islam in Europe.

'Some of the topics discussed,' said May, 'were sharia finance, the dhimmification of school and university textbooks, and the processes through which the European Union aids and abets all of these pernicious trends.'

Copenhagen hosted the following conference. A wealthy-looking British evangelical called Alan Lake turned up and chatted to Norwegian blogger Fjordman about the need to get the message out on the British streets. Lake wanted to expand the counter-jihad beyond middle-class types in lecture halls into a broader front of African Christians, working-class Britons and anyone else butting heads with Islam. Fjordman wished him luck, but privately thought Lake controlling.

The movement continued to grow. New blogs emerged and died like mayflies, but enough stuck around to make an impact. Organisations came out of nowhere with demonstrations and protests. The Center for Vigilant Freedom turned into the International Civil Liberties Alliance. Trykkefrihedsselskabet launched the International Free Press Society, an umbrella group for press freedom with a strong counter-jihad flavour.

Across the Atlantic other people were getting involved. Some belonged to a grassroots organisation trying to do for the US what the Brussels conference had done for Europe. Others were fellow travellers: conservatives with book deals, left-leaning feminists, Bible-thumping religious types. Two of them drew a poorly animated cartoon with foul-mouthed children and the Prophet Muhammad in a bear suit. The counter-jihad was easing its way into popular culture.

10

MIDDLE EASTERN SOCCER MOMS IN FORT HOOD

Action on the American Home Front, 2009

Brigitte Gabriel looked like she should have been shimmying out of an SUV in a high-school parking lot inspiring lustful thoughts in teenage boys. Lebanon's answer to the soccer mom was all dark eyes, bright teeth and gym figure. Gabriel would have fitted easily into the world of school runs and mall trips. Instead she ran America's biggest counter-jihad non-profit.

The crusade began when she was eleven years old and called Hanan Qahwaji. The French had carved Lebanon out of the Ottoman Empire's corpse after the First World War. The rigged political system benefited local Maronite Christians, who claimed descent from a fourth-century saint. The Muslim minority got symbolic but empty roles.

Tensions between Christian and Muslim outlived independence in 1943 and led to a brief civil war fifteen years later. In the early 1970s demographics changed when King Hussein of Jordan expelled the exiled Palestine Liberation Organisation from his kingdom. He supported their struggle against Israel but not attempts to overthrow his monarchy. Guerrillas and refugees crossed borders and moved into Lebanon. Soon the PLO controlled the western districts of Beirut. Their presence encouraged native Muslims politically left towards Moscow. Lebanese Christians moved further right.

In the spring of 1975 a dispute over fishing rights escalated into riots, shooting and massacres. A new civil war began in April. Qahwaji was Christian. She later told audiences in America horror stories of Palestinian militia groups blowing up the family home in Marjayoun. There were long years where the family seemed to spend every day hiding in a bomb shelter.

'The Muslims bombed us because we are Christians,' her father explained. 'They want us dead because they hate us.'

The family welcomed the Israeli invasion of Lebanon in 1982, hoping for peace, and couldn't understand the visceral hatred Muslim neighbours had for the new arrivals. Two years later Qahwaji was in the Israeli sector of Jerusalem using the name Nour Semaan and working as a news anchor for Middle East Television, a station owned by American televangelist Pat Robertson's Christian Broadcasting Network. Southern Baptists got a thrill watching broadcasts direct from the holy land. Qahwaji married an expat camera operator and moved to the US where another name change turned her into Gabriel Tudor. She lived a quiet life in Virginia Beach and ran a production company with her husband connected to Robertson's conservative media empire. The 9/11 attacks changed everything.

'I was struck by the same fear that I experienced during the war in Lebanon,' Qahwaji said. 'As I watched, words instinctively came from my mouth as I spoke to the TV screen: "Now they are here."'

Her Middle Eastern background and Christian faith made her an instant expert on the region for religious-right types. Qahwaji set up the American Congress for Truth in 2002 and the United America Committee two years later, both small-scale operations to promote Qahwaji as an expert on national security. The committee was co-founded with Jesse Petrilla, a twentysomething game designer who had got himself on talk shows with first person shooters like *Quest for Al-Qa'eda* and *Quest for Saddam*. California National Guard member Petrilla had ambitions to be a Republican politician. He soon left the committee behind for a tour in Afghanistan and a new set of worries.

'They train us how to fight the bad guys should we have to,' he told a reporter on the way over, 'but there is much less that can be done should a coward blow the road up from under you. That is the coward's way of fighting. Other than that, I am apprehensive that I may not have good high-speed internet all the time.'

Qahwaji stayed in the US where another name change turned her into Brigitte Gabriel. The lecture circuit became her battlefield.

She didn't hold back and conference organisers sometimes had to apologise for her views on Arabs. Despite this, she had support from some influential figures on the scene, including former CIA director James Woolsey and military man turned Fox News analyst Paul E. Vallely.

The United America Committee's ideology was uncomplicated. No Bat Ye'or, no Oriana Fallaci, no Eurabia. Just the constant message that Islamisation was happening to America through front groups, through Saudi-funded university courses, through Muslim migrants. America was under threat, Israel was at war, and liberals had no stomach for the fight. Gabriel had a polished speech for all occasions that started with her experiences during the Lebanese Civil War and ended knee deep in conspiracy theory.

'America has been infiltrated on all levels by radicals who wish to harm America,' she told audiences. 'They have infiltrated us at the CIA, at the FBI, at the Pentagon, at the State Department. They are being radicalised in radical mosques in our cities and communities within the United States.'

For those with long memories, it was an anti-Islamic twist on the John Birch Society, a fanatically anti-communist group that made a lot of noise back in the 1960s. Birchers thought the reds were taking over America and called anyone who denied it an enemy agent. Gabriel felt the same about Muslims. Her book titles gave a précis of her politics: *Because They Hate: A Survivor of Islamic Terror Warns America* and *They Must Be Stopped: Why We Must Defeat Radical Islam and How We Can Do It.*

By 2007 her reputation as a fiery speaker on Islam had attracted attention from important people. A senior Pat Robertson advisor called Guy Rodgers helped her transform the United America Committee into ACT! for America, a grassroots campaign opposing sharia law in the US. The absence of anything even close to a local sharia system didn't stop Gabriel creating websites, forming local chapters, and making enough noise to reel in big-money donors on the conservative and religious right. ACT! claimed 50,000 members the next year. Guy Rodgers saw the group as another missile in the conservative arsenal against the presidential campaign of Democrat senator Barack Obama.

Gabriel took part in a documentary called *Obsession: Radical Islam's War against the West*, which reached 200,000 people as a free

DVD during the election campaign. The glossy film had been made by the Clarion Fund, a pro-Israeli non-profit founded by Raphael Shore, a Canadian rabbi who spent his time creating propaganda movies and building scale models of the Second Temple to speed up the Messiah's return. Other pro-Israel groups like the Endowment for Middle East Truth helped distribute *Obsession*, with help from evangelical Christian organisations sympathetic to Zionism and convinced a Biblical apocalypse was on its way.

No one knew who gave Clarion the $17 million to make the film or follow it up with *The Third Jihad* but rumours centred on an enigmatic Chicago businessman. Others suspected Jewish millionaire software developer Aubrey Chernick, well known for using the Fairbrook Foundation to funnel money into the David Horowitz Freedom Center, which in turn trickled it down to ACT! for America, Jihadwatch and other anti-sharia groups.

Counter-jihad films were in the air that year. In Hollywood ex-naval man turned film producer Steve Bannon had come up with a proposal for *Destroying the Great Satan: The Rise of Islamic Fascism in America*, a documentary that looked at the supposed alliance between Islamic groups and American liberals to introduce sharia law to the US. Big counter-jihad names like Robert Spencer and Steven Emerson, a journalist who'd been campaigning against radical Islam since the 1990s, got pencilled in as talking heads, but the film never got made.

All the free DVDs and behind-the-scenes activism couldn't stop the right losing the 2008 election. A biracial politician with impeccably liberal views and charisma to spare moved into the White House. ACT! activists were among many on the right who thought Obama secretly a Muslim.

Brigitte Gabriel continued her campaign on the American home front. She gave a lot of speeches, jumped on a lot of bandwagons, and encouraged members to patrol their cities and note mosque locations. Most of the organisation's time was spent persuading various legislatures to pass anti-sharia law bills aimed at stopping possible Muslim plots against the constitution.

Membership grew in the American heartlands. Then in late 2009 something happened that convinced Gabriel and a lot of other people that ACT! had been right all along.

*

There was so much blood on the floor that nurses fell over as they tried to reach the victims. They had jammed the door shut and the gunman was still killing people outside.

In the early afternoon of 5 November 2009, a thirty-nine-year-old military psychiatrist of Palestinian descent called Major Nidal Malik Hasan entered the Soldier Readiness Processing Center in Fort Hood, Texas. He had eyebrows like black caterpillars and a glassy stare. Staff had seen him around a lot recently. Hasan's unit was deploying to Iraq.

On this visit Hasan had a FN Five-Seven automatic pistol with a twenty-round magazine and laser sights in one pocket of his fatigues and a .357 revolver in another. He had wrapped extra FN magazines in paper towels to stop them clinking. Soldiers attended the Center for vaccinations and check-ups. They were not allowed to carry weapons.

Hasan sat at a desk, prayed briefly, then stood up and pulled out the FN.

'Allahu Akbar,' he said and started shooting.

Soldiers got hit or dropped to the floor or tried to run. Hasan shot dead a doctor who charged him with a folding chair then went through the Center killing anyone in uniform. He spared five civilians crouched under a desk before exiting the building and getting into a gunfight with Fort Hood police officer Sergeant Kimberly Munley that left her on the ground with a broken femur. Nurses and medics still inside used a belt to tie the door closed. Hasan shot at the injured soldiers who had made it out.

Fortysomething African American police officer Sergeant Mark Todd ran into Hasan reloading his pistol. Todd put five bullets in Hasan's spine and ensured his death row cell would need a wheelchair ramp.

When it was all over there were thirteen dead, thirty-two injured, and a court martial with a predictable result. An investigation showed Hasan to be a socially isolated but devout Muslim, deeply disturbed by American involvement in Iraq and Afghanistan. In early 2001 he had attended a Virginia mosque at the same time as two of the 9/11 hijackers. In the months before the shooting Hasan had been in touch with Anwar al-Awlaki, a Yemeni-American imam under investigation by the FBI.

'I can't wait to join you,' he emailed al-Awlaki, referring to the afterlife.

The FBI and other agencies knew about the emails but didn't regard Hasan as a threat. Prosecutors declined to charge him with terrorism, preferring psychological explanations for the killings. The counter-jihad didn't agree.

'They still don't know why the military promoted Hasan and didn't act on "concerns",' Pamela Geller wrote on her blog. 'What concerns? His devotion to Islam? What would have been done had he been reported for his pious and devout love and devotion to Islam? Not only would he still have been promoted, anybody who reported him would have been demoted, a racist! An Islamophobe! An anti-Muslim bigot!'

Hasan's rampage was the deadliest attack on American soil since 9/11. Attitudes to Islam hardened across the country. ACT! for America's membership increased and the donations rolled in. Other evangelical groups joined the crusade. The Florida Family Association went after television programmes that showed too much sympathy for ordinary Muslims. Internet and television evangelist Bill Keller, who had done time for fraud before turning to religion, shot down any hope of interfaith understanding.

'How could you build bridges with people,' said Keller, 'who ask their Muslim brothers to fly a plane into the Twin Towers and killed thousands of innocent people?'

The Family Research Council attacked Muslim loyalty to America, along with liberalism, President Obama ('he seems to be advancing the idea of the Islamic religion') and homosexuality. Senior Council member Lieutenant General William Boykin was a former deputy Under Secretary of Defense for Intelligence and full-time hardcore evangelist. He ran a think tank called Team B II, named for an old Cold War reference, which looked for ways to combat 'stealth jihad' and 'creeping sharia'. It had a deep bench of members including Jewish historian Daniel Pipes, founder of the Middle East Forum and campaigner for American interests in the Arab world since 1994; Tom Trento, evangelical Christian leader of the United West group; and David Yerushalmi, a Jewish lawyer who had founded the Arizona-based Society of Americans for National Existence (SANE) back in 2006 to stamp out any hint of creeping sharia in the US.

Yerushalmi acted as counsel for Frank Gaffney, a prominent anti-Islamic campaigner who ran the secular Center for Security

Policy and believed the Muslim Brotherhood secretly controlled most of the mosques in America as part of a plot to replace the constitution with sharia law. Gaffney had spent time in the Reagan administration but got kicked out for not being enthusiastic about reducing nuclear arsenals. He donated $364,000 to Yerushalmi's SANE to help it prove sharia amounted to a criminal conspiracy against the US government. Activists measured imams' beards and counted how many worshippers wore hats, without coming to any legally binding conclusions.

Another big name was the Center for the Study of Political Islam run by Bill Warner, a seventysomething retired physics professor who had taught at Tennessee State University under his real name of Bill French. He took the position that Islam was incompatible with Western ideas of human rights, and 'political Islam' would not rest until the entire world had submitted.

The anti-sharia organisations slithered over each other like snakes in a pit, sharing funding sources and members. Sometimes they came together. A 2009 coalition called the American Public Policy Alliance united ACT! for America, the Middle East Forum, SANE, and the Center for Security Policy. The alliance did a lot of talking about 'stealth jihad' and the traitors in Congress, and got anti-sharia legislation passed in five states.

By the end of 2009 Brigitte Gabriel's ACT! had operations across America and in ten foreign countries, and an annual budget of $1.6 million. Gabriel drew a $180,000 annual salary. The group had enough money to dip its fingers into other conservative causes, getting excited over the idea of patriotic textbooks for school kids. Counter-jihadist bloggers focused on Europe looked enviously at the well-stuffed bank accounts of ACT! and its friends. The two wings of the counter-jihad generally remained separate but there were occasional crossovers. The Middle East Forum hired Paul Beliën as director of its Islamist Watch side project. David Yerushalmi represented Geller and Spencer's AFDI (American Freedom Defense Initiative) in various legal issues. Austrian activist Elisabeth Sabaditsch-Wolff started an ACT! Vienna chapter and addressed a 2010 conference in Washington. Edward May attended the event and went away impressed.

'Elisabeth Sabaditsch-Wolff was the last speaker of the afternoon, and gave a brief account of the accelerating Islamization of Austria and the rest of the EU,' said May, 'and why it matters to the United States. She struck a chord with the audience, and a lot of listeners approached her afterwards to ask questions and offer their assistance. One of my major goals is to help Americans understand why the European Counterjihad is important to the United States, and Elisabeth's efforts are a valuable part of that process.'

May had his own connection with Brigitte Gabriel through the International Free Press Society, the umbrella group that had originated in Denmark's Trykkefrihedsselskabet. Gabriel was an advisory board member when May worked as its Outreach Co-ordinator. Bat Ye'or was also a member, alongside Frank Gaffney; Gates of Vienna correspondent Paul Weston played a role, as did Canadian broadcaster Ezra Levant and his friend, journalist Mark Steyn.

Act! for America had the money, Gates of Vienna had the ideology, and talking heads like Steyn had their mouths close to the mainstream media megaphone. Not everyone was happy with the set-up. Some counter-jihadists grumbled that a well-known figure like Steyn should be more positive in pushing their cause. He seemed convinced the battle for Europe was already lost.

II

CRUSHED BY THE WHEELS
OF HISTORY

*A Brief History of Western Civilisation's Unstoppable
Decline, 1918–Present*

Money was worthless in Germany after the First World War. Locals used it as wallpaper and burnt bundles of the stuff to keep warm. Hyperinflation had hit hard. By 1923 a dollar bill could buy you 4,210,500,000,000 marks. An armful of notes might get a loaf of bread. Women and boys whored themselves on the street for a cheap meal.

In a Hanover army barracks, a fox-faced war hero wrote to his brother for a new edition of a book that seemed to explain the society collapsing around him. Captain Ernst Jünger was a twenty-eight-year-old veteran of the Western Front trying to hold together his inner life in a defeated Germany. He'd been wounded fourteen times, got the Iron Cross and the Pour le Mérite, and had seen entire battalions of young men fed through the mincing machine. He came home to a society that didn't care about his sacrifices.

Jünger spent his time off duty searching for something to give life meaning – the occult, entomology, nationalism, drugs, women. He took long midnight walks through the empty streets and wrote obsessively about his experiences in the trenches. In July 1923 he asked his brother for a recently published two-volume edition of *Der Untergang des Abendlandes*.

'Don't disappoint my decline-hungry heart,' Jünger wrote.

He'd already read the book but wanted the new, revised edition. Oswald Spengler's *Decline of the West* gave Jünger something that made Germany's collapse explicable: an absolute pessimism that things could only get worse.

The author of *Decline* was a fortysomething former high-school teacher who thought he'd cracked the code of history. Spengler rejected the linear idea of time flying forward like an arrow, bringing progressively superior technology, morality and culture. To him, the modern Western world was not the culmination of all human effort to date, but just the latest in a series of disconnected societies rising and falling over the centuries, inevitably and unstoppably.

Others had tried the same approach. An admirer once asked Voltaire why the Roman Empire fell. He expected a long and complex discussion. He didn't get it.

'It fell,' said Voltaire, 'because all things fall.'

End of discussion. That was Spengler's philosophy boiled down to six words.

The German's talent was to serve his pessimism with some science on the side. Spengler put important societies like Babylonia, the Egypt of the Pharaohs, early Chinese dynasties, India, the Aztecs, the Greco-Roman world, Arabia and Western Europe under the microscope. He found a common pattern. All started as cultures wriggling in native soil, exhausting their creative capital as they battled to establish unique art, social structures and goals. When there was nothing left to create, the cultures transformed into civilisations and directed all their energies outwards towards imperialism and technical achievement. The dimming of those energies opened the gates to carcinogenic elements like equality and liberalism. At that point the end was near. Spengler had no time for democracy.

In the last stages, members of a dying civilisation would follow any charismatic leader who promised to reverse the decline, then abandon them when the attempt inevitably failed; return to religion after a long period of unbelief; and watch helplessly as a former underclass took control and tried to recreate the civilisation's past glories but produced instead a crude parody. Then the civilisation died, a new culture arose somewhere, and the cycle continued.

Men like Jünger lapped up a book that explained Germany's defeat as an inevitable part of the Western world's decline. Less predictable was the enthusiasm for Spengler from readers on the victor's side. That roaring twenties celluloid montage of champagne, chorus lines and fluttering dollar bills concealed a thick vein of pessimism among the

Allies. Newspapers talked of falling birth rates, the break-up of the family, the destruction of the countryside by industrialisation, votes for women, trouble in the colonies. Many felt the ground beneath their feet was crumbling and turned to a book that explained it all. T. S. Eliot alluded to *The Decline of the West* in his poem *The Waste Land*; F. Scott Fitzgerald was a fan; H. P. Lovecraft used it as the backdrop to his novella *At the Mountains of Madness*; and decades later Ernesto 'Che' Guevara would have a copy on his bookshelf in Marxist Cuba.

'When the first volume of *The Decline of the West* appeared in Germany a few years ago,' wrote a *Time* journalist in 1928, 'thousands of copies were sold. Cultivated European discourse quickly became Spengler-saturated. Spenglerism spurted from the pens of countless disciples. It was imperative to read Spengler, to sympathize or revolt. It still remains so.'

The book was an intellectual grenade hurled at the public. Captain Jünger read and re-read the two-volume edition in his Hanover barracks and took from it a philosophy that would last the entirety of a long life.

'In many things Spengler has truly removed the scales from my eyes,' he said. 'His approach, after a second reading, has also become familiar to me, a sort of intellectual pearlthreading or a melody of the analogical...'

Others were less delighted to learn the decline was irreversible. In the modern counter-jihad world, this kind of pessimism was the black dog of depression they had to fight off every day. Yet Spengler kept turning up in counter-jihad thought. Paul Beliën's *The Brussels Journal* ran a three-part series on Spengler's philosophy, Gates of Vienna commenters discussed his work, and *Asia Times* journalist David Goldman, who was respected by counter-jihad types, used the pseudonym Spengler in tribute to his hero. Even Samuel Huntington's *Clash of Civilizations* had Spengler references.

Bloggers tried not to believe the prophecies and pushed back against anyone who got too comfortable with the idea of decline. Counter-jihad maven Robert Spencer got a spanking from his friends at *Frontpage* in late 2008 for 'intermittent lapses in Spengler'. Others shook their heads at Mark Steyn, whose views on demographics were deeply pessimistic.

The Canadian journalist had a higher media profile than most in the movement. He'd appeared in magazines on both sides of the Atlantic and made a nice side income as a television talking head. Counter-jihadists admired his public advocacy of their cause but didn't like where he was going with the gloomy predictions about demography and Islam. Even mainstream magazine *The Atlantic* called his thought 'Spenglerian'.

Steyn didn't care. Every humourist had a dark side.

*

Mark Steyn was a bearlike fortysomething Canadian who had started his journalistic career young after dropping out of a private school in Britain and heading for Fleet Street. He worked as a theatre critic before expanding into film reviews and conservative politics. Steyn's work was published in *The Daily Telegraph*, *The Spectator* and a raft of right-leaning publications in Britain and America.

His first books were on musical theatre, then the usual standby of collected columns. The Clinton years provided easy targets and by the end of the 1990s Steyn was living well in New Hampshire with his wife and children. He called himself a 'right-wing bastard' and peppered enemies with shotgun blasts of invective and wit. Liberal heroes like Clinton and Bob Dylan got it with both barrels: '[Bob Dylan] was at the Vatican not so long ago and, although we do not know for certain what the Pope said as the leathery, wizened, stooped figure with gnarled hands and worn garb was ushered into the holy presence, it was probably something along the lines of, "Mother Teresa! But they told me you were dead!"'

Then 9/11 hit and things got serious. Steyn watched the growing Muslim population in Europe with horror, then pessimistic acceptance. In 2005 he wrote the book *America Alone*. It took a central thesis from 2001's *Death of the West* by former Nixon aide Pat Buchanan, a Christian-right take on Spengler that predicted the destruction of Western civilisation within fifty years thanks to low birth rates among Europeans and high ones among migrants. Steyn's book took the decline idea and ran with it:

> Most people reading this have strong stomachs, so let me lay it out as baldly as I can: much of what we loosely call the Western world will not survive this century, and much of it will effectively disappear within our lifetimes, including many if not most Western European countries. There'll probably still be a geographical area on the map marked as Italy or

the Netherlands – probably – just as in Istanbul there's still a building called St. Sophia's Cathedral. But it's not a cathedral; it's merely a designation for a piece of real estate.

He predicted Islam would conquer Europe with a dual-prong strategy of outbreeding and attacking the natives. The battle would be fought through terror attacks and maternity wards. Eventually the West would surrender, weakened by the outsourcing of many family responsibilities to the state, the erosion of self-reliance, and myopic concentration among the liberal establishment on promoting diversity and combating racism. America would hold out the longest, thanks to its small Muslim population, and remain a lighthouse of freedom and democracy in the medieval murk until it too was swamped by the demographic tide.

America Alone was a deeply negative book, rivalling Oswald Spengler for its bleakness of vision. The demographic talk made a big impact on the counter-jihad world, but the dark nothing-to-be-done tone did not go down well.

'Critics would claim that Mr. Steyn isn't contributing to maintaining Western willpower by suggesting that we've already lost,' wrote Fjordman in a Gates of Vienna review.

The blog's commenters agreed. A laudable book but too pessimistic. They didn't want to believe birth rates had doomed their fight against Islam before it started; some pointed out that Steyn had left out important facts, like the slowing of Muslim population growth and the ageing nature of Islamic nations. They quoted Dr Koenraad Elst, a Flemish academic sympathetic towards the hard right and Hinduism: 'Islam is in decline,' he told *The Brussels Journal*, 'despite its impressive demographic and military surge.'

Counter-jihadists took that to heart and pretended not to hear Elst's follow-up comments that the decline might not take effect until after Europe had become majority Muslim. Steyn started work on a sequel called *After America: Get Ready for Armageddon*, which would take an even bleaker approach, with the claim the USA would collapse sooner than anyone expected thanks to debt and bureaucracy. Again, demographics lay at the heart of the argument. The global Muslim population had increased from 19.9% per cent in 1990 to 23.4 per cent in 2010, with a projection of 26.4 per cent by 2030. The Pew Research Centre estimated the Muslim population of Europe, including Russia and the Balkans, would rise from 6 per cent in 2010 to 8 per cent in 2030. Muslims in America would increase from 2.6 million to 6.2 million over the same period.

It was grim stuff for counter-jihadists but Steyn never lost his sense of humour. At public appearances he led audiences in a singalong to a self-penned tune called 'My Sharia Amour'. Pajamas Media described his work as 'Mort Sahl Meets Oswald Spengler'.

On 22 March 2010 Steyn was hacking away at *After America* on the laptop when news came in that the University of Ottawa had decided criticising Islam came close enough to hate speech for the lawyers to get involved. For once, he wasn't the man in the crosshairs. A fellow conservative journalist from south of the border had riled up Canadians with talk about Islam, terrorism and camels. Protesters were swarming the campus looking to shut down a planned lecture and the university vice-president was talking about helping along their crusade with legal action. Steyn immediately got involved. He cared about a lot of things, but being able to speak your mind came top on the list.

'This is the pitiful state one of the oldest free societies on the planet has been reduced to, and this is why our free speech campaign matters,' he wrote, 'because those who preside over what should be arenas of honest debate and open inquiry instead wish to imprison public discourse within ever narrower bounds – and in this case aren't above threatening legal action against those who dissent from the orthodoxies.'

The target of Ottawa's threatened legal action was Ann Coulter, a leggy, horse-faced blonde in her mid-forties with a thing for miniskirts. Her father had been an FBI agent who hero-worshipped Joe McCarthy and other red-baiters. Coulter inherited his politics and work ethic. She studied history at Cornell and law at Michigan, and moved into private practice specialising in corporate law before quitting to advise Republican senators on the easiest ways to deport illegal immigrants. A smart blonde with high heels and right-wing opinions had to fight hard in those days not to appear on television. Coulter was soon a media face. The 1990s saw her and conservatives like Mark Steyn going after President Bill Clinton and his sex scandals. She had the sharpest lines but Steyn got all the best jokes.

'If the president's penis is straight,' said Steyn, 'it is the only thing about his administration that is.'

The election of President Bush ended the easy anti-establishment jokes. Coulter turned author with books like *Slander: Liberal Lies about the American Right* and *How to Talk to a Liberal (If You Must): The World According to Ann Coulter.* She made wittily offensive appearances on television, gave radio interviews and wrote columns for David Horowitz's *Frontpage* site. On 11 September 2001 Coulter's friend Barbara Olsen died on the American Airlines flight that hit the Pentagon, spending her last minutes on the phone, huddled terrified in a seat telling her husband she loved him. It lit a flame of hatred for Islam in Coulter that never went out.

'It is preposterous to assume every passenger is a potential crazed homicidal maniac,' Coulter said. 'We know who the homicidal maniacs are. They are the ones cheering and dancing right now. We should invade *their* countries, kill their leaders and convert them to Christianity. We weren't punctilious about locating and punishing only Hitler and his top officers. We carpet-bombed German cities; we killed civilians. That's war. And this is war.'

She took part in Horowitz's 2007 Islamo-Fascism Awareness Week, promoting right-wing views on American campuses, but the counter-jihadists never saw her as more than a fellow traveller. Coulter was a conservative Republican who opposed Islam from a position of personal loss and an ideology that placed equal importance on low taxes, big business and the War on Terror. Enough common ground existed that the Canadian chapter of the International Free Press Society organised her 2010 speaking tour of local universities.

Coulter took podiums to talk about conservatism, the problems of Barack Obama's presidency, and methods to combat Islamic terrorism. A student at the University of Western Ontario asked how they could travel if Muslims got banned from flying.

'Take a camel,' said Coulter.

The next lecture at the University of Ottawa got cancelled when crowds of leftist protesters occupied the campus. IFPS member and lawyer Ezra Levant blamed university vice-president François Houle for riling everyone up with an email threatening legal trouble if Coulter went too far with the camel jokes. The American journalist pretended she didn't care and carried on with the lecture tour. Mark Steyn took up the battle.

'Lots of Americans loathe Ann Coulter,' he said, 'but it takes a Canadian like François Houle to criminalize her. The strictures he attempts to place around her, despite his appeal to "Canadian law", are at odds with the eight centuries of Canada's legal inheritance. Canadians should point that out to him politely, and explain that, although he lives high off the hog courtesy of the Canadian taxpayer, he does not speak for them.'

He printed Houle's email address and encouraged readers to let the vice-president know how they felt about freedom of speech and where it fitted with discussions about Islam. The row outlasted Coulter's stay in the country. When the arguments about Islamic theology and camel riding finally ended it looked like the University of Ottawa had won. Students, professors and large chunks of the Canadian media agreed that criticising Islam was racism. And freedom of speech stopped where racist talk began. That was bad news for conservatives who believed in freedom of speech, but catastrophic for a counter-jihadist trying to tell the world about demographics.

Not for the first time, Steyn was grateful he lived in America, where the First Amendment allowed some interesting people to say things about Islam that would have given François Houle a heart attack. Steyn and Coulter's aversion to Islam came from the conservative right. Others opposed the Muslim world from different positions: late-night talk-show hosts, libertarian cartoonists, apocalyptic Christians and feminists proud of their breasts. Counter-jihad ideas were starting to replicate in some strange places.

12

BREASTS, BEARS, BIBLES

Soft Counter-Jihad in Popular Culture, 2010

Iranian greybeard Ayatollah Kazem Seddiqi ran the Friday prayers in Tehran and was legendarily dull at it. Rumours suggested the job had been arranged by the country's supreme leader mainly to annoy a political rival. No one would ever accuse Kazem Seddiqi of being a vibrant speaker, but on 20 April 2010 he surprised connoisseurs of orthodox droning by saying something interesting. In a talk at Tehran University campus mosque he warned that revealing clothes on women could lead to seismic activity.

'Many women who do not dress modestly lead young men astray, corrupt their chastity and spread adultery in society, which increases earthquakes,' he said. 'What can we do to avoid being buried under the rubble? There is no way other than taking refuge in religion and adapting ourselves to Islamic behaviour.'

The Western media had fun with the story. 'Iran: Fashion that Moves the Earth,' ran a *New York Times* headline. Mockery of Kazem Seddiqi bounced around the internet until it reached a biology student at Indiana's Perdue University prepping for a PhD in Genetics. She wrote a quick blog post outlining an experiment to test the ayatollah's hypothesis.

'In the name of science,' said Jennifer McCreight, 'I offer my boobs.'

She wanted to see whether a group of cleavage-baring women parading around could cause an earthquake. A Facebook page went up called 'Boobquake'. McCreight thought she might get a small campus crowd interested. The post went viral. On 26 April over

20,000 women marched in Boobquake events across America wearing revealing tops and carrying signs: 'Science in Progress', 'God hates Boobs', 'Cleavage for Science'. Men turned up in solidarity, or with cameras. The media loved it. The next day McCreight announced that seismic activity had been lower than average during Boobquake, if you ignored a 6.5 quake in Taiwan. Kazem Seddiqi's theory had been disproved.

Not everyone was happy with the event. A rival Brainquake event put its emphasis on everything above the shoulders. Fewer people attended. Some feminists saw only hatred of Islam in McCreight's march and weren't surprised Boobquake got support from counter-jihad blogs like Historyscoper ('The #1 Blog for Serious Islam Watchers') and Gates of Vienna friend Vlad Tepes ('Objects in history may be closer than they appear').

'I was initially intrigued by the idea as a sort of campy and playful way to collectively disprove an idea,' said someone at Feministing. com, 'but after about 5 minutes of perusal, it became glaringly apparent that this North American response to an Iranian cleric was more about Islamophobia and ethnocentrism than the rights of Muslim women. The events are a vector for the co-option of feminist rhetoric to further objectify women, and a demonstration of the smug North American sense of moral and developmental superiority over those "other" brown folks in the Middle East.'

Boobquake had got itself mixed up in an ideological shootout. McCreight protested she was just a geeky, nerdy, atheist feminist whose opposition to Islam owed more to Christopher Hitchens than Islamophobia. Atheism was a growing movement in America, closely connected to a growing army of sceptics committed to dismantling any kind of received wisdom. British biologist Richard Dawkins gave lecture tours to promote his book *The God Delusion*. Magicians Penn and Teller had just wrapped up their *Bullshit!* debunking television programme after seven years, and Youtube channels mocked everything from prayers to UFOs. Hitchens was the movement's grand priest, all over the media attacking faith and belief.

Feministing and other left-leaning sites insisted they could smell racism in white Westerners critiquing a religion big in the Middle East. Dawkins didn't help the cause with a social media outburst.

'Islam,' he tweeted, 'is the greatest force for evil in the world today.'

The fallout from Boobquake illustrated growing fault lines on the left, between those who argued Muslims were victimised people of colour and others who saw only misogynistic crypto-fascists. One well-known atheist with a lucrative career as a comedian turned television host knew exactly where he stood. Bill Maher was a sleek streak of late-night talk show with slicked-back hair and all the right opinions. He voted Democrat, supported animal rights and cannabis legalisation, and fitted in with the usual liberal suspects who made a living on HBO and ABC. Before 9/11 his antagonism towards the spiritual aimed itself at all belief systems. Al-Qaeda persuaded him Islam was uniquely dangerous. Barbara Olsen had been flying out to appear on his show *Politically Incorrect* when she died. He kept the chair empty for a week.

Maher had no time for anyone who claimed all religions contained extremist elements. He gave that view both shotgun barrels.

'What's facetious about that argument,' he said, 'is that the kooks and the terrorists in the Christian and the Jewish world are truly just a little fringe. And in the Muslim world they draw from a vast pool of support, which is not in any other religion. So don't try and feed me that line.'

His attacks on Islam continued over the next decade. Eventually *The Guardian* ran an article called 'A History of Bill Maher's "Not Bigoted" Remarks on Islam' that stirred up some trouble. Feminists opposed to Boobquake managed to drag Maher's name into it, finding his dislike of Islam almost as hard to accept as his revolving door of younger girlfriends.

'Liberal dudes are the majority of the people upholding the Boobquake as a good idea,' was one comment on the iblamethepatriarchy blog. 'You know, dudes who are for abortion so that they have more access to pussy without the consequence of children. Bill Maher, etc.'

Most Maher fans didn't want to know. Their hero hated Republicans and loved President Obama and that was all that mattered. Opposition to Islamophobia, a term gaining traction over recent years, was not yet something that defined liberals or leftists. It soon would. The arguments continued: atheism versus feminism, sexual freedom versus sexual exploitation, valid critiques versus racist caricatures. The real counter-jihad floating out in internet cyberspace watched leftists tear each other to pieces over a diluted version of its anti-Islamic ideas.

A month after Boobquake came Everybody Draw Mohammed Day. A popular cartoon had caused a scandal by testing Islam's tolerance for freedom of speech. Soft counter-jihadism was entering mainstream culture.

*

If you liked poorly animated children who swore a lot then *South Park* was the programme for you. Comedy Central's biggest money-maker was into its fourteenth season by April 2010 and still spewing satire. Targets so far included abortion, David Caruso's career, the War on Terror, global warming, gay dogs, scientology, Paris Hilton, kids in wheelchairs and anything else America held sacred. It had made creators Trey Parker and Matt Stone millionaires.

On 14 April 2010 *South Park* broadcast its 200th episode. Parker wrote a script in which all the celebrities who've been ridiculed by the programme threaten a lawsuit unless film star Tom Cruise gets to meet the Prophet Muhammad. Subplots involve ginger terrorists, concerned townsfolk and a pantheon of religious figures. Animators put the Prophet in a bear suit to parody network concerns about offending Muslims. They kept quiet about a previous season which included an image of Muhammad with turban, yellow robe and fiery hands.

About 2 per cent of the population tuned in, making *South Park* the most watched cable television programme that night. The Muhammad storyline continued into the next week, but a few days before the 201st episode hit screens everyone was talking about a post that had gone up on a website called Revolution Muslim.

'We have to warn Matt and Trey that what they are doing is stupid,' said the site, 'and they will probably wind up like Theo Van Gogh for airing this show.'

Then the site gave Parker and Stone's addresses. The police got involved over what seemed a clear death threat. Revolution Muslim's Zachary Adam Chesser was picked up heading for Somalia to join the jihadists of al-Shabaab; Jesse Curtis Morton aka Younes Abdullah Muhammad got arrested in New York. A failed May 2010 car bomb in Times Square was blamed on the group but turned out to be the work of a lone wolf Islamist from Pakistan. Investigators eventually decided Revolution Muslim wasn't much of a threat, with only ten members pushing an amateur homegrown variant of Islamic extremism under the leadership of two white converts, one born to a New York Jewish family. That didn't stop the network blurring out Muhammad and his bear suit when it showed the 201st episode.

A survey found 71 per cent of Americans disagreed with the censorship. *Doonesbury* creator Garry Trudeau was one of many cartoonists who signed a supportive letter:

> We, the undersigned, condemn the recent threats against the creators of South Park, Matt Stone and Trey Parker, by the extremist organization, Muslim Revolution. Freedom of expression is a universal right and we reject any group that seeks to silence people by violence or intimidation. In the United States we have a proud tradition of political satire and believe in the right to speak or draw freely without censorship.

The death threats and censorship enraged a lot of other cartoonists who saw themselves as fearless satirists. At the end of April, Seattle's Molly Norris posted a mock-poster online for an Everybody Draw Mohammed Day. She claimed the event had been sponsored by the 'Citizens Against Citizens Against Humor or CACAH (pronounced ca-ca)' and drew on the poster household items like a box of pasta and a coffee cup all claiming to be a true likeness of Muhammad.

The idea morphed from satire to reality. LGBT sex-advice columnist Dan Savage publicised it and someone set up a Facebook page that got 100,000 members. Norris dropped out when she received death threats, some from Anwar al-Awlaki, the Yemeni-American imam who had been in touch with the Revolution Muslim gang and Fort Hood shooter Nidal Malik Hasan. The FBI advised her to go into hiding. The event still went ahead and on 20 May 2010 hundreds of Prophet Muhammad images went up on the Facebook page. Judges chose a connect-the-dots picture as the winner.

Online Americans had made it clear they placed more value on freedom of speech than hurt religious feelings. A group down in Florida who stood for the flag and knelt for the cross decided to push things further. They wanted to barbecue some Qurans.

*

Pastor Terry Jones was a battered fifty-eight-year-old with handlebar moustache and a wispy cloud of white hair. He liked to patrol the 20 acres of his Dove World Outreach Center compound with a pistol strapped to his hip. Jones was one of those military macho types who'd never served in the army.

Jesus Christ entered his life in the late 1970s when Jones was working as a hotel manager. He got involved with Maranatha Campus Ministries, an evangelical church mostly concerned with persuading university students to stop drinking, dating and doing drugs. It attracted some disillusioned flower children and short-haired types who didn't like the way the world was going.

In the early 1980s Jones moved to Cologne, Germany, on missionary work and founded his own church. Locals grew increasingly unhappy as what started as a hard-line slice of Christianity mutated into bullying and brainwashing run by a man whose Biblical scholar credentials weren't as rigorous as some might have liked. In 2008 the congregation rebelled and forced Jones out. He relocated to Gainesville, Florida and joined the Dove World Outreach Center, an evangelical church with a large compound, fifty members, a dislike of homosexuality and strong views on Islam.

Jones fitted right in and soon ran the place. In early 2010 he published *Islam is of the Devil: Know the Spiritual Truths That Will Bring the Christian Church Back to Its God-given Position.* An uncompromising comparison of Christianity and Islam, it dismissed Muslims as heretical unbelievers revving up for a war with the West. Jones claimed that the Quran was authored by humans and not God, that Muhammad had never existed, and that Islamic law was a totalitarian ideology similar to communism and national socialism. His counter-jihadism had no connection with the ACT! for America crowd or the smooth, well-funded evangelicals holding meetings in Washington state. Jones had a tougher type of God as his co-pilot.

The Dove Center took its message to the world. A large sign saying 'Islam is of the Devil' was parked on the Center's front lawn. Jones printed up t-shirts with the book's title and organised protests when a local school sent two students home for wearing them. The spring of 2010 saw Boobquake and Everybody Draw Mohammed Day. Pastor Jones decided to divert some attention his way and took to social media with an announcement that he would burn a few Qurans on 11 September. No one paid much attention until the story was picked up by a news agency. The 8,663 fans of the International Burn a

Quran Day page on Facebook found themselves swamped by a wave of international outrage.

President Obama asked Jones not to go through with the Quran burning, as did the governments of Canada, France, Germany and most of the Muslim world. The army claimed its soldiers could be put at risk in Iraq and Afghanistan.

'It is precisely the kind of action the Taliban uses and could cause significant problems,' said General David Petraeus. 'Not just here, but everywhere in the world we are engaged with the Islamic community.'

The pastor had a poster of the Mel Gibson film *Braveheart* on his office wall. He was not the type to back down even after death threats, attacks on his property, his insurance being cancelled and a mortgage called in for immediate repayment. The press reported Jones intended to go through with the book burning, and riots broke out in Afghanistan, Pakistan, Indonesia, Gaza, Somalia, Iran and among Muslims in India. News reports claimed anywhere from twenty to ninety dead.

International Burn a Quran Day came and went without any barbecue. Jones had changed his mind. Cuban dictator Fidel Castro apparently believed the FBI had threatened the pastor into silence but the real story seemed to be that Jones had got involved in a Pamela Geller campaign against a planned Islamic centre near the World Trade Center footprint and convinced himself negotiations would go more smoothly if he put down the firelighters.

A few Pastor Jones fans went rogue on 11 September and burned their own Qurans. Someone in Knoxville, Tennessee stuffed the holy book with bacon before setting it on fire. Other charred copies turned up in the driveways of Islamic centres across the country. The media kept quiet to prevent more riots. Towards the end of December 2010 a British organisation invited Pastor Jones to fly over and speak at a rally in Luton. A new wave of counter-jihadism had appeared across the Atlantic that liked flag waving, confrontation and going toe-to-toe with Muslims. The English Defence League was on the march and looking to make friends with anyone who shared its opposition to Islam.

The government in London started working up excuses to stop Jones entering the country. It was saved the trouble when the EDL disinvited him after learning Jones' acerbic views on homosexuality and anyone non-white.

They got a right-wing surfing rabbi instead.

13

SURFING WITH THE CASUALS IN LUTON

Taking the Message to the Streets, 2010

Most mornings he drove a station wagon down the Pacific Coast Highway to catch the waves at Malibu's Surfrider Beach. Everyone knew him – no one else rolled up in a dark suit and fedora. He would stab his longboard into the sand and murmur prayers over the Torah in the shade cast by a lifeguard station. Then the suit got swapped for a wetsuit and Norman Shifren was out there striding into the sea with his hair cropped and a grey beard frothing over his chest.

'God didn't all of a sudden abandon you when you left the synagogue or the church,' he said to a reporter. 'He's with you wherever you go and this body of water that we see out here reminds us of him and allows to reflect on just the awesome might of his creation.'

Shifren was born to a well-off Jewish family in 1951 and spent his youth bouncing around California and Hawaii. The Beach Boys were on the radio and the ocean was always close. Shifren surfed, avoided school and work, and went full beach bum. By his early twenties he'd become a Malibu lifeguard, living the dream. Conflict in the Middle East burst his solipsistic bubble.

The 1973 Yom Kippur War saw a coalition of Arab states attack Israel. Shifren felt a primal call of the blood and quit surfing to head for Tel Aviv. The Jewish state didn't have much use for a lanky surfer dude and put him to work on a kibbutz picking fruit. Shifren got bored and came home but found nothing to live for in California's endless summer. He got a degree in Spanish and returned to join the Israel Defense Forces as a physical fitness instructor. He brought his longboard with him.

Two failed marriages and some vagabond travelling opened the door to the spiritual life. Shifren created the *Surf and Soul* newsletter to spread the word about Judaism and hanging ten. In 1990 he became a rabbi, as orthodox as they came.

'Surfing and religion are transformative,' he said. 'Both require a lot of discipline. I trained for hours riding the big waves, I was a long-distance paddler, and I was a lifeguard. It rolled right over into the world of Torah.'

By the next year he was back in California teaching kids in some of the state's toughest schools. He called himself Nachum Shifren, married again and had four kids, and drove to the beach in a station wagon with a 'Forgive Me Father for I Have Surfed' decal in the back window. Colleagues knew him as hard-working, devout and apolitical. He didn't tell them about time spent driving for far-right extremist Meir Kahane or getting thrown out of a rabbinical convention for heckling guest speaker Jesse Jackson. 'My politics are not germane to what I'm doing,' he told journalists who tried to dig deeper. 'All I'm about is surfing.'

He took Orthodox youth groups out to the beach. The girls wore modest wetsuits and everyone gathered round a bonfire in the evening for kosher food and Kabbalah. Shifren became a respected local figure and in 2010 someone persuaded him to run for a Senate seat in West Los Angeles. The election brought his politics out into the open. Shifren was a counter-jihadist.

'The Muslim onslaught is at the gates,' he said. 'They are weary of our self-indulgence and they abhor our eroding social mores and valueless culture. They are sharpening the long knives, knowing that their time will come shortly.'

Shifren opposed gay marriage, allied himself with the Republican hard-right and praised the Tea Party, a populist grassroots movement campaigning for lower taxes and the repatriation of illegal migrants. He claimed to be the only candidate who'd pledged opposition to sharia law. His polling numbers stayed low and even the local Jewish community seemed embarrassed by his stand against Islam.

The rabbi took time out from election campaigning to look for others prepared to stand up to Muslims. An internet search turned up a group called the English Defence League protesting the pro-Palestinian policies of a library in Luton, England. An email exchange with a woman called Roberta Moore revealed the League was organising a Jewish wing. Shifren invited himself over.

In October 2010 he was in London addressing a gathering of patriotic football hooligans who hated Islam. My enemy's enemy is my friend.

*

When you're working class you've got your mates, the pub, clubbing at the weekend, a job if you're lucky, the football, the hairdressers, the shopping centre, that place with the cage fighting night on Wednesdays, two weeks somewhere sunny, some debt, some weed, some kids who get in trouble at school, some pills and powders when you're doing it large.

You try to make money to move on up but it doesn't happen. You were born around here, grew up around here, and you couldn't leave even if you wanted to.

That's why the local football team is important and it's okay to smash the fuck out of anyone who supports another one; why you fly the St George's cross and know patriotism will always mean more than having money in the bank; and why it wasn't a good idea for a Muslim group from Luton to demonstrate on 10 March 2009 against British troops just back from Iraq.

The police tried to argue them out of it. The demonstrators wouldn't listen. Islam4UK was a relaunch of al-Muhajiroun, a banned Islamist group which had hidden under the names Saviour Sect and al-Ghurabaa for the last few years. Supporters had protested outside the Danish embassy a few years back. Now they wanted to have a go at troops parading through Luton town centre.

The streets were lined three or four deep with locals cheering the boys home. Police cleared a square of pavement for a dozen protesters to wave placards saying 'Anglian Soldiers Go to Hell' and 'Butchers of Basra'. It did not go over well. Scuffles kicked off and threats got screamed. Police struggled to keep the two sides apart. Someone got on the roof of a building and dropped strips of bacon on Islam4UK. A chant of 'Bin Laden's Mother is a Whore' went up, started by a man with a face like a belligerent potato and a sunbed business doing nicely in the suburbs. Stephen Lennon loved his wife and kids, making money, and Luton Town FC.

The man who'd end up as Britain's most notorious counter-jihadist was born in 1982 as Stephen Christopher Yaxley. Divorce and his mother's remarriage changed his surname. The teenage Lennon was smart enough to get eleven GCSEs at school and an engineering apprenticeship at Luton airport. He was set for a decent life at the tougher end of the class system.

His road to early adulthood was fairly typical for a white boy from Luton. Family always around; Sikh and Bosnian best friends growing up; bombing through the estate on a motorbike; first confrontations with Muslim gangs in Bury Park when Lennon and his mates went to Kenilworth Road for Luton FC; girlfriends and school and a few fights; members of the family involved with Luton football hooligans the MiGs (Men in Gear) and drifting into that world; seeing local Pakistani gangsters in flash cars; getting mugged by a Muslim gang who called him a white pig; the adrenaline of a football riot then regretting any involvement when the police started kicking doors in; vowing to stay out of trouble; settling down to mortgage and marriage and playing it safe.

He lost everything after a fight with an off-duty policeman during a domestic dispute. Lennon served twelve months and got banned from working at any British airport. He left prison angry and re-joined the hooligan scene, organising transport and meet-ups on a path that everyone could see was heading straight back to prison. A mate threw him a lifeline with a job in the plumbing business. Lennon discovered a talent for making money and put the plumbing profits into a tanning salon with English and Polish signs in the window. Polish girls liked a good tan. The money came rolling in.

Lennon went to March's army parade with his mum's cousin Kevin Carroll, a towering ginger fortysomething carpenter with the neck of a bull. Carroll tried to provide some adult supervision to his almost-nephew but had a mild form of OCD that made it a miracle they ever got anywhere on time. 'If you go pick Kev up from his house,' said Lennon, 'he'll walk out the door, then walk back in again to check something or other, then back out, then back in.'

The pair came to cheer the boys in green and instead saw Islamists abusing British soldiers on the streets of their home town. Lennon and Carroll started up some chants and taunted the protesters until police escorted the Islam4UK group away. The next day Lennon and Carroll found out the organiser's home address and decked it out in British bunting and English flags. The man's car got set alight later. Lennon denied any involvement.

Muslims had only been in Britain in significant numbers since the Second World War, with a jump in the 1960s when the government welcomed workers from its former colony of Pakistan. By 2001 there were 1.6 million Muslims in the country, making up 3 per cent of the population. Eight years later the number was nearly 5 per cent at 2.7 million. Many settled in Luton. Muslims made up about 24 per cent of the town, and whites 54 per cent. Tensions had been high for a while. Back in 2002 al-Muhajiroun put up 'Magnificent Nineteen' posters round Luton glorifying the 9/11 hijackers. MiGs and local Muslims had a few fights over that.

Lennon knew which side he was on. Even before prison he'd produced a leaflet claiming local Muslim men groomed underage white girls and got a few mates to burn a home-made Islamist flag in the town centre. An early attempt to get different hooligan firms to link up and oppose Muslims got shut down by the police. The Islam4UK stunt at the parade relit the flame.

The local council had planned a St George's Day march later that month but cancelled it on police advice. Lennon and Carroll organised an unofficial replacement event protesting radical Islam. They got together some fellow Luton FC casuals who knew how to take care of themselves and a local counter-jihad blogger called Paul Ray, who shared their views and had some useful contacts in America. The marchers called themselves the United People of Luton (UPL). The rally got shut down by police kettling that kept everyone penned up for hours and forced female supporters to urinate in the road. Lennon and Carroll refused to give in and planned more events.

The police diagnosed the UPL as a cause of local tensions, not a symptom. Supporters started getting hauled down the station at 2 a.m. for questioning. Lennon stayed in the shadows and let a series of impromptu frontmen take the spotlight. A nineteen-year-old lad gave a few well-received speeches until his mum found out and grounded him. Black and Sikh activists with their own anger at Islam turned up and spoke at rallies. No one lasted long. Lennon was forced to take a more public role, and the UPL discovered it had a charismatic leader who said what they all thought.

He used a few different pseudonyms in the early days ('Wayne Kerr' got a laugh when journalists quoted him in the newspapers) but Tommy Robinson was the one that stuck. The original Robinson was a fake name used by a Luton hooligan for his 2006 beer and violence memoir *MIG Down*. Lennon got a passing mention as one of the new generation of hooligans. Not happy about appearing in the book, the UPL leader borrowed the author's name for a few rallies. It stuck.

The marches got bigger. Cardiff City fanatic Jeff Marsh brought along his Casuals United crowd of hooligans recruited from across the country. Birmingham-based British Citizens against Muslim Extremists got involved. A UPL march down in London forged links with the capital's football firms. Men who usually spent their Saturday afternoons biting off each other's ears near stadiums found they had a common enemy in Islam. A lot of shaven-headed figures with patriotic t-shirts and Stone Island jackets began converging on Luton for a few pints and some flag waving.

There were Facebook pages and Twitter accounts and videos on Youtube. Soon the UPL was attracting news coverage of the worried middle-class persuasion. Opinions tolerated from Melanie Phillips or Oriana Fallaci looked a lot more disturbing coming out the mouths of working-class men on street corners.

'Chaotic alliance stirs up trouble on streets,' said a *Guardian* headline.

By August, the group had gone nationwide. The English Defence League was born.

*

Two narratives exist about the EDL's birth. One involves a conspiratorial meeting in a Barbican flat where rich counter-jihadists moulded Lemon and Carroll into the puppet leaders of a street army. The other is the story of Luton lads defying the establishment and taking orders from no one. Either could be true.

The conspiracy version centres on a millionaire IT consultant called Alan Ayling, a well-preserved fiftysomething evangelical Christian who managed Oracle databases for the European Bank for Reconstruction and Development. He used the name Alan Lake for his counter-jihad adventures and knew the value of keeping things hidden.

'You've got to have pseudonyms,' Ayling told a meeting of the far-right Sverigedemokraterna (Swedish Democrats). 'You've got to have, you know, five email addresses, one for your friends, one for your counterjihad, one for your really extreme counterjihad comments, and all the rest of it.'

Ayling had spent the last few years searching for a cause to give his life meaning. He campaigned to free Tibet from Chinese occupation but lost interest and moved on to religion at Notting Hill's evangelical Kensington Temple. Christianity changed his life, but it wasn't until he met some African refugees that his moral compass found its true north. Long conversations with them about Islamic persecution and burning villages turned Ayling from a middle-aged man searching for meaning into a counter-jihad crusader on a Manichean battlefield. Good versus evil, right versus wrong. Christianity versus Islam.

The IT millionaire was no elitist. He saw the counter-jihad as a mass movement spreading its message on the streets, with some discreet guidance from people like himself. He connected with March for England, a small anti-Islamic group run by football fans out of Portsmouth. It organised events in southern England and turned up at a 2008 Stop Islamisation of Europe rally near Lambeth Palace. The relationship was short-lived. March for England was lucky to get a hundred people for a demonstration. Ayling had bigger plans. He found the cadre for his own mass movement when a contact told him about the United People of Luton. Ayling invited the top men to his Barbican flat to talk tactics.

Ayling introduced Lennon, Carroll and Ray to a group of shadowy counter-jihadists that included wealthy property investor and Brussels Counterjihad Conference attendee Ann Marchini, a man from Bristol known as Wurzel, and goateed, chubby-faced Christopher Knowles. In this narrative Ayling creates and funds the English Defence League as his own private army, with Stephen Lennon as frontman.

The Luton narrative is very different. It agrees the Barbican meeting took place but downplays the significance. In this version the English Defence League is already up and running when Lennon and Carroll get Ayling's invitation. The decision had been made months earlier to turn the UPL into a nationwide organisation under a fresh name; it boosted numbers by absorbing Casuals United, British Citizens against Muslim Extremists, and groups of politicised football supporters round the country. The new organisation retained a working-class leadership who liked a few beers and did whatever they wanted. Lennon didn't take orders from anyone but felt curious enough to meet Ayling and friends.

'Early on,' he said, 'we were called to a meeting of what I can only call London intelligentsia by Alan Lake, a very bright chap who was supportive of us.'

The meeting was too intellectual for Lennon and Carroll. They didn't understand the high-level conversation and never went back; Ayling never offered any money. The only thing that made an impact was meeting Colin Dye, a well-connected evangelical who claimed to have heard the queen asking a leading Baptist how long her country had left before Islam took over.

'No more than sixty years, ma'am,' was the reply.

Lennon's version of the English Defence League creation myth didn't explain why Ayling would turn up at marches calling himself 'events director' and tell a Norwegian journalist he'd bankrolled the organisation in its early days. Ayling's version didn't explain the underfunded disorganisation of the EDL. Most of the football casuals marching through Luton didn't care which narrative was true. Whoever was in charge, the English Defence League had ambitious plans for spreading the counter-jihad message that involved linking up with important Americans. The Pastor Jones visit fell through, but a Californian rabbi was interested in visiting.

The transatlantic relationship was back on. Not everyone in the League was happy about it.

14

CANNIBAL DOGS AND CONQUERING SIGNS

The English Defence League on the March, 2010–2011

The Israeli embassy was a coffee-coloured building in a leafy part of South Kensington with a Star of David flag over the front door. Security was tight. Twenty years back Palestinian terrorists exploded a car bomb that blew the frontage off the embassy and injured twenty people. Since then guards had kept an eye on anyone suspicious strolling through the area. On 25 October 2010 they were working overtime when the Surfing Rabbi and 300 members of the English Defence League gathered outside.

Nachum Shifren stood on a makeshift platform with a megaphone, surrounded by men with short hair and crusader cross t-shirts. English Defence League and Israeli flags fluttered behind him. Left-wing protesters on the fringes screamed abuse. An EDL girl waving a Star of David got called a Nazi as police struggled to keep the two sides apart. Shifren ignored all the noise. He had strong opinions about the chances of peace with Islam and wanted the League to hear them.

'I'm still waiting for Arabs and Muslims to have peace with each other,' he said. 'Sunni versus Shia. The al-Qaeda versus the Hamas. Hamas versus Al-Fatah. Like the dogs that they are, they eat each other alive.'

The Shifren connection had begun earlier in the year when Luton town council joined an international campaign to boycott Israeli goods and support the Palestinians. This annoyed English Defence League boss Stephen Lennon enough to start his own counter-campaign against the council. He made headlines and attracted the attention of a counter-jihadist rabbi over in California doing a Google search. Shifren flew in to join an EDL protest in Luton, refused to take a car on the Sabbath, and walked the whole way into town surrounded by football casuals and confused police officers.

The protest went well enough that Shifren stuck around for another rally outside the Israeli embassy down in London. Police banned Lennon from attending but he slipped in dressed as a rabbi with the League's newly created Jewish division, a group headed by petite Brazilian-born Roberta Moore. A Rio de Janiero native in her late thirties, Moore had no time for anyone who thought the League was using her to appear more diverse. 'They think the League is exploiting us,' she told a reporter from *Haaretz*, 'while it is really we who initiated the Jewish division. If anything, we are exploiting them.'

She claimed the division had 100 members. Moore was often seen in a Jewish Defense League t-shirt (black fist on yellow star), an extremist far-right New York City group founded by Rabbi Shifren's friend Meir Kahane that had some terror attacks in its past. She was an enthusiast for community self-defence but didn't like the Jewish Division being labelled violent.

'Our members are not hooligans,' said Moore. 'We are educated people with jobs. If we defend ourselves is that hooliganism? The Jewish community sit in their houses and do nothing. They will enjoy the benefits of our action.'

The Jewish division was not the only bit of diversity in the English Defence League. Mixed-race Joel Titus ran the youth division until some trouble at the football earned him a court order. Guramit Singh headed up the Sikh division; a Hindu division also existed. The LGBT mob waved rainbow flags on marches. Critics wondered at the sincerity of it all and pinned Alan Ayling as the man behind the multicultural outreach. The millionaire's attitude toward the League's core membership of football casuals was ambivalent:

> Working with our street people, from the working class, can be very frustrating but also very satisfying. These are individuals who care about the freedom of the British people: ninety-nine percent of the intellectuals are a total waste of space. These workers don't know how to run a meeting or debate persuasively, but they are people who are doing something, people I respect. If there is anyone who will save this country, it is the ordinary soldiers from the working class.

Ayling's ordinary soldiers had the Knights Templar cross as their emblem and used the slogan '*In hoc signo vinces*' (Under this sign you will conquer), words seen written in the sky by Constantine I, the first Christian emperor of Rome. Medieval imagery seemed appropriate for a crusade.

The English Defence League had been going for over a year by the time of the Israeli embassy rally. The first demonstration under its new name had taken place on 8 August 2009 in Birmingham. Over 900 people turned up. A left-wing group called Unite against Fascism held a counter-demonstration with local Muslims. There were chants, harassed-looking police officers trying to hold the line, English flags, men in t-shirts with scarves wrapped around their faces. Someone threw a bottle and it all kicked off.

'It was chaos,' said a woman caught up in the violence. 'I had only come up to do a bit of shopping, and found myself in the middle of a full-blown riot. People with small children were running into shops for cover. The whole city centre just descended into some kind of war zone.'

Another demonstration in Birmingham the next month saw ninety arrests, with thirty in Manchester that October. League marches were human rivers of St George's flags, crusader crosses, placards with angry words about sharia law and rape, Israeli flags, rainbow flags, pints of beer and drunken songs: 'Give me bullets for my gun/and I will shoot the Muzzie scum/No surrender to the Taliban.'

The League established Welsh, Scottish and Ulster branches. European activists organised their own versions, as did supporters in America and Australia. The Norwegian Defence League made the biggest impact with its marches and demonstrations; an early member was a quietly fanatical man called Sigurd Jorsalfar whose views worried the leadership. Other leagues did little more than post memes on Facebook. A balding fiftysomething who called himself Steve Simmons, but whose real name was Chris Redmond, formed the European Freedom Initiative to co-ordinate all Defence Leagues across the continent.

Other foreigners showed an interest in Lennon's group. Muammar Gaddafi's Libya offered £5 million in funding as long as it got a say in the League's direction. Lennon turned it down: 'It felt like treason.' He wouldn't have known what to do with the money anyway. There was no master plan.

'You have to understand that this was an ad hoc street movement in the purest sense of the word,' Lennon said. 'We posted dates of demos and protests on Facebook. We acted on a whim – my whim usually – in response to being offended at some piece of political correctness or other [...] People wanted to protest against another mega mosque, others saw their young people being attacked or poisoned with drugs. We went to help them complain about it.'

League ideology lacked the Eurabia theorising of Bat Ye'or, the demographic apocalypse of Mark Steyn, the Manichean religious war of ACT! for America. Members had street-level concerns. They worried about Muslim gangs, intercommunal violence, heroin dealing, unwillingness to integrate, and the breaking scandal over Rotherham's Labour council looking the other way while Pakistani men groomed white children for sex. The media showed little enthusiasm for these kinds of stories, so the League took to the streets with flags and megaphones, convinced that all publicity was good for their cause.

At the Israeli embassy demonstration in October, Shifren gave his speech and got applause and chants. Lennon jumped on the platform, whipped off his rabbi disguise, then made a run for it as police ploughed through the crowd after him. He shook them off by going through a nearby Indian restaurant and out the back door. Afterwards there were scuffles at Speaker's Corner in Hyde Park and a police escort to the train station.

Shifren emailed Pamela Geller when it was all over. He was clearly impressed.

'When I was introduced at the demo,' he wrote, 'I got a minute-long standing ovation, with shouts of: "Rabbi, Rabbi, Rabbi." Never in my life have I been appreciated so much. The love was overflowing, they were so grateful for me thinking of them and supporting them. Of course, it was I that was grateful. Today was a shot heard round the world!'

The English Defence League went into 2011 with flags flying high. It all went wrong in seven months.

*

The year started well. A rally in Luton on 5 February saw 3,000 march along St George's Mall past barriers, boarded-up shops and riot police. The previous evening Prime Minister David Cameron had made a speech in Germany that blamed Islamic extremism in Britain on the failure of multiculturalism. Cameron was no fan of the English Defence League ('terrible people, we would always keep these groups under review and if we needed to ban them, we would ban them') but his words seemed to show that counter-jihad talking points had penetrated the mainstream.

The next day saw League members collecting in pubs round Luton. Pints were downed, a few lines snorted in the toilets, and then they were moving off with their St George's flags, placards ('We Demand a Vote on the Building of Mosques in Britain'; 'Sharia Law Oppresses Women'), chants of 'No Surrender' and 'E-E-EDL', and lots of ski masks and scarves to hide identities. Members with hi-vis jackets stewarded the spaces between marchers and watching police.

Stephen Lennon, Kevin Carroll and representatives of Defence Leagues from across Europe gave speeches from a stage in St George's Square. The sound system was poor, the wind strong, a helicopter hovering overhead too loud. Few heard much and those further away preferred to chant and sing. Eventually everyone drifted away to catch coaches and trains or go for a beer and a chat about Islam.

'They can't live like us cos they are not evolved for it,' said one drunk on a barstool. 'They are simple, made for backward villages in the mountain where they can sit around eating stinking curries and raping chickens. They come over here and ruin England, I mean, would you want to live next to them? I don't, but they are taking over. That is why I want them gone.'

The next day the march was all over the newspapers. New members flooded in. Roberta Moore reached out to foreign friends and persuaded the Jewish Defense League of Canada, an over-the-border cousin of Rabbi Meir Kahane's group, to hold a demonstration to support Lennon's group. The Canadians had links with the counter-jihad. They'd been behind a solidarity rally for Geert Wilders the previous year.

The Dutch politician had been making a name for himself in the counter-jihad world with a film about Islam. *Fitna* was seventeen minutes of Quran quotes juxtaposed with media clips of Islamic terror. It borrowed elements from the Clarion Fund's *Obsession: Radical Islam's War Against the West*. Wilders had been touring it round private showings since 2008, with Paul Beliën of *The Brussels Journal* at his side as a newly employed advisor. The film was controversial enough for Wilders to be refused entry to the UK, although the United States Senate proved more welcoming. In Italy, the film got Wilders the Oriana Fallaci Free Speech award from the Associazione Una Via per Oriana. When he took a bathroom break during the ceremony in Rome thirty-five policemen guarded the door.

The English Defence League hadn't got any awards yet but the marches and rallies had confirmed it as a power player in the counter-jihad. It didn't have long to enjoy the prestige. Things blew up in the summer when Roberta Moore quit. Lots of rumours flew around about her defection, including gossip about links with some very dodgy people in New York. Moore had a simpler explanation.

'I sincerely hope that the leaders will get the strength to squash the Nazis within,' she said. 'They will destroy this movement if allowed to remain.'

She joined the British branch of the Jewish Defense League. The accusations of anti-Semitism panicked Pamela Geller into disavowing Lennon's group. It didn't surprise Melanie Phillips, who had condemned the English Defence League as far-right from the start. Gates of Vienna stayed loyal but even Rabbi Shifren lost some of his enthusiasm. The League denied everything, but it was a weakened position after some recent revelations about Lennon's past.

An anonymous video had gone up on YouTube exposing Tommy Robinson's real identity. Lennon's car got firebombed; his next-door neighbour's house got the same treatment when arsonists misread the address. No one took responsibility for the YouTube leak but rumours blamed a plot aimed at forcing Lennon to hand over the League to rivals.

Suspicion fell on Paul Ray, who'd left the group in the summer of 2009, taking his connections to the Gates of Vienna and the 910 Group with him. Threats from Luton Muslims had rattled him enough to head off for a long holiday to the sunny rock of Malta, where gossip claimed he made friends with some far-right types who cooked up a blackmail scheme to get their hands on the English Defence League. Lennon never publicly accused him of anything, but he made his feelings clear.

'Paul Ray is a nutter,' he said. 'A 100 per cent bona fide, right-wing fruitcake from Dunstable.' Lennon refused to give up control of the League and was doxed. Journalists armed with his real name quickly discovered he was a former member of the far-right British National Party.

The BNP had been around since 1982 as a neo-Nazi group but officially dropped its anti-Semitism after 9/11 to focus its rage on Islam. Supporters claimed the change was a genuine response to a bigger threat; opponents saw a cosmetic modification to make the BNP more electable. Mainstream opinion leant towards the latter option. A 2004 poll found seven out of ten respondents would never consider voting for the party. Five years and several terror attacks later, things had changed. The BNP was on the rise, gobbling up local council seats in racially tense areas. In October 2009 party leader Nick Griffin appeared on the BBC political show *Question Time* after the BNP won two seats in the European elections and fifty-five seats in local councils.

The party's time in the sun was short-lived. By the time the English Defence League established itself, Griffin's group was going through splits and dissent after failing to capitalise on its earlier success, the start of a slide into lost votes and obscurity. Many supporters transferred their loyalty to the United Kingdom Independence Party, whose leader Nigel Farage had expanded from anti-European Union activism into opposing mass immigration, Islamic fundamentalism and the wearing of burqas in public. The respectable image of UKIP attracted more voters than the BNP could ever manage. Farage's party got 2.5 million votes in the 2009 European Parliament elections, the first stage of a rocket-fuelled rise to major-party status. The BNP lost any hope of breaking through to the mainstream and remained toxic in the popular imagination.

Moore's accusations of anti-Semitism on top of revelations about Lennon's past proved disastrous for the English Defence League's image. Lennon claimed his membership only lasted long enough to discover party activists didn't like his black friends. Not everyone believed him. The League boss tried to demonstrate some anti-racist credentials by expelling far-right types and shutting down the edgy Welsh Defence League, which predated the parent body and had been born as an internet group under Casuals United boss Jeff Marsh, whose politics were on the white side of nationalist. Marsh didn't share the leadership's view of the League as a multicultural movement. He refused to support the Surfing Rabbi and watched Shifren's speech from the other side of the road among some left-wing protesters.

'The EDL had invited some crazy Rabbi over from America and were having a demo in London with him speaking,' said Marsh. 'A lot of people kicked off over the Jewish thing again and said they were fed up of Tommy constantly promoting it.'

Marsh remained loyal enough to accept the closing down of the Welsh Defence League and the expulsion of the hard-line military veterans who made up a League group called the Combined Ex-Forces. He stayed out of a conflict between Lennon and the Infidels, a group of supporters from the north who leaned far to the right. Infidel leader John Shaw had a conviction for animal cruelty after an unsuccessful go at llama farming and kept recommending all 'true British patriots' read the anti-Semitic *Protocols of the Elders of Zion*. Lennon kicked them out after a fistfight over either politics or money, depending on who was telling the story.

Marsh's loyalty was all the more surprising as Lennon had never liked him. The low point in their relationship had been a Cardiff demo organised by the Welshman where local hooligans decided they preferred battering the English contingent to demonstrating about Islam.

'Marshy, as it quickly became clear, was a complete and utter arsewipe,' said Lennon. 'Even his own so-called friends couldn't stand him.'

Despite all the grumbling and internal dissent, the BNP revelations, and the accusations of extremism, the League remained battered but alive. Lennon's housecleaning persuaded Pamela Geller to come back on board, and made it easier for the Gates of Vienna to justify its support. Critics refused to believe the English Defence League was any less far-right; fans that it had ever been far-right in the first place.

The League's main Facebook page still had 100,000 members by the middle of July 2011 and had seen a lot of celebrating down the pub when Osama bin Laden got shot dead by an American Navy SEAL team. The League got another boost when a survey found that 58 per cent of non-Muslims in America, Russia and Western Europe thought Muslims fanatical, while 53 per cent of Muslims returned the favour. Fifty per cent thought Muslims violent and 66 per cent of Muslims felt the same way about non-Muslims. Not all opinions were negative (41 per cent of Americans, Russians and Western Europeans told pollsters Muslims were generous) but it was a long way from the months after 9/11 when everyone blamed Osama bin Laden and not his religion.

Then a Norwegian started his own private war and the English Defence League, along with everyone else in the movement, got accused of inspiring a mass murderer. Anders Breivik was a vain mummy's boy with a rich fantasy life and an internet connection. After his business ventures collapsed, he retreated to his mother's Oslo flat and shut the door on the world. At first he focussed his obsessions on online game *World of Warcraft*. Then he found the counter-jihad.

15

THE GREATEST MONSTER IN OSLO

Anders Breivik's One-man War, 2011

The white Volkswagen transit van parked outside was making Annelise Holter nervous. The fifty-one-year-old secretary worked reception at an eighteen-storey office building known as H Block that housed the Prime Minister's Office, the Law Courts and the rest of the Norwegian government's beating heart. Oslo was a relaxed, low-crime city, but Holter decided not to take any chances.

She rang security and asked them to take a look, explaining the van had been there for twelve minutes. They promised to send someone. The phone was barely back in its cradle when a timer in the back of the van reached its detonation point and exploded a homemade 950-kilogram fertiliser bomb in a roar of white light and flame. The blast smashed every window in the government district and could be heard 7 kilometres away.

Shrapnel and glass killed Holter at her desk. Seven other people died in the explosion. It was 3.25 on the afternoon of 22 July 2011.

Police and ambulances scrambled to the scene. In the blizzard of phone calls and panic someone rang the police line to report having seen a man in a police uniform climb out of the transit van and get into an unmarked civilian car nearby. The witness had the licence plate number. Someone noted the call and left the note on a desk at the police operations centre. It was forgotten in the chaos.

An hour and a half after the bombing, a policeman called Martin Nilsen boarded the MS *Thorbjørn*, a rusty black-and-red former military landing craft converted into a ferry. The *Thorbjørn* belonged to the Arbeidernes Ungdomsfylking (Workers' Youth League – AUF), the youth wing of Norway's Arbeiderpartiet (Workers' Party), and was used to transport guests over to the annual summer camp on the party's privately owned island of Utøya.

The Arbeiderpartiet had been around since the late nineteenth century. After a brief flirtation with Marxism in the 1920s it flipped over into the mainstream and had managed to keep its hands on the levers of power ever since. Critics liked to call it socialist but whatever radicalism the Arbeiderpartiet once possessed had been rinsed out by the realities of government and replaced by a more mainstream social democrat approach. In 2011 it was the biggest party in Norway and ruled the country as part of a coalition.

Like most youth movements, the AUF was more radical than its parent body. Members liked to lecture their elders about Marxism, open borders and a new multicultural Norway that would sweep away the reactionary past. Arbeiderpartiet politicians smiled tolerantly. The party hierarchy saw the AUF as an incubator for the next generation and had created the summer camp on Utøya to get a closer look at promising young activists. The day before the bombing, Foreign Minister Jonas Gahr Støre sat on the grass, casually dressed in trainers, and tried to persuade AUF members it would be counter-effective to boycott Israel. Everyone agreed to disagree. Støre was a big enough supporter of immigration and multiculturalism that he could be forgiven for his views on the Palestinians. He had supported AUF measures to recruit among ethnic minorities, a plan that had borne fruit with the current generation on Utøya, which contained a number of Kurds, Chechens and other immigrants among the nearly 600 teenagers and adults. The AUF banned pork and alcohol on the island to make them feel at home, and segregated the previously unisex shower and toilet arrangements.

Police officer Nilsen took the ferry across with forty-five-year-old camp leader Monica Bøsei, who was on board to supervise anyone leaving or arriving at the island. Nilsen was carrying several bags and explained he had to make a routine check on the camp after the Oslo bombing.

The pair disembarked at Utøya and Nilsen retold his story to island security officer Trond Berntsen, a fifty-one-year-old off-duty policeman and stepbrother of Crown Princess Mette-Marit. Berntsen's ten-year-old son was among the campers. Nilsen wanted everyone to assemble in the centre of the island for a briefing and the trio walked towards an office building to arrange everything. It was 5.22 p.m.

As they walked, Nilsen drew his pistol and shot dead Bøsei and Berntsen. He walked further into the island, put down his bags, and ordered campers in a nearby cafe to approach him. As they did he pulled a semi-automatic rifle with a laser sight from the bag and started shooting.

For the next hour Nilsen stalked the island killing campers. They ran, hid, swam to escape. Those who played dead were shot in the head anyway. Some were so paralyzed with terror they stood still as he approached, not even running when he ran out of ammunition. He persuaded a group on the island's western coast that he had arrived to evacuate them by boat then killed them as they approached. He used a telescopic sight to pick off others as they climbed down a cliff. Nilsen was silent for most of the rampage but a girl who survived the killing of her friends heard him speak as he aimed the rifle.

'You are going to die today, Marxists.'

The police were delayed by bad logistics and frightened campers who sailed the ferry to an isolated spot and refused to move. When officers reached the island at 6.25 p.m. Nilsen had already called the police emergency number twice to surrender. When no police appeared he continued killing.

Sixty-nine people died, all shot except two who died trying to get away. Thirty-six of the dead were adults from eighteen to fifty-one years old; thirty-three were younger. The youngest was fourteen years old.

Nilsen dropped the rifle when the police arrived. They searched his bags and found fake identification papers, a Ruger Mini 14 .233 semi-automatic rifle, a Glock 9mm automatic pistol and a Benelli Nova shotgun. Nilsen was wearing a custom-made pendant with the cross of medieval crusader order the Knights Templar in red enamel around his neck.

His real name was Anders Behring Breivik.

*

Breivik came from a long line of desperation and coldness. His mother had grown up in a dysfunctional household: dead father, bullying half-brother, lunatic mother who blamed her partial paralysis on her daughter and dragged herself around the house on two stools, clumping on the wooden floor. Breivik's mother became a nurse, had a daughter from a brief affair with a Swede, then hooked up with an emotionally repressed Norwegian diplomat who could barely bring himself to acknowledge his existing three children and didn't seem to care when Anders was born a year into the marriage.

The family spent some time in London, with expensive flats, diplomatic functions and no love. The marriage broke down and Breivik's mother took her two children back to Norway and poverty. She made a few efforts to dump her children on the state but never went through with it.

Social workers thought she might be mentally ill and made efforts to remove Breivik and his half-sister. Nothing came of it. Neighbours watched a string of boyfriends visit the flat while the children took care of themselves; they endured the mother's rambling conversations on the stairs that hovered between constant double entendre and a sexualised fear of men.

Breivik's father had a new wife in Paris and little contact with his son. Breivik grew up without him. Sometimes his mother seemed normal and loving, other times harsh and violent. He coped, although those around him noted his closed-off nature and how he only slowly warmed to others. There was some bullying of others, and some killing of insects sadistic enough that other parents kept him away from their family pets. It only seemed significant in retrospect.

As a teen he got into hip hop and tagging. His handle was Morg, the henchman cum executioner of Galactus, a god in the Marvel comic universe. Breivik had a Pakistani best friend and adopted the Norwegian street style: baggy trousers, hoody, gelled hair, headphones, speech littered with slang picked up from the local Arabic street gangs. Breivik managed to be orderly in his lawbreaking, refusing to steal spray cans and lining up the ones he bought in neat rows by colour.

There were some arrests, some counselling sessions, but ultimately it was ostracism from peers that pushed him out of the lifestyle. He tried too hard and wasn't cool enough.

'He belonged to the cool gang for a while, even though he wasn't cool,' said a fellow tagger. 'He was basically a fifth wheel. In the end we wouldn't put up with him any longer.'

After tagging and hip hop he reinvented himself with bodybuilding – not a mainstream activity then – and began to dress preppy in Lacoste polo shirts. Vanity crept in. He had an operation to straighten his nose and looked into transplants when his blond hair began to thin. A part-time job in telesales brought in good money and Breivik started seeing himself as a thrusting entrepreneur. His schoolmates went off to university but Breivik stayed in Oslo and set up a string of businesses in advertising, telecommunications. Most failed but a few made enough of an impact to be sold on to larger companies.

He joined the Fremskrittspartiet (Progress Party), a neoliberal conservative political group around since the early 1970s. Pro-market and pro-American, it suited Breivik's new image as a junior businessman. He held some minor positions in its youth branch; other activists found him competent and organised but so uninterested in talking about himself that he barely seemed to have a personality. The Fremskrittspartiet took a strong stand against immigration. By the mid-1990s that had morphed into an opposition to Islam, triggered by the murder of a Norwegian translator working on Salman Rushdie's *The Satanic Verses*. In 1980 Norway had just over 1,000 Muslims; ten years later it had 54,000; by 2010 there were 144,000.

Breivik got a girlfriend who also supported the Fremskrittspartiet. Lene Langemyr had been brought up by adoptive Norwegian parents but was of Middle Eastern background. She had no time for Islam or cultural ghettoes. It angered her when Muslim men in Oslo assumed she was one of them and told her to wear more conservative clothes and stop hanging with whites.

'Get dressed!' they said if she walked around town in a sun dress.

Breivik became a keyboard warrior, spending hours debating with others on Fremskrittspartiet message boards and urging boldness in their political message. He saw himself as some kind of self-help guru, offering advice on practising speeches by rehearsing in front of a mirror, dressing well, taking the party's message to the public. No one seemed very impressed but he was moderate enough in his views and criticised more extreme voices like Oriana Fallaci. One comment on Islam was a model of tolerance: 'It's important to make the point that Islam is a great religion (on a level with Christianity),' he wrote, ten months after the 9/11 attacks, 'and that Muslims are generally good people (on a level with Christians).'

He avoided national service with an exemption to look after his mother when she was sick. A herpes infection had got complicated and led to a drainage cup and meningitis. Breivik overcompensated for avoiding the army with a detailed knowledge of weapons. He and Lene both joined a shooting club. Breivik hoped for a position on the Fremskrittspartiet list in forthcoming elections but was never chosen. Too strange, too much of an outsider. More ostracism from his peers. He left party activities, drifted away from Lene and returned to the world of making money. In one of his last posts on the Fremskrittspartiet message boards he stopped being tolerant and told others he predicted civil war when Muslims became the majority in Norway.

Back in the business world he came up with a scheme printing fake university diplomas in Indonesia and shipping them all over the world. The fakes were ostensibly to replace lost originals but everyone used them to claim non-existent degrees. The money rolled in. He started playing the affluent young professional, clubbing with friends, wearing designer clothes. He was fond of Lacoste and its green alligator logo. There were few girls in his life after Lene. Friends thought he might be gay. Breivik denied it, claiming the vanity and occasional spot of makeup were just part of being a modern metrosexual man. He fantasised about having an obedient Slavic wife who would mother seven children, but a brief attempt with a mail-order girlfriend from Belarus failed when it became obvious her real goal was financial.

He begged a relative to get him into the local Masonic lodge. The man promised to do his best although privately thought Breivik too strange. Breivik seemed to see the Freemasons as a place for backroom deals to help his business.

The diploma business shut down when some newspaper journalists came sniffing around. Breivik had plenty of money, a lot of it invested in shares, but refused to get another job. Eventually finances got tight. He moved into his mother's small apartment and they reverted to the usual toxic relationship of cold distance alternating with inappropriate closeness. When she broke up with a boyfriend Breivik bought her a vibrator and quizzed her about using it.

The money dwindled to nothing and soon Breivik was spending whole days in his room locked into the internet. He discovered *World of Warcraft*, an online multiplayer roleplaying game set in a world of dragons and magic. It became his whole life.

The game was globally popular and Breivik joined international raiding parties. Online he was enthusiastic, sociable and well liked.

Out in the real world his Freemason relative had finally got him accepted, but Breivik barely seemed to care. He reluctantly attended the initiation ceremony and then only turned up to a few more meetings, where he seemed bored. The Freemasonic hall had suits of armour and Christian iconography and crusader murals but Breivik preferred online fantasy battles.

His character, a mage called Andersnordic, became leader of a guild but it all turned sour when Breivik started expelling anyone who could not spend twelve hours at a time playing the game. He abandoned his old friends and moved on to a more powerful guild, but was mocked by its experienced players for his desperate need to be liked. He was not cool enough again and the game soured.

World of Warcraft faded out of his life. He had found something else that gave him meaning.

16

A VERY POSITIVELY MINDED INDIVIDUAL

Breivik's Vision for Europe, 2011

Anyone who stumbled across Anders Breivik's YouTube channel a few hours before the massacre on Utøya would have seen a freshly uploaded video that felt it had something important to say. Music from the *Age of Conan the Barbarian* online game soundtracked a slideshow of memes and text divided into sections about Cultural Marxism, Islamic Colonisation, Hope, and A New Beginning. It didn't make much sense until news reports about a shooting spree started coming in.

Breivik wanted to get his message out there. The video was for everyone, but he hoped to reach the counter-jihad intelligentsia with a book.

He was still hunting teens on the island with his rifle when 1,003 email addresses harvested from counter-jihad and right-wing sites received a pdf copy of something called *2083: A European Declaration of Independence*. The book claimed to be written by Andrew Berwick but the man in the photographs at the back was the same one killing people on Utøya. Breivik's final task before he put on his fake policeman's uniform, booked a hire car and headed for Oslo had been to click send on the automated email programme. He'd spent the last few years alone in his room swallowing the views of the counter-jihad, and now he was vomiting it all back up.

The signs of self-radicalisation include social isolation, unwillingness to engage with those of different views, the use of different identities, and spending too much time online. Anders Breivik ticked all the boxes.

His deep dive into the counter-jihad began with the usual suspects. The Gates of Vienna, Robert Spencer's Jihadwatch and Pamela Geller's blog got regular visits. Bat Ye'or and Norwegian right-winger Fjordman became heroes. The online world dragged Breivik out of his depressive hibernation and gave him new purpose in life. Old friends who occasionally sought him out learned to avoid talking politics if they didn't want a rant about dhimmitude. Breivik had shown a willingness to criticise Islam during his time with the Fremskrittspartiet but this time the rhetoric was different, more intense.

'If a pipe is leaking in your bathroom, what do you do?' he said, channelling dead Dutch politician Pim Fortuyn. 'It's not very complicated after all. You go to the source of the problem, the leak itself! You don't mop it up until after you have fixed the actual leak. Needless to say, our regime is the leak, the Muslims are the water.'

His mother proudly told neighbours her son was writing a book. Breivik called his opus *2083: A European Declaration of Independence* but never made any effort to get it published. He had other plans. The text was a cut-and-paste compilation of other people's writings, some taken from sources far off the grid. He was spending time on Stormfront, a neo-Nazi site around since the 1990s. Stormfronters did not much like Islam but feelings were complicated by Muslim anti-Semitism and wartime support for the Third Reich. Photographs of Bosnian Muslims wearing Totenkopfs on their fezzes turned up on the kind of far-right sites that tried to massage Nazi racism into something less transgressive. When Stormfront commenters discussed Islamic immigration the agreed solution was usually deportation. If they posted drunk, it was gas chambers.

Breivik understood the contradictions in bouncing between a neo-Nazi site and Jewish counter-jihad blogs, but felt Stormfronters could be useful allies in the fight. Everyone was on the same side when the pipe was leaking. Breivik tried to cross-pollinate the deportation idea into the Gates of Vienna comment section but saw his plan dismissed as unworkable.

He transferred his posting to document.no, a conservative Norwegian site run by journalist and former leftist Hans Rustad. Breivik jumped into the conversation and threw out ideas like sparks from a Catherine wheel: publish a conservative newspaper, push Norwegian culture to the right with a local version of the American Tea Party movement, start a Norwegian branch of the English Defence League. The last came to fruition in 2010 thanks to the efforts of local counter-jihadists but Breivik's only input was to become a member under the name Sigurd Jorsalfar when it was already up and running. He was kicked out the following March during a purge on extremism.

By then his counter-jihadist beliefs had metastasised into dreams of suicidal glory. At some point between *World of Warcraft* and the Norwegian Defence League, Breivik came to believe that a terror attack on the heart of power could turn a failed thirty-two-year-old businessman living with his mother into a hero. His rationalised it as the punishment of those responsible for the Islamification of Norway, justified by an unwillingness to wait for the mainstream creep of slow political change. Somewhere in the cold dark of his subconscious lay the understanding that the real motivation was to escape his isolation, ostracism and lack of direction.

In 2009 he failed to buy weapons on a trip to the Czech Republic but legally obtained a Glock handgun back home through a shooting club. A hunting licence got him the Ruger rifle. He took steroids and hit the gym. The same year he set up a farming business that would provide cover for obtaining the fertiliser to make a bomb when his plan got rolling two years later. Explosive primer was ordered from an online Polish shop; the Oslo police launched a brief investigation but uncovered nothing suspicious.

Breivik added some material to his book about the preparations and posed for pictures, making sure to work out for a week before the sessions and carefully combing his thinning blond hair. He resembled Volkert van der Graaf, the assassin of Pim Fortuyn, with his chilly, quiet Northern European fanaticism. In the photographs he wore a fake dress uniform with unearned medals; a frogman's outfit; a Freemason's apron. Breivik hoped to control his image after the attack by preventing the media printing unflattering pictures.

In his downtime he binge-watched American television shows like *The Shield* (corrupt cops in Los Angeles), *Rome* (pop-culture sword and sandals), and *True Blood* (brooding vampires). He played *Call of Duty: Modern Warfare 2* as training material. He wallowed in self-pity over what would happen if he got taken alive.

'When I wake up at the hospital,' he said, 'after surviving the gunshot wounds inflicted on me, I realize at least for me personally, I will be waking up to a world of shit, a living nightmare.'

*

Counter-jihadists were always writing books. Bat Ye'or, Melanie Phillips, Oriana Fallaci, Mark Steyn, Pastor Jones, Pim Fortuyn and Fjordman all believed that readers would understand the truth if only they knew enough about Islam. Breivik had little original to add to the conversation but dived in anyway.

2083: A European Declaration of Independence was a 1,518-page collage of English text. Breivik lifted material from the Gates of Vienna, a Jeremy Clarkson column from the *Daily Telegraph*, a Melanie Phillips column from the *Daily Mail*, the Belgian Hinduism expert Koenraad Elst. He quoted Mahatma Ghandi, George Orwell, Karl Marx, Barack Obama, Anwar Shaaban, Yasser Arafat, Osama bin Laden, Plato, American poet Bruce Bawer and others as standalone text or nested within someone else's work. Pamela Geller, Robert Spencer, Bat Ye'or and Daniel Pipes got hailed as major inspirations. Breivik said positive things about German-Jewish journalist Henryk Broder, Ayaan Hirsi Ali, Hindu nationalists and Serbian paramilitaries. Large chunks of Wikipedia acted as connective tissue.

A chapter about political correctness reprinted a pamphlet originally produced by Washington-based conservative think tank the American Free Congress Federation. Another section came from the manifesto of Ted Kaczynski, the radical environmentalist Unabomber who parcel-bombed academics for twenty years until the media agreed to run his *Industrial Society and Its Future* text. Breivik swapped out Kaczynski's mentions of 'leftists' and 'black people' for 'cultural Marxists' and 'Muslims'.

The biggest influence on the manifesto was homegrown. The *Declaration* included hundreds of pages taken from Gates of Vienna regular Fjordman. The Norwegian writer had all the usual counter-jihad beliefs: support for Bat Ye'or's Eurabia theory, cheerleading for Israel, opposition to multiculturalism, the claim that leftists encouraged Islamic immigration out of 'white masochism', contempt for feminism, certainty that Islam was a religion focused

The World Trade Center in New York burns during the 11 September 2001 terror attacks orchestrated by Osama bin Laden. (Courtesy of Wally Gobetz)

Above: Controversial politician Pim Fortuyn was assassinated in the car park of a Dutch radio station during a heated election campaign. (Courtesy of Dick van Ageelen)

Left: A statue of Pim Fortuyn in Rotterdam, showing the impact his murder had on the Netherlands. (Courtesy of M. M. Minderhoud)

A young Theo van Gogh, in the days when the Dutch film director cared more about making movies than attacking Islam. (Courtesy of the Nationaal Archief)

Somali migrant turned Dutch media star Ayaan Hirsi Ali. (Courtesy of Gage Skidmore)

Left: Career politician Geert Wilders continued the legacy of Pim Fortuyn in the Netherlands. (Courtesy of Wouter Engler)

Below: Formidable Italian journalist and early counter-jihad influence Oriana Fallaci. (Courtesy of GianAngelo Pistoia)

Right: French philosopher René Guénon 's ideas proved popular with both Muslim converts and counter-jihadists. (Public domain)

Below: Wealthy New Yorker and prominent counter-jihad activist Pamela Geller. (Courtesy of Pamela Geller)

Above: American conservative media firebrand Ann Coulter. (Courtesy of Gage Skidmore)

Left: An early counter-jihad rally in Washington DC, 2007. (Courtesy of Raphael1)

The more pessimistic members of the counter-jihad agreed with German philosopher Oswald Spengler's theories of historical decline. (Courtesy of the Bundesarchiv under Creative Commons 3.0)

Left: English Defence League leader Stephen Lennon. (right) with Rabbi Norman Shifren. (back, centre) and Roberta Moore. (front). (Courtesy of London BDS)

Below: An English Defence League march in Newcastle, dominated by the controversial Infidel wing. (Courtesy of Gavin Lynn)

Right: Norwegian mass murderer and counter-jihadist Anders Breivik in an idealised self-image from his manifesto. (Courtesy of *2083: A European Declaration of Independence*)

Below: A memorial at the Utøya Learning Centre on the island to those killed during the rampage by Anders Breivik. (Courtesy of the Human-ethical Association)

Russian writer Elena Chudinova published a cult novel in which Islam takes over Europe. (Courtesy of Dom Kobb)

Misanthropic novelist Michel Houellebecq wrote a bestseller that predicted an Islamic France. (Courtesy of Fronterias do Pensamento/Luiz Munhoz)

A rally in Brest to show solidarity with dead of *Charlie Hebdo* magazine. (Courtesy of Photographix)

German Chancellor Angela Merkel, whose actions during the European migrant crisis caused controversy. (Courtesy of Arno Mikkor)

Pegida activists demonstrate in Germany, with the motto on one man's jacket reading 'Our Government, Our Tradition'. (Courtesy of Bündnis 90)

Pegida movement leader Lutz Bachmann. (Courtesy of Lutz Bachmann)

The first wave of Syrian migrants arrives in Greece during 2015. (Courtesy of Georgios Giannopoulos)

Migrants escorted through Slovenia in 2015. (Courtesy of Borut Podgorsek)

Steve Bannon, Trump's right-hand man and political fixer who tried to bring together the counter-jihad and alt-right movements. (Courtesy of Gage Skidmore)

British journalist and gay counter-jihad icon Milo Yiannopolous. (Courtesy of KMeron)

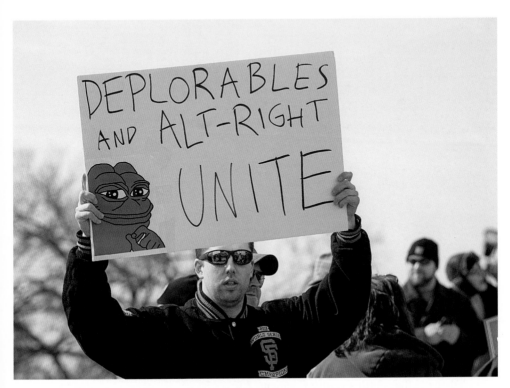

An alt-right protester in Portland brandishes a sign featuring the ubiquitous Pepe the Frog. (Courtesy of Fibonacci Blue)

Donald John Trump is sworn in as forty-fifth president of the United States of America. (Courtesy of the White House)

Thousands protested against President Trump's Executive Order 13769, a counter-jihad measure that banned immigration from several Muslim nations. (Courtesy of Fibonacci Blue under Creative Commons 2.0)

on destroying all other faiths and had been engaged in a global war against them for fourteen centuries. Fjordman dug up a 2008 quote by Norwegian anthropologist and Miljøpartiet De Grønne (Green Party) candidate Thomas Hylland Eriksen that resonated with Breivik.

'Our most important task ahead is to deconstruct the majority,' said Eriksen, 'and we must deconstruct them so thoroughly that they will never be able to call themselves the majority again.'

Eriksen claimed the quote only looked threatening out of context but Fjordman and his readers interpreted it as a call by a major political figure to destroy the white majority of Norwegian society. Breivik saw it as proof the government used Islamic immigration as a weapon against people like him. Now he was fighting back.

The book provided a cross-section of counter-jihad thought filtered through Breivik's outsider viewpoint. Its patchwork nature made coherence a problem but the main message seemed to be a call for the restoration of an anti-feminist patriarchy that would destroy 'cultural Marxism' and expel all Muslims from Europe in a similar manner to the Beneš Decrees, which kicked German civilians out of Czechoslovakia at the end of the Second World War. Breivik believed this would be achievable by 2083, a symbolic 400 years after European forces broke the siege of Vienna and ended the Ottoman threat to Western Europe.

Only the last section of *2083: A European Declaration of Independence* was mostly Breivik's own work. He gave recipes for homemade explosives, a detailed diary of his preparations for the attacks, and photographs in various costumes. He recommended studying the enemy and provided reading lists, cribbed from elsewhere, of books on left-wing and Islamic themes. A section on motivational music namechecked Helene Bøksle (Norwegian folk), Clint Mansell (atmospheric film soundtracks), and Saga (neo-Nazi ballads). The preparations revealed he originally planned to take former prime minister Gro Harlem Brundtland prisoner and decapitate her on film then post footage to the internet. Brundtland saved her own life by leaving the island before the rampage began. Breivik thought her gory murder would have inspired future generations.

'I'm an extremely patient and a very positively minded individual,' Breivik said. 'I have obviously changed my ways over the years and am now driven by idealistic goals and work for the interests of my countrymen and all Europeans. Most people would not acknowledge the work yet (nor are they likely to appreciate it during my lifetime) but this is an irrelevant fact for me. With time they will understand what is going on around them and that what we are trying to accomplish will benefit not only them, but most importantly their children and grandchildren.'

Breivik didn't want history to remember him as a loner. He claimed membership of the Pauperes commilitones Christi Templique Solomonici, a new version of the medieval crusader Knights Templar allegedly formed at a 2002 London meeting. The order was just a fantasy amalgamation of the guilds from *World of Warcraft* jumbled up with Breivik's brief time in the Freemasons, intended to give a nod to the international nature of the counter-jihad. He had never visited London.

Counter-jihad, nationalism, Zionism, crusader rhetoric, elements of neo-Nazism, and the deed by terrorism of Al-Qaeda all came together in Breivik. The largest ingredient was narcissism. He had more in common with the school shooters of Columbine or Jokela than standard political terrorists. Breivik wanted people to remember his name.

'I'm the greatest monster since Quisling,' he told police when interrogated, referencing the notorious wartime collaborator.

The trial began on 16 April 2012. A few months earlier a psychiatric report had found Breivik a paranoid schizophrenic. The court, the Norwegian public and Breivik all objected. A second report found him sane. Norway wanted justice. Breivik wanted to parade his beliefs. He announced his intention to call an eclectic group of defence witnesses to show Norway the danger of Islam.

Summons went out to anthropologists, prominent Islamists, leftist politicians, Arne Tumyr of Stop Islamisation of Norway, Tore Wilhelm Tvedt of far-right group Vigrid, and a number of counter-jihadist writers. Some protested, some tried to wriggle out of it. The court told them they had no choice. The counter-jihad was going on trial alongside Breivik.

17

PERFECTION OF WRITING BY MEANS OF AN ASSAULT RIFLE

The Counter-Jihad in Court, 2012

Anders Breivik had two groupies. One was a blonde German from Stuttgart who tried to push her way into the court, claiming to be his girlfriend and brandishing photographs on her phone that journalists recognised as downloaded from their own news reports. Police ushered her away for an interview and eventual deportation.

The other was a literary man. Fifty-eight-year-old Richard Millet was a fixture in the Paris establishment of expensive flats and long lunches and book talk. This success was a triumph of assimilation for the square-faced, glasses-wearing Gallimard editor and novelist. Born in south-west France, Millet grew up in Lebanon where his father worked in the Beirut Ministry of Public Works. Back in France at fourteen years old, tanned and speaking Arabic, Millet's new classmates called him 'Ahmed'. He wondered if he was really French. Eight years later he quit a post-university job digging graves and returned to Beirut when civil war broke out in Lebanon. As a young Brigitte Gabriel cowered in a bomb shelter, Millet went to war.

The main Christian forces were Pierre Gemayel's Kataeb al-Quwwat al-Nizamiyah (Kataeb Regulatory Forces – KRF), the military wing of the Kataeb Party, or Phalange. In its early days the Phalange had critiqued French imperialism and pushed for independence. It softened its views once Lebanon gained self-rule, soothing the consciences of French right-wingers who wanted to admire Gemayel's mix of Christianity and authoritarianism. When the Lebanese Civil War began a handful of Frenchmen joined the KRF. Millet was one of them.

'I had to kill men sometimes,' he said, 'and also women, old people, perhaps children.'

The Phalangist veteran prepared to risk death for a foreign country had a contradictory thirst for the comforts of a more mainstream life in France. Back home after a tour of duty, Millet started the literary revue *Recueil* in 1984, parlaying it into an editorial job at the heart of the French literary establishment. He stood out among the wine-and-cheese parties and stuffy editorial meetings with his obsession with violence, suicide, contemporary decadence. Millet compared himself to Ernest Hemingway, Ernst Jünger and other writers who had experienced war; he described the manuscripts on his desk at Gallimard as sandbags. Years later he would admit that he spent only a few months in the Phalangist ranks, blindly spraying an assault rifle over barricades at an enemy he never saw.

Millet wrote complex novels about generations of families moulded by their home towns and home lands, overlaid with the dark Catholicism of sacrifice, guilt and sexual desire. Modernity is never positive in Millet's novels. Progress brings only poverty and despair and death.

Critics pinned him as a conservative Catholic, although his suicide attempt after a failed marriage didn't fit the profile, or one of establishment-friendly 'new reactionaries' like Renaud Camus, a gay right-winger who pushed the idea of a Eurabia-style great replacement in which the establishment waged demographic war against the French people. Millet preferred to see himself as a literary rebel. He talked about his Phalangist adventures in Beirut, praised Osama bin Laden and Syrian dictator Bashar al-Assad, and criticised multiculturalism, but never poked the bear hard enough to lose his comfortable job.

A book that came out in August 2012, a few months after the verdict in the Breivik trial, changed everything. Millet's *Langue fantôme suivi de Éloge littéraire d'Anders Breivik* (Phantom Language Followed by Literary Praise for Anders Breivik) conjoined an essay on linguistics with an analysis of the 'literary' aspect of Breivik's killing spree interpreted as 'formal perfectionism'. The seventeen-page essay contained sharp criticism of what multiculturalism and modernity had done to Europe, coupled with jabs at what Millet saw as Breivik's low-brow manifesto and taste for typical Western decadence.

'He is heterosexual,' wrote Millet, 'he likes snowboarding, Budweiser, Chanel perfumes, Lacoste shirts (the company swiftly protested against the photos in which Breivik, being arrested, sports, with a strange smile, a polo shirt featuring that horrible little crocodile, one of the emblems of contemporary infantilism).'

Millet saw the Norwegian murderer as a symbol of the West's decline rather than its champion. Breivik was just another spree shooter who didn't understand his actions were a product of multicultural modernity rather than a protest against it. Readers could accept that part of the argument, even if they didn't agree; it was the kind of road the Frenchman often drove down. Then Millet praised the 'literary beauty' of the attack and talked about 'perfection of writing by means of an assault rifle', and the essay went through the barriers and off the bridge as the argument morphed into something between the post-modernism of Jean Baudrillard (author of *La Guerre du Golfe n'a pas eu lieu* – The Gulf War Did Not Take Place) and ambiguous support for Breivik's motives.

'Breivik is without a doubt what Norway deserved,' Millet wrote, 'and what is awaiting all our societies, which continue to blind themselves in order better to deny themselves, particularly France and England.'

A firestorm of controversy caught hold, both in France and abroad. Some hated Millet for not condemning Breivik; others for treating the deaths of sixty-nine people as a subject for post-modern literary gymnastics. The reaction caught Millet by surprise. He had been spicing up his establishment position with a bit of right-wing radicalism for years and no one had ever done more than look shocked. Now the media was denouncing him as a Nazi and a mass-murder groupie.

Millet refused to apologise. He was pushed out of Gallimard. Former friends lined up to condemn him. His career took some hard body blows and newspaper columns filled with angry opinion pieces about his politics and morals, real and imagined. From now on he would be known as the man who excused Breivik, not the novelist who worked hard at his craft.

'I'm one of the most hated French authors,' he said. 'It's an interesting position that makes me an exceptional being.'

Defiant words, but he was wounded. Millet retreated behind the barricades, having learned the hard way what a lot of counter-jihadists already knew. Being associated with the Anders Breivik trial was not good for business.

*

The Norwegian state had charged Breivik with 'destabilising or destroying basic functions of society' and 'creating serious fear in the population'. After the usual preliminaries and search for lawyers prepared to represent a killer, the trial launched into forty-three days of photographs, videos, diagrams, endless reports and statements split into neatly numbered lines. Breivik cried the first day, seemingly with embarrassment, when his YouTube video was shown. Then he packed his emotions away and remained chilly and self-contained as teenagers described seeing their friends killed.

He got five days to defend himself. Breivik used the time to cross-examine opponents about cultural Marxism, make long speeches urging European nationalists to work together, and coax witnesses into describing the evils of Islam. He had planned for important counter-jihadists to appear but the people he'd cut-and-pasted into *2083: A European Declaration of Independence* were not keen on appearing in the witness box.

Theodore Bruce Bawer was bald and heavy-lidded, with eyebrows like two slashes of black marker pen. The fifty-six-year-old New Yorker had lived in Oslo for thirteen years. He combined a delicate literary sensibility with hatred for Islam that burned hot as napalm. Breivik's legal team wanted him in the witness box but Bawer saw them as puppets in a conspiracy orchestrated by the government.

'The real reason for dragging some of Norway's most prominent critics of Islam into court,' said Bawer, 'was to establish guilt by association – to link all of us, in the minds of Norwegians, with the most reviled creep in modern Norwegian history – and to send out the message that if you publicly criticize Islam in Norway, you can end up being dragged into court.'

Bawer had written poetry and literary criticism back in New York and was tough-minded enough to combine homosexuality, right-wing politics, Christian faith and some libertarianism. He moved to Oslo at the end of the 1990s to do travel journalism and translation work. The 9/11 attacks radicalised him, as so many others.

His 2002 article 'Tolerating Intolerance: The Challenge of Fundamentalist Islam in Western Europe' in the *Partisan Review* was an early shot in what would be a long war. Three years later he wrote *While Europe Slept: How Radical Islam is Destroying the West from Within*, a text that fitted neatly into the counter-jihad. Bawer claimed Islam would destroy European liberal values and threaten homosexuals, women and Jews; that rising Muslim birth rates would lead to domination of Western Europe in thirty years; and that political correctness and multiculturalism had to be destroyed to prevent this happening. The book got nominated for a National Book Critics Circle Award and became a *New York Times* bestseller.

In 2009 came *Surrender: Appeasing Islam, Sacrificing Freedom*, which had Bawer arguing that Europeans censored themselves in response to Islamic violence to avoid provoking any more of it. Bawer rarely self-censored; indeed, he wanted all Muslims in Europe deported. Then came the Breivik massacre. An article Bawer wrote for the *Wall Street Journal* condemned Breivik but put some blame on the Norwegian government for not doing enough about Islamic immigration.

'In Norway, to speak negatively about any aspect of the Muslim faith has always been a touchy matter,' Bawer said, 'inviting charges of "Islamophobia" and racism. It will, I fear, be a great deal more difficult to broach these issues now that this murderous madman has become the poster boy for the criticism of Islam.'

Fellow witness Fjordman went into hiding after journalists exposed him as Peder Are Nøstvold Jensen, a chubby, curly-haired thirty-six-year-old from a left-wing family who studied at the American University in Cairo. His scepticism about Islam began when Egyptian neighbours threw a party to celebrate 9/11 and deepened after a tour with a monitoring team in the Middle East. Jensen began blogging as Fjordman in February 2005 while back in Oslo running a day-care centre and doing a master's degree. He didn't want to appear in court and was getting legal advice from American contacts. Jensen claimed no connection between Breivik and his own worldview.

'I have read Breivik's so-called manifesto closely, as well as some of the letters he has sent to the media from prison,' said Jensen. 'My view is that Mr. Breivik is a nutcase who is probably medically insane.'

Conservative commentator and author Hanne Stine Nabintu Herland, Norway's answer to Ann Coulter, also refused to take the witness stand. She preferred prison to participation.

'I refuse to be dragged around the circus ring,' she said, 'like another clown in the perpetrator's bizarre delusion.'

Counter-jihadists outside Norway had their own fallout from Breivik's rampage. The Gates of Vienna shut down its comments sections for a while and posted a statement that it had never advocated violence. The media went after bigger names, leaving some teeth marks in Pamela Geller's normally thick hide when she unwisely told journalists the AUF camp had been a left-wing indoctrination centre. Even Bat Ye'or and Melanie Phillips took flak. Little Green Footballs happily attacked former friends, with Charles Johnson's blog posts lifting the lid off the counter-jihad world for any passing journalists. Robert Spencer was one of many who had their names smeared all over the media as an inspiration to Breivik. The man behind Jihadwatch dismissed the accusations. 'I'm no more responsible for Breivik's murders,' Spencer said, 'than the Beatles are for Charles Manson's.'

On the other side of the Atlantic, the English Defence League saw support haemorrhage away. It issued a statement through Facebook.

> We can categorically state that there has never been any official contact between [Breivik] and the EDL, our Facebook page had 100,000 supporters and receives tens of thousands of comments each day. And there is no evidence that Breivik was ever one of those 100,000 supporters. Even so, anyone who expresses any extremist beliefs of any kind, be it white supremacist, Christian fundamentalist or Islamic extremists, they all get banned from the site.

Any links Breivik may have had with the League remained murky. He knew members as internet contacts, and Paul Ray admitted the Norwegian might have been inspired by his blogging but knocked back any suggestion of closer contact. Ray suggested Alan Ayling had been a friend to Breivik, got sued for libel, and had to pay the IT millionaire €5,000 in damages. Claims Breivik had visited England for a League march seemed plausible but police couldn't find any proof.

It all damaged the English Defence League. A march through the heavily Muslim area of London's Tower Hamlets in September 2011 only attracted 1,000, a third of the number for the rally in February. Things got worse. Pakistani hackers calling themselves Z Company Hacking Crew got into the English Defence League Facebook page. They posted abuse and personal details of League members.

> LOL bare pussyhole edl scum licking ass so they so they don't get rushed by there fellow skin heads.. All ya lots can do is act

bad on facebook u don't get out ya yards ur too busy cleaning the dishes ir drinkin piss down the pub and ur acting thugish on a facebook group!

Then Stephen Lennon was arrested trying to enter America using the passport of a lookalike friend after being banned from the country as an undesirable. He got ten months in prison back in the UK but served most of it at home wearing an electronic tag.

'But I was still left regretting one big media opportunity,' Lennon said, 'the chance to take our message to the American mainstream. I really screwed that up.'

The prison sentence came after numerous other problems with the law: a conviction for 'threatening, abusive or insulting behaviour' at a Luton vs Newport match in 2010; a week in prison for breaching bail conditions the next year; another suspended conviction for assault the same year for headbutting a man Lennon claimed was a neo-Nazi; three days in prison for protesting at FIFA headquarters in Zürich over the banning of remembrance poppies on the English kit.

By 2012 Lennon was sick of it all. Six Muslim men tried to car-bomb a League rally in June. They failed but the lack of public sympathy for potential victims was disheartening. Lennon and the rest of the leadership were burned out after pushing hard but achieving little. Rallies didn't change election results. Many lads just saw them as a good day out. Get some beers in down the pub, snort some coke, look for a row. Lennon didn't know how to extend the message. Even Jeff Marsh agreed.

'There's only so many times,' he said, 'people are prepared to be stood in a field surrounded by the old bill, pushed about and kettled, listening to the same old speeches.'

The counter-jihad was in trouble. Seeing prominent members forced into a photo opportunity with Anders Breivik in front of the global media would only make things worse. Bawer and Jensen went looking for loopholes after Breivik's lawyers requested the counter-jihadists attend as expert witnesses. Both men were determined to avoid the courtroom after the Norwegian judges made it clear they viewed them as extreme-right figures whose testimony would not be broadcast, to avoid inciting susceptible viewers. They got help from Legal Project, an off-shoot of Daniel Pipes' Middle East Forum. Digging through the law books unearthed the arcane point that only actual witnesses to a crime, not those giving expert opinions or background, could be compelled to give testimony. Bawer and Jensen had barely cracked open the champagne when they heard the trial judges had reclassified them as regular witnesses.

'Too many people involved in this case have proven themselves incapable of grasping a very elementary point,' said Bawer, 'namely, that in a democracy, you don't haul writers into court to be grilled about their political views.'

Legal Project got involved again and convinced Breivik's lawyers the reclassification was absurd and probably illegal. The lawyers reluctantly agreed to drop some of the summons but made sarcastic comments about propagandists who didn't want to be heard. Counter-jihadists who did turn up, like Ole Jørgen Anfindsen of the Honestthinking.org blog, found no one had any questions to ask them anyway.

The trial finished on 22 June 2012 and the guilty verdict came down two months later. Breivik got the maximum sentence of twenty-one years with a minimum of ten to be served, and the proviso that the sentence could be extended if he remained a danger. Breivik's attempt to give a speech about taking the fight to Islam during sentencing was shut down by the judges. He was taken away to serve his time in a three-room cell with a PlayStation.

In the aftermath, the media seemed convinced that Breivik and many in the counter-jihad were fascists. Few actual fascists rushed to embrace them. Even an activist like Frenchman Dominique Venner had little positive to say in a brief blog post about Richard Millet's controversial book on Breivik.

'No one dwelt on the first part (deploring the evils of the French language),' wrote Venner on his blog. 'Everyone threw themselves on the eighteen pages of curious literary praise for a *serial killer*.'

He used the English term for mass murderer, although those italics contained more hidden depths than the Mariana Trench.

Nine months later Venner walked into Notre-Dame Cathedral in Paris with a gun in his hand and a mission to wake France to the dangers of Islam.

18

IT ISN'T EASY BEING LOVED BY IDIOTS IN PARIS

Francophone Approaches to Islam, 2013–14

In the late afternoon of 21 May 2013, a seventy-eight-year-old Frenchman, bald and unwell and wearing glasses, entered the medieval cathedral of Notre-Dame in Paris and pushed through the crowds to the altar. The place was full of tourists. Around 1,500 of them were shuffling between wooden pews, necks craned at the layers of pale grey stone arches arcing towards the sky, gawping at the kaleidoscopic stained-glass rose window in the north.

Dominique Venner placed a sealed envelope on the altar. He took out a FN Herstal 9mm pistol, put it in his mouth, and pulled the trigger. The tourists stampeded out and a security guard knelt in a pool of blood for twenty minutes failing to save Venner's life. The seventy-eight-year-old suicide died lying on the stone floor of the cathedral.

'We will pray for this man,' said cathedral rector Monsigneur Patrick Jacquin, 'as we pray for so many others who are at their wits' end.'

It was all over the internet as a shock piece until the journalists discovered Venner was a controversial historian with a far-right past. The story went political. Venner's last blog post had been a long essay against gay marriage, legalised in France three days earlier despite mass protests by Catholic groups. The headlines wrote themselves.

'*Suicide d'un anti-mariage gay dans Notre-Dame.*'

Venner's political engagement began in the mid-1950s when he joined the army. Most young Frenchmen were doing their best to avoid the vicious colonial war raging with the Front de Libération Nationale (National Liberation Front) for the future of Algeria. Venner was making a statement by embracing the uniform.

He got back to France in October 1956, radicalised and right-wing and blaming leftists for failing to keep the tricolour flying in North Africa. He got work as a journalist and joined Jeune Nation, a far-right group popular with Paris students. There were marches and speeches and rows in the street with communists. A few years later he was cursing Charles de Gaulle for finally giving Algeria its independence. The French president knew his country couldn't hold on to that baked slice of desert and feared the consequences of even trying. At a time when the far-right cared more about imperialism, De Gaulle worried about demographics.

'Do you believe that the French nation can absorb 10 million Muslims, who tomorrow will be 20 million and the day after 40 million?' he asked a crony. 'If we adopt integration, if all the Arabs and Berbers of Algeria were considered as Frenchmen, what would prevent them from coming to settle in mainland France where the standard of living is so much higher? My village would no longer be called Colombey-les-Deux-Eglises, but Colombey-les-deux-Mosquées!'

A disillusioned Venner spent the next decade sliding slowly out of the extreme-right. He initially supported the Organisation de l'armée secrete (Secret Army Organisation), a terror group of white settlers and rogue army officers who tried to keep Algeria French; later he denounced OAS violence and went for power through the ballot box; when that failed he supported the cultural change pushed by intellectuals of the Nouvelle Droite. By the early 1970s Venner had distanced himself from politics enough to be taken seriously as a writer on firearms, hunting and military history. In 1981 the Académie française gave him the Broquette Gonin Price for a book on the Red Army. The left insisted he was still fascist but Venner's books sold well and other historians took him seriously.

Muslim migration and terror attacks of the early twenty-first century reawakened the political animal. Venner began writing articles for his blog and other far-right websites; he got involved with Printemps français (French Spring), a group of Catholics and far-right activists campaigning against gay marriage, although Venner remained a pagan. Then he got sick.

He never talked about the illness, just wrote some political testaments in the forms of letters and a final blog post, said goodbye to a family who knew nothing of his health problems, and headed for the cathedral at Notre-Dame. Most journalists believed he had died to protest gay marriage. A few who dug deeper noted the existential boilerplate in his last writings.

'It is by deciding, truly willing one's destiny, that one conquers nothingness.'

They all overlooked the real message in Venner's final blog post. At its core was a simple argument: France was undergoing a great replacement at the hands of 'Afro-Maghreb immigration' and this, not gay marriage or liberal thought, was the true threat. The new immigrants held values and belief systems utterly alien to Europeans of all political views. You could have mass Muslim migration into Europe, argued Venner, or you could have a Europe with liberalism and gay marriage. You couldn't have both.

*

Notre-Dame de Paris was a suicide spot rich in symbolism. Architects thought it the greatest French Medieval Gothic building; Catholics loved the cathedral as one of the most famous churches in the world; patriots saw it as an embodiment of French culture and history. Back in 1931 an axe-faced Mexican feminist shot herself at the altar after an unhappy love affair.

Fans of obscure dystopian Russian literature saw another kind of significance in Notre-Dame. Elena Chudinova's Мечеть Парижской Богоматери (The Mosque of Notre-Dame) was a 2005 Russian-language novel about a future France where Islam has taken control. The book won a sci-fi award and sold around 100,000 copies over the next decade. A Serbian edition came out in 2006, a French one in 2009, and Polish and Bulgarian versions in the years after. A bootleg Turkish translation was out there somewhere and ultra-traditionalist American Catholics were prepping an English edition.

Chudinova was a big-smiling blonde from Moscow, a forty-five-year-old devout Russian Orthodox Christian when she wrote the novel. Her parents were palaeontologists but their daughter preferred poetry and journalism. Under the Soviet regime she wrote samizdat underground books about the White Armies on the losing end of the Russian Civil War. The fall of communism freed her to write openly; ongoing wars in Chechnya focused her attention on Islam. In 2004 she shared the horror when Islamic militants took over a Beslan school in the Republic of North Ossetia-Alania and killed 334 people, many of the victims children. Authorities alleged a British jihadist had been involved in the planning. The next year Chudinova began work on a novel set in the Western European nation with the largest number of Muslim citizens.

'I did not choose France,' Chudinova said. 'She, herself, decided that I needed to write about her. I am a mystic not a realist. I believe that a country can say "do so" and a person will hear her will. Honestly, I had no other choice... Why did La Belle France need me, a Russian, is not for me to decide. I had the obligation to write.'

Muslims first entered France in the seventh century when Umayyad Caliphate armies conquered Spain and kept heading north. Charles Martel stopped them at the Battle of Tours in 732 but it took another 200 years to push them out of France and hundreds more years to expel the remnants from Europe. The imperial flow reversed itself in the centuries that followed as French soldiers made an empire in North Africa. Muslim subjects got the Grande Mosquée de Paris as thanks for dying in the First World War but by the fifties colonies like Algeria were fighting for independence. The imperialist dream faded away and France's small Muslim population was soon bolstered by economic migrants who preferred low-wage jobs in a former oppressor to unemployment in their homelands.

The government in Paris was never keen on noting things like race and religion on census reports. Everyone was French and *vive la république*. Cautious estimates put Muslims at 4.7 million in 2000 (8 per cent of the population) and 6.2 million a decade later (10 per cent). Chudinova saw the figures growing into a majority in the near future. Her book took the idea and ran with it.

Мечеть Парижской Богоматери opens with some winemakers stoned to death by a Muslim mob near the Arc de Triomphe. Europe belongs to a new Islamic Caliphate, the Basilica of St Peter in Rome has been demolished, and America is distracted by civil war. In France, the cathedral in Notre-Dame is now a mosque and Christians who refuse to convert live in squalid ghettoes. The novel follows a rag-tag militia movement of secular French guerrillas, traditionalist

Catholics from the Society of St Pius X who live in the Parisian catacombs and a heroine partly based on Italy's Oriana Fallaci. When the Muslim authorities announce their intention to liquidate the Christian ghettoes, the resistance rises up and takes back Notre-Dame Cathedral in a symbolic suicide mission.

The book was a good read but critics thought it baggily structured and too long. Character is sacrificed to polemic and realism to heroics. Chudinova was a Russian nationalist proud of how little she knew about Islam, happy to paint Muslims as shadowy oppressors motivated by intolerance and hate. The book reflected the author's real-life worldview of Islam and Christianity locked in a battle to the death. Western hate speech laws forced Chudinova to dance round her intentions during interviews.

'My novel does not make inter-religious strife,' she said, 'but rather invites Christians to come back to Christ.'

This proud Russian nationalist may have appeared far-right by Western standards but she hated both Venner and Russians closer to home who flirted with fascist thought and iconography, like political theorist Alexander Dugin and his bookshelves full of Julius Evola and René Guénon. She had equal contempt for those with different kinds of failings who couldn't live up to the high standards of her Christian crusade. Few were surprised by her reaction to the news that a famous French writer with a bad reputation was working on a book with similarities in theme and setting to her own.

'Anti-Islamic activism does not consist of stealing the idea of someone else's book, and Houellebecq undoubtedly took the idea of my book,' she said. 'Many people noticed this, by the way.'

Michel Houellebecq was bringing his own brand of scabrous pessimism to the counter-jihad.

*

Some women just like meaningless sex with hundreds of partners. They like anonymous *queues* thrusting into *chattes, bouches, et culs* in swingers' clubs, dark car parks, tree-lined avenues quiet at night.

'I was carried by the conviction that I rejoiced in extraordinary freedom,' said Catherine Millet, an art critic who voyaged the sexual underground of Paris. 'To fuck above and beyond any sense of disgust was not just a way of lowering oneself, it was to raise yourself above all prejudice. There are those who break taboos as powerful as incest. I settled for not having to choose my partners.'

Michel Houellebecq thought Millet was fooling herself. Meaningless sex provided a minimal distraction from the horror of existence; people attended sex clubs because the alternative was worse, not because they enjoyed it. He knew from first-hand experience. The sex clubs can't have been picky. Houellebecq looked homeless, with a face like a mouldy peach and scuzzy blond combover. His clothes belonged in a plastic bag outside a charity shop.

The writer wouldn't admit to liking much about life. He told interviewers he hated Nietzsche, Viennese Actionists, ecologists, adolescents, hippies and Satanists. Houellebecq claimed to like Stalin but no one knew if he was being serious or not. He might have been telling the truth about liking American protopunk band The Stooges. He disliked Islam. In 2002 he called it the stupidest of the world's religions while promoting his novel *Plateforme* and narrowly squeaked out of a conviction for spreading racial hate.

'I didn't think Muslims had become a group that took offense at everything,' Houellebecq said. 'I knew that about the Jews, who are always ready to find a strain of anti-Semitism somewhere, but with the Muslims, honestly, I wasn't up to speed.'

Houellebecq was born Michel Thomas in 1956 on La Réunion, a French island east of Madagascar. His parents divorced; his communist grandmother raised him after his mother headed for Brazil with a boyfriend to live the hippy dream. There was a boarding school in Paris, agronomy at university, a marriage, a son, a divorce, depression, swingers' clubs, savage eczema, periods of institutionalisation.

He was working as a computer administrator at the National Assembly in Paris when his first poems were published under his grandmother's name of Houellebecq. The first full-length book was a 1991 look at H. P. Lovecraft, the American author of cosmic horror stories.

'I am not very proud of being a human being,' said Lovecraft. 'In fact, I distinctly dislike the species in many ways.' The Frenchman could understand. The tentacles and eldritch horrors and cultists in Lovecraft's work camouflaged a profoundly nihilistic understanding of humanity's unimportance in the universe. Houellebecq's book took a deep dive into Lovecraft's philosophy and created a hybrid monster of the two men, helped by the French author making up some of the supposed quotes. A real H. P. Lovecraft quote he missed seemed plenty ironic in light of what would happen later.

'If religion were true, its followers would not try to bludgeon their young into an artificial conformity,' said Lovecraft, 'but would merely insist on their unbending quest for truth, irrespective of artificial backgrounds or practical consequences.'

H. P. Lovecraft: Contre le monde, contre la vie (Against the World, Against Life) was a minor success and opened the door to novel writing. *Extension du domaine de la lutte* (Extension of the Battlefield) was a 1994 account of loneliness and being locked out of the sexual marketplace; *Les Particules élémentaires* (The Elementary Particles) a 1998 bestseller about a search for meaning through the decay of Western society seen through the eyes of two brothers; 2001's *Plateforme* (Platform) celebrated sex tourism in Thailand and got Houellebecq his first taste of controversy over its depiction of Islamic terrorists; *La Possibilité d'une île* (The Possibility of an Island) was a 2005 sci-fi novel about cloning in a post-apocalyptic France; and *La Carte et le territoire* (The Map and the Territory) was a more playful 2010 novel in which Houellebecq turns up as a character and gets murdered.

His books dissect modern France in chilly, clear-eyed detail. Mothers are flighty and selfish, hippies murderous, Americanisation an existential threat, and neither right or left have any answers. The novels sold well and got translated around the world, less for their pessimism and more for the direct line Houellebecq had open to the zeitgeist. *Les Particules élémentaires* appealed to readers seeking answers as the twentieth century closed; *Plateforme* anticipated the 2006 New Year's Eve terror bombings that killed three in Bangkok. The Frenchman had a knack for fictional narratives on themes readers didn't know they cared about until publication day.

In late 2014 the press was full of reports he'd written another book, dark and topical as ever. Houellebecq's piece of dystopian sci-fi about an Islamic France would sell millions and put him centre stage at a real-life terror attack in the heart of Paris.

19

A DRAWING NEVER
KILLED ANYONE

Michel Houellebecq and Charlie Hebdo, 2015

A thick cloud of incense and mysticism floated over Belle Époque Paris. Hidden behind the political scandals and saucy cabarets was an occult world of black magic, warring magi, reborn Cathar cults, Rose + Cross salons, Egypt fetishes, astrology, tarot and Kabbalah. Young men with independent incomes gathered in cafés to discuss the latest article by Gérard Encausse aka Papus, the godfather of modern occultism. Braver ones joined esoteric cults like the Martinists and the Hermetic Brotherhood of Light to search for eternal truths and pull back the veil of death.

The late nineteenth-century French public regarded the whole scene with suspicion. Mystical themes and bohemian lifestyles looked a lot like Satanism when seen from the respectable side of the street. In 1891 the bourgeoisie got a closer look when Joris-Karl Huysmans lifted the lid with his fifteenth novel and confirmed all their fears. A crop-haired civil servant with bushy goatee and a writing sideline, Huysmans was notorious for quitting worthy social commentary mid-career to turn out books about aesthetes and decadents. *Là-Bas* (Down There) took things further. The book's protagonist is a novelist researching fifteenth-century serial killer Gilles de Rais who stumbles on a Satanic ring in contemporary Paris.

The book scandalised readers, got banned from kiosks at railway stations, and sold well. Huysmans claimed it was all based on fact and had enough contact with practitioners of the black arts to sound convincing. Others thought the author's recent return to devout

Catholicism made him gullible to horror stories. *Là-Bas* smeared the reputations of many Parisian mystics but the occultist scene lumbered on long enough to intrigue René Guénon a decade later. Huysmans would die an oblate at a Benedictine monastery near Poitiers, still convinced Satanism had its claws deep in his contemporaries.

A century later, Michel Houellebecq chose Huysmans as the focal point of his new novel. *Soumission* (Submission) was due out on 7 January 2015 but a lot of people had already had an illegal preview. No one could remember a major novel like this ever being pirated before publication. The controversial subject matter surprised Houellebecq fans who remembered the storm over *Plateforme*. Houellebecq had made his feelings clear in interviews at the time.

'When people ask me about Islam for example,' he said in 2008, 'it's not something I think about at all. I thought about it once. I thought it was the stupidest religion and didn't think about it again. And I'll probably never think about it again in my life.'

He changed his mind. *Soumission* is a first-person alternative-reality narrative in which France turns to Islam. François is professor of literature at a Paris university who specialises in the work of Huysmans. He is directionless and spiritually dried up, directing his energies towards seducing students into meaningless affairs with no future.

The France outside his window is in chaos. Marine Le Pen's far-right Front National (FN) is on track to win the elections and the panicking political establishment has joined forces with an Islamic party run by the charismatic Mohammed Ben-Abbes. Muslims and far-right activists fight on the streets. Following the death of his parents, François takes refuge from the chaos in a monastery, hoping to experience the same return to Christ as his hero Huysmans.

The original plan had been for the narrator to embrace Catholicism. Houellebecq had been hit hard by the recent death of his own parents (and his dog, which seemed to upset him more) and wanted *Soumission* to parallel his spiritual search. The book rebelled. Houellebecq couldn't bring himself to write a conversion scene and François leaves the monastery still an atheist to drive aimlessly around France as the establishment rigs the elections and keeps out the Front National.

Ben-Abbes becomes president with plans to expand the European Union across the Mediterranean into a reborn Holy Roman Empire. Right-wing Catholics discover they have more in common with the ascendant Muslims than they realised. Burqas become a common sight in the streets, unemployment drops as women are banned from working, and crime in Muslim ghettoes disappears. The novel ends with the smooth-talking director of the newly Islamic Sorbonne, a white French convert, convincing François to embrace Islam in exchange for professional advantage and a gaggle of submissive young wives.

'My book describes the destruction of the philosophy handed down by the Enlightenment, which no longer makes sense to anyone, or to very few people,' said Houellebecq. 'Catholicism, by contrast, is doing rather well. I would maintain that an alliance between Catholics and Muslims is possible. We've seen it happen before, it could happen again.'

Those words hinted at the René Guénon style Traditionalism that some claimed to see woven into the book. Right-wingers ('nativists') suddenly abandoning their fight against immigration to become happy Muslims makes little sense unless they're followers of Guénon, or even Evola, able to slide into the most spiritually virile religion on offer. Others just saw a play on France's wartime collaboration with the occupying Germans. But the whole idea of Islam reinvigorating France, and by extension the West, echoes Guénon's belief in spiritual renewal, although Houellebecq clearly had little interest in the technicalities of faith. Islam in *Soumission* means little more than moral certainty, opposition to decadence, and multiple wives. Everyone still drinks wine.

The book didn't even seem much concerned with the workings of a religious coup. Houellebecq glosses over the power games with the creaky mechanic of having his narrator without Wi-Fi at critical moments, or watching a television wrecked by static and tuned to a foreign channel.

After hearing the buzz surrounding the pirated copies, Elena Chudinova became convinced *Soumission* borrowed shamelessly from her novel. Houellebecq had been accused of plagiarism in previous books. Critics had noticed *La carte et le territoire* copied sections from Wikipedia and its title from a 1999 novel by Michel Levy. Houellebecq claimed the borrowing was just part of his style, which didn't convince many. He had a better defence against Chudinova. *Мечеть Парижской Богоматери* and *Soumission* shared a theme but little else. Chudinova's book was a proudly Christian call to arms against an imminent dystopia. Houellebecq's atheism luxuriated in the pleasures of defeatism and the calm, cool river of surrender. The Russian eventually accepted the differences, but still thought her book had a more realistic view of any Islamic future.

In the week before *Soumission* officially came out, satirical magazine *Charlie Hebdo* had a caricature of the author on the cover. He looked even more decayed than in real life.

'Predictions of Houellebecq the Mage,' ran the cover line. 'In 2015 I lose my teeth ... and in 2022 I celebrate Ramadan!'

Houellebecq didn't much care. Everyone knew *Charlie Hebdo* cartoons were meant to be offensive. That was the point.

*

Charlie Hebdo was sixteen pages of left-leaning weekly satire out of Paris that shifted 30,000 copies an issue. The magazine appealed to the kind of middle-aged leftists old enough to remember the 1960s and naive enough to think freedom of speech could be taken for granted in a Western European democracy.

The publication had started with the satirical magazine *Hari-Kiri Mensuel* ('a stupid and bad paper' according to its masthead), launched in 1960 by a gang of disaffected leftists and Indochina veterans taking aim at French conservatism. After the social upheaval of May 1968, when students saw a strike by workers as catalyst for revolution and everyone got beaten by riot police, *Hari-Kiri* launched a more vicious weekly edition: *Hari-Kiri Hebdo*.

Hebdo got shut down for satirising the October 1970 mourning over the death of former president Charles de Gaulle. The headline 'Tragedy at Colombey Ball: 1 Dead' reminded everyone that 145 people died at the Club Cinq-Sept disco fire a week earlier. The Minister of the Interior suddenly remembered that naked cartoons from previous editions of *Hari-Kiri Hebdo* looked vaguely pornographic and shut it down. A gang of staff relaunched the weekly as *Charlie Hebdo*. Depending on who you asked, the name referenced either De Gaulle or comics monthly *Charlie Mensuel*, best known for running the French-language version of *Peanuts*.

Charlie Hebdo lasted twelve years then closed for financial reasons, a relic of a more radical past. It clawed itself back out of the grave in 1992 when French leftists rediscovered their hatred for America and anything right-wing in the wake of the Gulf War. The reborn magazine found a new audience which loved vicious swipes at capitalism, conservatism, nationalism, religion and good taste. Opponents saw a firehose of obscenity which soaked the wrong targets as often as the right ones.

The magazine's selling point was its sloppily done cartoon covers aimed at famous faces. Popes, politicians and Jesus Christ all got the *Charlie* treatment. Marine Le Pen was a popular target, drawn in an incestuous clinch with her even more right-wing father, then with pubic hair shaped like Hitler's moustache or modelling for John Galliano, the British designer recently convicted of anti-Semitic abuse. The dislike of the Front National was heartfelt. In 1996 *Charlie Hebdo*'s editors organised a petition to ban the party. Its failure didn't discourage attacks on the far-right or absolve the magazine editors from accusations of hypocrisy when they ran cartoons showing the Prophet Muhammad with a bomb in his turban. The Grande Mosquée de Paris sued them under hate speech laws in 2007 but didn't get anywhere.

Other covers featured Muslim Brotherhood activists being shot in Egypt ('The Quran is shit, it doesn't stop bullets'); Muhammad in tears at his fundamentalist followers ('It isn't easy being loved by idiots'); and some anti-Catholicism with John Paul II blessing an over-excited local crowd under the headline 'The French: Stupid as Negroes'. *Charlie Hebdo* didn't do political correctness.

The magazine occasionally acknowledged it had gone too far. Cartoonist Siné aka Maurice Sinet got sacked for a drawing that satirised rumours President Sarkozy's son intended to convert to Judaism. Siné sued his former employers and got €90,000 damages for unfair dismissal, along with some death threats from America's Jewish Defense League after journalists unearthed comments made by the cartoonist in the past.

'Yes, I am anti-Semitic and I am not scared to admit it,' Siné said back in 1982. 'I want all Jews to live in fear, unless they are pro-Palestinian. Let them die.'

In November 2011 the magazine renamed itself *Charia Hebdo* for an edition that satirized Islamic extremism and featured a cartoon of Muhammad telling readers, '100 lashes if you don't die of laughter.' Someone firebombed their offices in response. Editor Stéphane Charbonnier installed a security door at the magazine's 20th Arrondissement offices and the police assigned a security detail. *Charlie Hebdo* ran more caricatures of Muhammad the next year.

'A drawing has never killed anyone,' said Charbonnier.

By this time the magazine had become a minor French institution, a foulmouthed grandfather who always managed to shock, even as family members convinced themselves his heart was in the right place. The two police officers with assault rifles prowling around outside seemed more for show. *Charlie Hebdo*'s first edition of January 2015 had the headline 'Still No Attacks in France This Year' over a cross-eyed jihadist.

'Wait!' says the jihadist, 'we still have until the end of the month to present our wishes.'

A funny joke. It would only take another week.

20

JE SUIS CHARLIE

The Attack on Charlie Hebdo, 2015

On 7 January 2015 two men wearing black military fatigues and masks ran into the wrong office. The Kouachi brothers were homegrown Islamic militants with Czech vz.85 assault rifles and a poor sense of direction.

'Is this *Charlie Hebdo*?' one of them shouted.

Number 6 rue Nicolas-Appert was home to the *Charlie Hebdo* archives. The magazine lived a few doors up at number ten. The brothers left when archive staff called the police.

Saïd and Chérif Kouachi grew up in a French orphanage after the deaths of their Algerian-born parents. The pair moved to Paris when younger brother Chérif turned eighteen and settled in the 19th arrondissement, a green lump in the north-east, home to North African migrants. The brothers lived off pizza delivery jobs, drugs and small-scale criminality. Saïd had curls of black hair tight to the skull and a wispy beard framing his face. Chérif was an aspiring rapper with a shaved head, dark eyes and skin the colour of milky coffee. They joined a local gang that hung around the Parc des Buttes-Chaumont.

Religion played no part in their lives until Chérif met Farid Benyettou, a long-haired and fox-faced type of Algerian descent who sometimes went by the name Abu Abdallah. Benyettou worked as caretaker in a local mosque and saw himself as a theorist of jihad. His influence radicalised the rest of the gang, who started military-style training in the park. A few members made it to Iraq to join al-Qaeda in its fight against American troops. Chérif and Benyettou were arrested in 2005 trying to leave Paris for Damascus, a popular gateway for al-Qaeda recruits. Chérif did three years behind bars and inspired the well-reviewed *Djihad!*, a TV movie loosely based on the case.

In prison he met Djamel Beghal, a Frenchman who had worshipped at London's notorious Finsbury Mosque and was doing time for terrorism offences, and Amedy Coulibaly, a black Frenchman of Malian descent who converted to Islam after getting six years for bank robbery. Chérif radicalised further under their influence.

The year after his brother got out, Saïd visited Yemen to study at the Sana'a Institute for the Arabic Language. He ran into Nigerian rich kid Umar Farouk Abdulmutallab, who would fail to blow up an American airplane on Christmas Day 2009 and get four life sentences for it. The next year both brothers were arrested for a plot to jailbreak a member of Groupe Islamique Armé, the Algerian terror group which killed eight people in France with a 1995 bombing campaign and tried to fly a passenger jet into the Eiffel Tower. Lack of evidence sunk the case and put the pair back on the streets.

Police kept an eye on them but the brothers lived quietly with wives and children in social housing, doing menial jobs and rarely socialising with outsiders. They may have slipped the surveillance long enough to visit Yemen for military training with an al-Qaeda affiliate but no one could prove it.

By the end of 2014 the Kouachi brothers were in their early thirties and secretly plotting to bring jihad to the streets of Paris. Their friend Coulibaly got a loan from consumer credit company Cofidis and approached a Brussels arms dealer from his bank-robbing days. The delivery took place near the Brussels-Midi railway station. Coulibaly's 5,000 euros got him vz.85 assault rifles, Skorpion machine pistols, a rocket launcher, Tokarev TT pistols and a pump-action shotgun. The arms dealer thought he was dealing with just another criminal.

In the first week of the new year, the brothers dressed in black combat fatigues and masks and loaded their weapons into a stolen car. They headed for the rue Nicolas-Appert.

*

Corinne Rey was thirtysomething cartoonist with a strong chin and waterfall of curly dark hair. *Charlie Hebdo* readers knew her as Coco.

She had just arrived outside the office at 10 rue Nicolas-Appert with her young daughter fresh from kindergarten when Chérif and Saïd Kouachi materialised beside her. It was 11.30 a.m.

'Two hooded and armed men brutally threatened me,' she said. 'They wanted to enter, go up the stairs. I typed in the code.'

Frédéric Boisseau was sitting at the reception desk. The big, cheerful Frenchman who trained Krav Maga on his days off and had two young daughters was doing maintenance work in the building. The brothers shot him dead. *Charlie Hebdo* staff having an editorial meeting in a first-floor room thought they heard firecrackers.

Chérif and Saïd headed upstairs, taking Rey and her daughter with them. They pushed along a narrow corridor lined with notice boards pinned up with cartoons, cards from absent colleagues, messages to staff. The editorial meeting was uncertainly continuing when the brothers burst in and shouted out Charbonnier's name. When he reacted they shot him and his police bodyguard Franck Brinsolaro.

'I have no kids, no girlfriend, no car, no credit,' Stéphane Charbonnier told *Paris Match* three years earlier. 'It probably sounds a bit pompous, but I prefer to die standing than to live on my knees.'

Brinsolaro had more to lose. A trim forty-nine-year-old with greying hair and stubble, he had just married long-term girlfriend Ingrid Brinsolaro, blonde and serious editor of *L'Éveil Normand*. They had an eight-year-old daughter and one-year-old son.

There were sixteen more people in the room. Only eight lived through the next five minutes. Laurent Léger and book designer Gérard Gaillard hid under desks during the shooting, along with Rey and her daughter. Publishing director and cartoonist Laurent Sourisseau, better known as Riss, was shot in the shoulder but survived. Journalist Fabrice Nicolino was shot in the leg but survived. Journalist and South America expert Philippe Lançon was shot in the face but survived. The gunmen spared crime reporter Sigolène Vinson as she crawled along the corridor because she was a woman, but warned her to read the Quran.

Everyone else died. Jean Cabut, seventy-six years old, one of the magazine's founders; Georges Wolinski, eighty, a cartoonist who first encountered comics when American soldiers introduced them to his

Tunisian home town during the war; Bernard Verlhac aka Tignous, fifty-seven, a darkly good-looking cartoonist with four children; Bernard Maris, sixty-eight, Banque de France economist who wrote a column for the magazine and was friends with Michel Houellebecq; Mustapha Ourrad, sixty, the copy-editor and Nietzsche enthusiast from Algeria; Michel Renaud, sixty-nine, a former journalist who had dropped in that morning along with Gaillard to meet Charb; white-haired cartoonist Philippe Honoré, seventy-three; and Elsa Cayat, fifty-four, a psychologist who wrote an advice column for the magazine and was killed for being Jewish.

The shooting lasted five minutes. The gunmen left the room shouting.

'Alluha Akbar!'

*

Policeman Ahmed Merabet was near the *Charlie Hebdo* offices on bicycle when the alert came in. He and a fellow officer cycled to the scene and split up. Merabet was a forty-two-year-old Muslim, married and about to leave patrol work to become a detective. He saw the two gunmen climbing into their car and opened fire with his pistol.

The Kouachi brothers clambered back out of the black Citroën C3 and fired back. One bullet hit Merabet in the groin and he fell to the pavement, moaning in pain by some parked cars.

'Do you want to kill us?' one of the gunmen asked.

'No, it's okay, boss,' said Merabet.

One of the brothers shot him through the head. The whole scene was filmed by a journalist in an overlooking building. As the Kouachis got back into the Citroën they shouted at the street.

'We have avenged the Prophet Muhammad. We have killed *Charlie Hebdo*!'

The car peeled off into Paris. It would be found abandoned near Porte de Pantin with jihadist flags, petrol bombs and an ID card in the vehicle. The brothers hijacked another car, ran over a pedestrian, and got into a firefight with police. Then they escaped.

When the siege hit the news Amedy Coulibaly went out into the streets of Paris to carry out his part of the plan. He shot and injured a jogger. No one saw him. The next day the Kouachi brothers robbed a petrol station; independently, Coulibaly murdered off-duty police officer Clarissa Jean-Philippe and injured a street cleaner. In the early morning of 9 January the Kouachis hijacked another car in Crépy-en-Valois in the greater Paris area but abandoned it after a firefight. They holed up in a local signage company. Shortly after, Coulibaly entered a busy kosher hypermarket in east Paris. Claiming allegiance to Islamic State, a fundamentalist army growing in the fractured state of Iraq, he told police he would kill his hostages if the Kouachi brothers did not go free.

Both sieges came to an end at around 4.30 p.m. when police commandos went in. The brothers ran out of their building and were shot down as they fired at the police. Coulibaly murdered four hostages before he died.

'What we saw today was an attack on the values of our republic,' said Paris mayor Anne Hidalgo. 'Paris is a peaceful place. These cartoonists, writers and artists used their pens with a lot of humour to address sometimes awkward subjects and as such performed an essential function.'

All major French cities saw huge demonstrations, as did New York, London, Sydney, Amsterdam and elsewhere. Emotional journalists did pieces live to camera in front of impromptu shrines: flowers, glowing pools of candles, photographs of victims. The media seemed hit hard that some of their own had died. More cynical ones who had history with Islam were less surprised.

'This is like groundhog day,' said Bill Maher, 'except the groundhog keeps getting his head cut off.'

The slogan '*Je Suis Charlie*' was everywhere. I am Charlie. Facebook allowed users to put a tricolour filter on their profile pictures to show solidarity. Right-wing types circulated '*Je Suis Charlie Martel*' memes.

*

Houellebecq's *Soumission* came out the same day the Kouachis killed twelve people at *Charlie Hebdo*. It became a global bestseller. Some readers expected a call to arms against Islamic immigration, like Eric Zemmour's 2014 non-fiction *Le Suicide français*. Instead they got a work of resignation that cautiously saw spiritual regeneration in a France transfused with Muslim values. Prime Minister Manuel Valls obviously hadn't read the book.

'France is not Michel Houellebecq,' he told journalists. 'It is not intolerance, hate, and fear.'

Shell-shocked survivors from *Charlie Hebdo* managed to put together another issue a week later. Centre-left newspaper *Libération* gave them a room in their building and *Le Monde* lent computers. The cover showed a cartoon of the Prophet Muhammad holding up a '*Je Suis Charlie*' sign with tears in his eyes.

'All is forgiven,' ran the headline.

French readers queued for hours at the newsstands to buy a copy. Belgian police raided a jihadist cell in the Wallonien town of Verviers and killed two men who had planned terror attacks on anyone selling the magazine. Muslim mobs in the Republic of Niger killed ten people and burned down churches when the new issue came out. It sold 7.95 million copies around the world.

The *Charlie Hebdo* attack cut through liberal certainties like a scimitar through a watermelon. Liberal French had to accept that *laïcité* meant nothing to jihadists; leftists found themselves wondering if Muslims really were the new proletariat. Michel Houellebecq got police protection in the wake of the attack. He lived in a working-class Chinese district of Paris, a location taken as eccentric by most journalists but which may have been wiser than they knew. The narrator of Houellebecq's *Soumission* also lives there.

'If ethnic fighting spreads within Paris itself,' says one character in the book, 'the Chinese will stay out of it. Chinatown may become one of the last safe neighbourhoods in the city.'

Not everyone supported *Charlie Hebdo*. Over 200 writers signed a petition of protest when literary organisation PEN International awarded the magazine a Freedom of Expression Courage Award at its May gala. The murders were abhorrent, went the logic of people like Wallace Shawn and Russell Banks, but *Charlie Hebdo*'s racism could not be ignored. Cartoonist Garry Trudeau gave the petition his support at a Long Island University award ceremony in April. The sixty-six-year-old New Yorker's satirical *Doonesbury* strip was the cartoon of choice for America's liberals and syndicated to over 1,000 newspapers worldwide.

'Traditionally, satire has comforted the afflicted while afflicting the comfortable,' Trudeau said. 'Satire punches up, against authority of all kinds, the little guy against the powerful. Great French satirists like

Molière and Daumier always punched up, holding up the self-satisfied and hypocritical to ridicule. Ridiculing the non-privileged is almost never funny – it's just mean.'

Trudeau did not mention his 2010 letter of support to *South Park*, but did blame *Charlie Hebdo* for radicalising French Muslims with its satire. He noted that freedom of speech came with a price. More radical figures than Trudeau agreed.

'If you want to enjoy "freedom of speech" with no limits,' tweeted Mohammed Junaid Thorne, an Aborigine self-styled imam with a bad complexion, 'expect others to exercise "freedom of action".'

Some exercised that freedom of action by heading for Iraq to join Islamic State, the brightest star in the jihadist firmament. Their opponents marched through chilly streets in Eastern Germany to protest a huge influx of Muslim migrants. A human tsunami was building off the southern coast of Europe. The demographics Mark Steyn had complained about a few years back were turning critical.

21

OPENING THE GATES IN DRESDEN

The Rise of Pegida, 2015

Germany perfected right-wing extremism in 1933, then perfected forgetting all about it twelve years later. Millions dead, Europe in ruins, and a whole segment of the political spectrum forever discredited. The East found itself under a communist dictatorship which had to build a wall to stop citizens leaving; the West was run by middle-aged men with straight backs and conveniently fuzzy memories about their activities in uniform. Everyone agreed the Third Reich had been an inexplicable anomaly but that orders had to be obeyed, and then got on with the business of post-war living.

That amnesia wore off within a generation. Young people grew up worrying that without eternal vigilance the National Socialist experiment would regrow like a lizard's tail. West Germans had the most to be concerned about, with neo-Nazis already exploiting the controversial subject of post-war immigration. In the 1960s Turkish *Gastarbeiter* (guest workers) arrived to help build the economic miracle. Four million had settled by the start of the twenty-first century. Other migrants made their way to the West as asylum seekers: 380,000 between 1986 and 1990. The open-door policy continued after communism ended and the two halves of the country reunited, with well over a million migrants flooding in to escape civil war in former Yugoslavia.

Not everyone in the new Germany was keen on multiculturalism. A far-right arson attack on an immigration hostel in Rostock in 1992 shocked the government into reducing migrant numbers. Racial tensions slackened until the figures swung back up in 2013, with many of the recent migrants Muslim. The far-right was too marginalised by this time to take advantage, but many ordinary Germans were not happy.

In October 2014, Lutz Bachmann was a forty-one-year-old PR man on the Dresden club scene. He was getting jowly, a little creased across the forehead, but held back middle age with a taste for expensive casual clothes and a sharp haircut. Bachmann grew up in Dresden under communism. Crumbling buildings, party propaganda, Stasi spies everywhere, jobs for life. The area was known as the 'Valley of the Clueless' because it was it was a rare slice of East Germany that couldn't pick up Western television broadcasts.

After unification Bachmann played as a low-level professional footballer for a while then moved into the shadowlands of nightclubs and crime. He had convictions for burglary, cocaine dealing and drunk driving. A 1998 arrest warrant had Bachmann absconding to South Africa and opening a Cape Town nightclub for black patrons. It annoyed whites mourning the end of apartheid.

'People were shouting at me,' he said, 'How can you do this as a German, as a white? How can you open a night club for blacks?'

The South Africans eventually extradited him back to Germany for a few years in prison. Time done, Bachmann moved into public relations for clubs and an apparently respectable existence. It took immigration to disrupt his life of late nights and throbbing bass. In 2014 the government announced plans to build fourteen refugee reception centres in Dresden; later that year Kurdish migrants marched through the town. News reports talked about clashes between rival Muslim groups elsewhere in Germany. Worried about Islam, Bachmann started a Facebook group: Patriotische Europäer gegen die Islamisierung des Abendlandes (Patriotic Europeans against the Islamisation of the West).

That page led to a small demonstration in Dresden that attracted little attention. Bachmann cared enough to repeat it every Monday. Ordinary Dresden residents began to take notice. Bachmann persuaded nightclub cronies to turn up. Connections with football firms brought in some hooligans, a traditionally anti-Islamic faction. Germany already had Hooligans gegen Salafisten, a small European Defence League adjunct that staged occasional marches. Numbers began to grow. Posts turned into marches, marches into a movement, and Bachmann found himself addressing thousands of people. At least 10,000 attended a march on 8 December 2014.

'Mostly white men over forty wearing shabby clothing,' said the man from the *Sydney Morning Herald*.

Left-wing counter demonstrators turned up and police fought battles to keep the sides apart. German chancellor Angela Merkel made sharp comments about marchers being used in the cause of xenophobia but stopped short of condemning Pegida. A December 2014 poll showed 30 per cent of Germans sympathised with the group, 26 per cent partially approved, with another 19 per cent being understanding of its aims.

Interior Minister Thomas de Maizière thought Bachmann's movement was a front for the far-right but couldn't find anything too extreme in the Pegida manifesto. Bachmann wanted stricter laws on asylum and guarantees that migrants would assimilate into German culture.

'In Idaho this would be mainstream,' said Gerald Praschl, political editor of popular magazine *SUPERillu*. 'But here it is considered right wing.'

In January, Pegida marched through Dresden and observed a minute's silence for the victims at *Charlie Hebdo*. The group's growth worried the German government enough for Maizière to publicly warn the group not to exploit *Charlie Hebdo* for propaganda. In happier times the French magazine would probably have stuck Bachmann on the cover in crude caricature. The old gang at rue Nicolas-Appert wouldn't have been keen on a man who hoped to change German politics through immigration activism.

'Well, there was already a revolution in 1989 coming from Eastern Germany,' Bachmann told *Time* magazine, 'and they know what we are able to do here if we keep on growing. But we'll see what happens. As we say in Germany, we don't know where this train is going.'

*

Pegida gave hope to a counter-jihad movement still badly damaged by the Anders Breivik killings. Elsewhere, membership remained down, activism minimal.

The offshoots of Stephen Lennon's English Defence League did little except update their Facebook pages. Stop Islamisation of Europe managed a few small demonstrations. Pamela Geller and Robert Spencer had created Stop Islamization of America back in 2010 but achieved little more than controversial bus adverts ('In any war between the civilized man and the savage, support the civilized man. Support Israel. Defeat Jihad') and protesting a planned thirteen-storey Islamic community centre near the World Trade Center site. Geller called it the Ground Zero Mosque and caused enough public uproar, along with Pastor Jones, that the developers decided to build some luxury condos instead.

The left-leaning non-profit Southern Poverty Law Center called Stop Islamization of America a hate group, and the invitations to speak on Fox News dried up. An attempt to unite everyone in Stop Islamization of Nations (SION) back in January 2012 didn't achieve much except the defection of the Norwegian division, whose 3,000 activists preferred their own path.

Pegida's success promised a fresh start for the counter-jihad. Branches opened in Scandinavia, Switzerland, Belgium and Canada. Over in England, it inspired Stephen Lennon to re-join street politics. The English Defence League founder had been through a rough few years. There had been death threats, the intimidation of his wife and kids, Kevin Carroll getting chased by a Muslim with a shotgun, the failed bomb attempt on an EDL rally, media ambushes, police pressure, and failure to move into conventional politics with the British Freedom Party, a supposedly centrist movement created by former BNP and UKIP members. The party's highpoint was Carroll coming fourth in the election for Bedfordshire police commissioner. Lennon was burnt out and wanted to quit the counter-jihad.

Public horror at the murder of soldier Lee Rigby on 2 June 2013 kept him onside for a while longer. Two Islamists of Nigerian descent murdered an off-duty soldier in south-east London. The news showed footage of them with bloody hands and a partially decapitated body just out of shot as they lectured passers-by about Islam. Nearly 10,000 people attended a League march in Newcastle. Students invited Lennon to debate opponents at the Oxford Union.

Public outrage at radical Islam soon dissipated. Not even the information that attacker Michael Adebolajo had been a familiar face at anti-League events could bring new members to the counter-jihad. A poll just after Lee Rigby's murder found 61 per cent thought the English Defence League's marches increased the likelihood of Islamic terror attacks.

'I couldn't believe that Britain could effectively just glance out of a car window at a passing accident and drive on,' said Lennon. 'A moment's curiosity and no more.'

His disillusion returned. He began privately meeting with Mohammed Ansar, a round-faced Muslim of Pakistani background who quit a career in banking to become a professional political pundit. Ansar was a familiar face at lectures, talk shows, and panel events. He had impressed Lennon at a BBC discussion programme on Islam, and an uneasy friendship blossomed. They rarely agreed on much but Ansar invited the League boss along to watch him debate London's Quilliam think tank. It changed Lennon's life.

Quilliam got its name from a nineteenth-century British convert to Islam, its money from the government, and leadership from British Muslims who had turned their backs on extremism. The foundation went after anyone preaching radicalism and saw Ansar as a fanatic hiding behind the pose of moderate Islam. During the debate Quilliam activists launched an onslaught of intellectual firepower at the pair, humiliating Ansar but impressing his guest. Afterwards, they advised Lennon to leave the English Defence League if he really wanted to tackle jihadism.

Lennon had been thinking along the same lines for months. Quilliam representatives offered £2,000 a month if he gave them the credit for the decision to leave. Lennon took the money. At a Quilliam press conference on 8 October 2013, he and Carroll announced they were quitting the English Defence League, claiming to be sick of the far-right infiltration that had already disillusioned Roberta Moore.

'I read more about Quilliam and I looked at what Quilliam has done,' Lennon said. 'They've actually brought change, which is what I want to do. I want to bring change. I want to tackle Islamist extremism, I want to tackle neo-Nazi extremism – they're opposite sides of the same coin.'

Douglas Murray interviewed him for *The Spectator*. Murray was a gay, conservative Oxford graduate just the right side of supercilious who'd been making a name for himself with well-spoken takedowns of radical Islam. His piece welcomed Lennon's escape from the street brawls of the English Defence League to a more civilised discourse. Privately, Lennon shook his head at a world where he got jail time and Murray a book contract (*Neoconservatism: Why We Need It* and *Islamophilia: a Very Metropolitan Malady*) for saying the same things.

Lennon's defection dropped the guillotine blade on the English Defence League. The organisation continued to march but no one paid much attention anymore. If Alan Ayling had been funding the

League, as critics claimed, then the money stopped. A few bitter League members got some grim satisfaction when everything went wrong for Lennon early the next year.

He had lent his brother-in-law the £20,000 deposit for a house; the brother-in-law lied about income on his application, so Lennon getting his money back after the house sold counted as fraud. He got eighteen months. In prison the governor put him on an open wing despite Muslim inmates threatening to kill him. Lennon went on the offensive by drawing burqas on *The Sun*'s topless page 3 girls to annoy Muslim prisoners next in line for the newspaper. Then he read the Quran. 'Obey Allah or burn in hell forever. Page after page of it. Sex slaves, the lot. The thing is horrific.'

The Quilliam monthly payments stopped. Lennon got out of prison to find himself friendless and directionless until Pegida's success in Germany offered up a model for a more respectable counter-jihad movement. No brawling, no police raids. He linked up with fellow counter-jihadists Paul Weston and Anne Marie Waters to discuss forming a British branch.

Former Gates of Vienna correspondent Weston had passed through the British Freedom Party before forming his own Liberty GB, a small pressure group calling itself a 'patriotic counter-jihad party for Christian civilisation, Western rights and freedoms, British culture, animal welfare and capitalism.' Anne Marie Waters was a lesbian NHS lawyer with a left-wing past who'd drifted across the political spectrum to UKIP and then the counter-jihad. She spent most of her time demanding mosque closures and setting up ShariaWatch, rumoured to have the support of prominent lawyers interested in secularism.

'I am, and have always been, very clear,' said Waters. 'Sharia tribunals represent a severe infringement of the basic civil rights of women, they have far overstepped the boundaries of arbitration, they are acting unlawfully, and they must be closed down.'

The trio believed Pegida UK could capitalise on its parent party's success. Then Lutz Bachmann got involved in a scandal that severely damaged the Pegida brand. It had all been going so well at the march for *Charlie Hebdo* when Bachmann looked out at the sea of French and German flags and asked for a minute's silence to remember Paris. A crowd of 25,000 had marched through the January cold in this Saxon town on the River Elbe to show solidarity with the dead of *Charlie Hebdo*. Some were Dresden locals, others sharp-dressed football casuals or bulky men who made their money in the nightclub business. Many were ordinary people who had found a movement that openly said what they privately thought. Pegida was Germany's fastest-growing political movement.

Not long after, something happened that made it look like Thomas de Maizière was right. A picture of the Pegida leader posing as Hitler had gone viral on social media. Opponents circulated it with the slogan '*Er ist wieder da*' (Look Who's Back) from a popular book and film, transgressively hilarious to Germans and mildly amusing to everyone else, about Adolf Hitler's return from the dead. That plus some Facebook posts calling migrants animals got Bachmann dragged into court.

He denied making the comments and his lawyers proved persons unknown had photoshopped a smear of Charlie Chaplin moustache onto an existing photograph. The court still fined him €9,600. Bachmann resigned from Pegida but re-joined the next month as chairman. Senior movement figure Kathrin Oertel, a Hitchcockian blonde, immediately resigned and created Direkte Demokratie für Europa, hoping to distance the counter-jihad from extremism. It went nowhere, but Pegida was now firmly attached to the far-right in the public imagination.

Bachmann's marches attracted less people as spring and summer came in. The *Charlie Hebdo* event with its French flags and posters of Angela Merkel in a headscarf and shouts of '*Wir sind das Volk!*' (We are the People – an old anti-communist slogan from the Berlin Wall days) had been the movement's last show of strength. Bachmann set up political party Freiheitlich Direktdemokratische Volkspartei (Liberal Direct Democratic People's Party) which failed to do much. Fiftysomething ultramarathon runner Tatjana Festerling ran for Dresden mayor but got less than 10 per cent of the vote. The only bright spot came from Pegida's informal alliance with Alternative für Deutschland (AfD), a fringe party making an awkward transition from euroscepticism to counter-jihad.

The situation changed dramatically in the last months of 2015 when a million migrants from mostly Muslim nations entered Europe. Cheerful blonde girls stood around train stations holding 'Refugees Welcome' signs; families opened their homes to strangers; Angela Merkel talked about the birth of a new Germany. The counter-jihad saw an apocalypse that would destroy Europe.

22

THE BRILLIANT BLUE OF THE AEGEAN SEA

Middle Eastern Migrants Head for Europe, 2015

Orange jumpsuit, sand dune, executioner in black. Another Islamic State beheading video spreading like a syphilitic rash over social media. Only a few years earlier Osama bin Laden had preached jihad from a cave with dubbed cassette tapes and poor-quality video. Things were different now. Islamic State videos had drone work, uninspired but semi-professional editing choices, and close-ups of blood spraying black out the decapitated neck. It was 'Jihad 2.0', in the words of French professor and political commentator Alexandre del Valle.

Islamic State had entered through a door opened in Damascus back in 2011 when pencil-necked dictator Bashar al-Assad found himself struggling against drought, crop failure and an angry population demanding democracy. Rolling protests across the region had already toppled regimes in Tunisia, Egypt, Yemen and Libya. The shaky Syrian regime looked next in line for the Arab Spring.

Protesters thought al-Assad would quickly cave in to their demands. They knew the dictator had never wanted to rule Syria in the first place. His elder brother had been raised for the job until a roundabout jumped in front of his speeding Mercedes. When the demonstrations started, al-Assad turned out to be less of a pushover than anyone expected. Secret police beat protesters off the street and dragged them into prison. Those who managed to get away fled Damascus for a new rebel movement in the provinces that brought together democrats, religious hardliners and defecting army units. By July the country was deep in civil war.

Western powers tried to stop the fighting but couldn't find anyone with clean enough hands to get behind. Syria had been at war for three years, and no one thought things could get any worse, when Islamic State appeared out of the desert.

The organisation had been around since the end of the previous century as Jama'at al-Tawhid wal-Jihad (Monotheism and Jihad), a gang of Jordanian jihadists so strict that even ally Bin Laden disapproved. Founder Abu Musab al-Zarqawi went to war against American forces in Iraq, recruiting locals and foreign jihadists to his cause. Over the next few years Jama'at al-Tawhid wal-Jihad went through several name changes, got bigger and more ambitious, broke with an increasingly marginalised Bin Laden, and expanded across the border into Syria. It now called itself ad-Dawlah al-Islāmiyah fī 'l-'Irāq wa-sh-Shām (Islamic State of Iraq and the Levant). To everyone else it was Islamic State or ISIS.

By 2015 Islamic State leader Abū Bakr al-Baghdadi, a doughy Iraqi with a paranoid stare, ruled a territory of 3 million people that stretched across Syria and Iraq. The group pushed an apocalyptic interpretation of Islam to the outside world with propagandist video executions that thrilled sympathisers but horrified everyone else. Knives and guns; desperate men in orange jumpsuits that referenced imprisoned jihadists in America's Guantanamo Bay; speeches warning foreign nations to stay out of the war; the flashing blade, the severed head. Islamic State even did interactive social media campaigns. Foreign supporters voted in a Twitter campaign, #SuggestAWayToKillTheJordanianPilotPig, on ways to murder a captured airman. They elected to burn him alive in a steel cage.

Millions of Syrians fled the war for refugee camps in neighbouring countries. News cameras panned down miles of tents, sacks of grain, miserable families sitting on folding beds. Some moved on to the West, paying people smugglers $1,000 a person to join the flotilla of boats and rafts breaking into the European Union through its soft southern belly. Greece got 68,000 migrants in the first six months of 2015, Italy 67,500. Soon everyone claimed to be a Syrian refugee, even those coming from Sub-Saharan Africa. Once on European soil the migrants moved north, heading for Germany and Sweden but silting up along the Hungarian border.

Viktor Orbán had a face like a mudslide and control of Hungary's centre-right Fidesz government. His nation was a conservative former Soviet satellite with no history of non-white migration. Orbán built a 325-mile-long razor-wire fence along the border with Serbia and Croatia, and began grudgingly registering migrants a few at a time even as he made doom-filled speeches about the death of European identity. Germany's Angela Merkel criticised the unfriendly welcome without being keen on accepting migrants into her own country.

The summer months ramped up the crisis. By August 250,000 had entered Europe on a dangerous journey over bad seas in leaky boats. They kept coming. Nearly 4,000 would die trying to make the crossing. Typical was a boat that got into trouble on 3 October. Sea water was coming over the gunwales, the crew was panicking, and 200 migrants packed the deck praying to Allah. Among them was a man carrying a Syrian passport in the name of Ahmad Almohammad. The captain told everyone to be calm, that a Greek navy ship was on its way.

The migrants kept praying. They remembered the horror stories about the boat that sank near Bodrum recently. No one had come to help that little boy.

*

The image that symbolised the migrant crisis was a small, dead boy face down in the Turkish sand. It made the front pages, the television news, the social media feeds. His name was Aylan Kurdi and he was three years old.

Kurdi and his Syrian family had been aiming for Greece via the Aegean Sea, part of the 1.2 million people who would claim asylum in Europe by the end of the 2015 and double the number from the previous year. In the early morning of 2 September a motorised inflatable boat carrying Kurdi and fifteen others had capsized five minutes out of Bodrum in Turkey. Five people died, three of them children. Local hotel workers found the bodies of two children floating in the water and carried them to the beach. A Turkish photographer snapped a picture of Kurdi lying bunched up and grey on the wet sand. Within days the picture was all over the world.

The media contrasted Kurdi's body with the riots and tear gas at the Hungarian border where Orbán was trying to stop the human wave moving north. Migrants claimed they wanted to live in nations with sparkling records of human rights; the Hungarians thought it was the fat welfare systems in Germany and Sweden that attracted them. The emotion around Kurdi's photograph sidelined difficult facts. The boy's father had snagged a good hotel job in Turkey, saving $5,000 in cash for the people smugglers, and had been piloting the boat himself.

The anguished public conversation over a child's death threw open the gates of Europe. Angela Merkel suspended EU regulations on immigration and welcomed 442,000 migrants to Germany, compared to the 19,000 who had applied for asylum back in 2007; Sweden took another 163,000, with the rest scattered across the western half of the continent. The former communist East refused to take any, and migrants showed no enthusiasm for poverty and snow. Asylum systems got to work deciding who got to stay and who had to return home. Official figures broke down the migrants as 58 per cent adult male, 17 per cent adult female, and 25 per cent minors. Most minors were male, with many claiming to be seventeen years old; most authorities didn't check claimed ages but a British government investigation into a sample group of child migrants found 65 per cent were actually adults.

The news showed images of young people in German cities greeting migrants with 'Refugees Welcome' signs in a public festival of charity. Some brought food, others opened their homes. The counter-jihad side couldn't believe what it was seeing. Baron Bodissey at the Gates of Vienna made his feelings clear.

'Commonly referred to as the "European migration crisis",' he wrote in August 2015. 'The word "invasion" is not generally used.'

Douglas Murray of *The Spectator* started research for a book about a Europe driven into demographic collapse by colonial guilt and capitalist thirst. Steve Bannon, the America media magnate in charge of right-wing Breitbart News, compared the situation to *Le Camp des Saints*, an apocalyptic 1973 novel about Third World immigration destroying Europe written by explorer, travel writer and traditionalist Catholic Jean Raspail. Over in America, Pamela Geller was equally horrified. She made a big deal of a blurry photograph where a brown hand held a piece of paper with 'Islamic State in Rome' in front of a possibly Italian street.

'The concept of immigration jihad goes all the way back to Muhammad,' she wrote. 'Al-Hijrah (immigration) as a means of supplanting the native population and reaching the position of power is a tenet of Islamic imperialism.'

Pegida got an infusion of new blood with the migrant crisis. By the autumn its Dresden marches were attracting 9,000 participants. Signs blasting Angela Merkel's open-door policy were common, often with Photoshop pictures of her in a Nazi-style uniform with the Euro sign replacing the swastika. Someone went to the effort of making a wooden gallows.

'Today we see an inner hardening among the movement,' said Professor Werner J. Patzelt, a Dresden University lecturer in political science. 'Participants have become angrier and more upset, which can be described as a radicalization.'

The anger was still rising. A 19,000-strong Pegida rally on 19 October caused outrage across Germany when a guest talked about garbage dumps, paedophiles and concentration camps. He was Turkish and usually wrote books about cats.

*

Akif Pirinçci was a drawn-looking fifty-five-year-old whose parents had emigrated from Istanbul to Germany as *Gastarbeiter* when he was ten. A brief career as an enfant terrible writer mixing high and low culture got him noticed on the literary scene but his 1989 book *Felidae* broke through to the mainstream. Its hero was a cat who solved crimes.

Cat lovers and crime enthusiasts had enough disposable income for Pirinçci to move his wife and son into an upmarket Bonn villa. Sequels to *Felidae* and other books like *Der Rumpf* (quadruple amputee plans a murder) and *Yin* (dystopian all-female world) made him a millionaire. The money failed to smooth Pirinçci's prickly character or stop him complaining about highbrow critics who refused to acknowledge his talent.

Around 2009 he began to appear in right-wing spaces, giving interviews to counter-jihad blogs and writing commentary for conservative newspapers. He called Islam a breeding ground for terrorism among immigrant communities and made other standard counter-jihad points, shocking a German media which preferred its celebrities liberal and guilt-ridden. The sexism that crept in after his 2013 divorce didn't help.

The next year Pirinçci published polemical bestseller *Deutschland von Sinnen: Der irre Kult um Frauen, Homosexuelle und Zuwanderer* (Germany Loses its Senses: The Crazy Cult of Women, Homosexuals and Immigrants) to sum up his views: Germany was on the slide, immigrants got too much tolerance, homosexuals waved their sexuality in everyone's faces, feminism was destroying the family, and Muslim demographics were waging a creeping genocide. The book sold a lot in the face of outraged criticism. Its success pushed Pirinçci further towards the counter-jihad world and he appeared at some Alternative für Deutschland events. In October a Pegida member and Facebook friend asked him to speak at a rally. He agreed.

Pirinçci gave a fiery speech. Germany was turning into a Muslim garbage dump; the leftist Grüne (Green Party) were child fuckers; Germany was a shit state; a prominent Muslim had as much to do with German culture as Pirinçci's anus did with the production of perfume; the government would be happy to arrest all Pegida supporters but the concentration camps were out of order. It all got too much by the end and the crowd booed and hissed until he wound up the speech. They preferred Bachmann's smoother approach.

By the next day journalists were selectively misquoting Pirinçci to give the impression the concentration camp remark was aimed at Muslim migrants. Publishers cancelled contracts and Amazon. de deleted all his books. Facebook blacked out his account. The government opened an investigation. Pirinçci left the country for a long holiday after journalists tried to blame him for the 196 arson attacks on migrant centres that year, many around Dresden. Police eventually admitted neo-Nazis rather than Pegida were responsible.

The migrant boats kept coming. The one carrying Ahmad Almohammad had been sinking out in the brilliant blue of the Aegean Sea when a Greek naval vessel slid alongside and rescued everyone as the water lapped around their feet. They headed for the island of Leros, all brown earth and white buildings under a sky bright and constant as enamel paint. Local authorities processed them, checked documents, took fingerprints and printed Greek-language papers for travel to the mainland.

Ahmad Almohammad was among the sixty-nine men from the rescued boat processed on the first day. The Greeks recorded him as twenty-five years old, 5 feet 7 inches tall, and born in Idlib. The photograph showed a man with slight stubble, badly cut brown hair, and a wall-eyed stare. He seemed calm and polite.

The next ferry to Athens was three days away. Almohammad and an angrier migrant who claimed to be his brother prowled Leros looking for a quicker route. They looked enough alike that the sibling claim might have been true, although the second man's passport was in the name M. al Mahmod. They told locals money was no problem. A private boat sailed them and four other migrants to nearby Kalymnos. From there a Blue Star ferry called the *Diagoras* took them to Piraeus in Athens.

On 7 October Almohammad and his brother turned up at the Macedonian–Serbian border. The next day they were in a Croatian refugee centre but didn't stay, crossing into Hungary and telling officials they were making for Austria. Then they disappeared.

Ahmad Almohammad would next be seen in Paris outside Le Stade de France on 13 November. It was the worst terror attack in Europe since the war.

23

WHEAT FIELDS IN
THE BATACLAN

The Heart of France Attacked, 2015

The crowd was bouncing, the band loud, the strobes flashing. Tonight's headliners had a singer with a handlebar moustache and a knack for writing the kind of trashy, scuzzed-up, sexy Americana that French hipsters loved. At least 1,500 Parisians had turned out this Friday 13 November to see the Eagles of Death Metal burn through a set at the Bataclan, an intimate 11th arrondissement venue popular with foreign bands.

When the shooting started at 9.40 p.m. the band was rocking out the country punk of 'Kiss the Devil'. Three gunmen walked in through the rear doors like they owned the place, looked around, and opened fire at the crowd waiting by the bar.

'First of all I thought it was part of the show,' said someone there, 'but then I turned around and saw someone who had just taken a bullet in the eye.'

The attackers reloaded their Kalashnikovs and kept shooting. The band ducked behind their guitars and ran off stage and the music stopped and the screaming started. Panicking fans nearest the gunmen shoved their way through those who still didn't understand what was happening.

'Like a gust of wind through wheat,' said an Eagles fan watching from the balcony.

People dropped to the floor but the gunmen just fired low. Some made it out through an emergency exit; some jumped the stage. Fifty made it on to the roof and others locked themselves in offices and toilets on the Bataclan's upper floors. A woman hung out a second-floor window. One gunman went up to the balcony for a better angle of fire down into the hall.

Then it was dead bodies and blood and screaming wounded. The gunmen shot anyone still moving. The floor was an inch deep in blood. Phones were ringing in dead pockets from friends and family with news about the suicide bombings at Le Stade de France up in Saint-Denis.

Islamic State had planned a three-part attack. The football stadium, the concert, the restaurant district. Twenty minutes before the Eagles of Death Metal went into 'Kiss the Devil' the man who called himself Ahmad Almohammad blew a hole in his ribcage outside Le Stade de France. Germany and France were playing a night-time friendly in front of 81,000 people. German Finance Minister Frank-Walter Steinmeier attended as guest of French President François Hollande.

Almohammad's role in the attack was to enter the stadium and detonate a suicide vest loaded with Acetone peroxide-based explosives. The panic would send crowds rushing towards two other bombers waiting outside.

Security was too good. Almohammad got patted down at a turnstile trying to enter after the match had started by a guard who couldn't understand the vest but wasn't taking any chances. He turned Almohammad away. The Islamic State soldier walked a few paces and pulled a wire. He took out a chunk of his chest and killed a passer-by.

Ten minutes later another turnstile guard refused entry to Bilal Hadfi, a twenty-year-old with gentle eyes and a forehead you could land a plane on. Hadfi blew himself into bloody mush near gate H. Both explosions could be heard in the stadium, but the match continued.

A twenty-minute drive away in the 10th arrondissement, three men with Kalashnikovs climbed out of a black Seat with Belgian plates in the rue Bichat. Locals knew the district as the haunt of well-heeled 'bobos'. The bourgeois bohemian hipsters were out in force tonight spending their money at Le Carillon bar and the Le Petit Cambodge restaurant. Glasses clinking, cutlery clanking, food, chatter, music, cigarette smoke hanging over pavement tables.

Le Carillon had an oxblood frontage and a board chalked with the word 'WiFi'. The gunmen opened fire at people sitting outside. An unbelieving passer-by watched the nearest attacker. 'He was left handed and shooting in bursts of three or four shots. It was fully intentional, professional bursts of three or four shots. He killed three or four individuals who were sitting in the chairs in front of the cafe. We saw them get shot down. They fell off their chairs onto the ground.'

The gunman entered the cafe and kept shooting. The other two turned and opened fire on Le Petit Cambodge. The shooting was over in less than thirty seconds. All three climbed back into the Seat and drove off. Fifteen people had died.

Seven minutes later, the Seat stopped in the rue de la Fontaine-au-Roi for a single gunman to spray the terrace of the Café Bonne Bière. Five died. The car screeched off to the south. Near the boulevard Voltaire the car stopped to let out Brahim Abdeslam, a Belgian bar owner of Moroccan descent. He left his Kalashnikov behind and trudged towards the Comptoir Voltaire café.

The others drove to La Belle Équipe restaurant on the rue de Charonne and shot dead nineteen people sitting on the terrace, before escaping into the Paris night. The man they left behind pushed his way into the Comptoir Voltaire through the cramped wooden tables and carafes of wine, put a hand over his face, and triggered the suicide vest. Whatever jihadist mechanic wired the explosives got it all wrong. The vest blew Abdeslam apart in a cloud of sparking smoke but no one else died.

At the same moment another jihad team climbed out of a grey Volkswagen Polo near the Bataclan concert hall. America's Eagles of Death Metal were playing.

*

It was chaos. Just before 10.15 p.m. a senior police officer and his driver ran into the Bataclan and fired at a gunman, who detonated his suicide vest and died along with whatever Eagles of Death Metal fans lying around him had survived the first assault. A mob of Brigade de Recherche et d'Intervention officers jogged into the hall with assault rifles and bulletproof shields. The last two gunmen were on the balcony with a group of twelve hostages, holed up in a corridor with a lockable door.

Reports were coming in of a third suicide bomber near Le Stade de France. Greek immigration would have recognised him as the angry man from Leros who claimed to be Almohammad's brother. He had wandered the outskirts of the stadium trying to avoid the swarming police before blowing himself up in the rue de la Cokerie. Back in the Bataclan it took an hour to sweep the hall and discover the gunmen's location. A hostage with a gun to his head relayed demands, others stood as shields in front of windows and doors. A jihadist agreed to talk by phone.

'You can thank President Hollande,' he said, 'because it's thanks to him you must suffer this.'

He blamed the attacks on French involvement in Syria, which had recently escalated into airstrikes and arming rebel groups; he threatened to decapitate hostages. The other gunman shot someone in the street from the window. Both smiled when they heard the crying of injured people downstairs.

At 12.20 a.m. the police turned off the lights and threw in stun grenades. One gunman blew himself up; a bullet storm turned the second into chopped meat. A total of 130 people had died, eighty-nine of them at the Bataclan, with hundreds more injured. The government declared a state of emergency. Carpets of glowing candles and cellophane-wrapped flowers spread outside the attack sites. Facebook brought back its tricolour filter. A big-nosed thirtysomething German pianist called Davide Martello, known to his fans as Klavierkunst, towed a grand piano up to the Bataclan doors and played 'Imagine' by John Lennon. The performance and its motivation moved onlookers but disgusted Gates of Vienna's French correspondent 'Madeleine'.

'We have a terrible problem with brainwashed masses,' she wrote. 'Look at this idiot, playing bloody "Imagine" by that horrid little socialist John Lennon. As an homage to those metal fans mowed down by machine guns in the Bataclan venue, it's more like a kick in the face.'

Her boss was even more direct. Edward May wanted to end Muslim migration into America.

'In the wake of last night's massacre in Paris,' he said, 'a petition has been filed at petitions.whitehouse.gov that seeks to place an indefinite moratorium on Middle Eastern refugee resettlement in the United States. The initiator of the petition says: "We know that jihadis have been using the cover of refugee resettlement to exploit our weak borders and commit acts of terrorism. Paris is proof of this objective."'

The petition didn't go anywhere, although an American presidential candidate would soon come along who took the idea seriously. In France, Alexandre del Valle supported extending that moratorium to Europe. The attacks had convinced the professor that Islamic State intended to divide and conquer the continent by combining terror attacks with mass migration; the group was using the liberal compulsion to defend Muslims against any accusations of extremism as a shield.

'So many of the brave migrants presented to all as victims, doctors and engineers, graduates, as "Chances for France",' he said, 'are in fact fake refugees, illiterates, seasoned offenders linked to trafficking networks, and even terrorist sympathizers. Indeed, out of 100,000 migrants, we can count, at least, a hundred radical Islamists likely to be linked to jihadist groups.'

Del Valle and the Gates of Vienna were part of a much bigger backlash against Muslims. It had the authorities worried. A Pew Research Centre survey on attitudes towards Islam after the attacks found 43 per cent of Europeans now held unfavourable views of Muslims. Figures were higher among countries in the frontline of the migrant crisis like Greece, Italy and Hungary, although only 33 per cent of Swedes and 29 per cent of Germans had given into negativity. A separate survey found 61 per cent of Americans looked unfavourably on Islam. Police got posted on security detail outside mosques across Europe, to counter-jihad disgust.

'The old definition of a nanosecond,' wrote a cynical Mark Steyn back in 2006, 'was the gap between the traffic light changing in New York and the first honk from a car behind. The new definition is the gap between a terrorist bombing and the press release from an Islamic lobby group warning of a backlash against Muslims.'

At least four attackers escaped: the two gunmen in the Seat, their driver, and another driver who chauffeured the suicide bombers to Le Stade de France. Police thought the last man might have ducked out of his own suicide assignment; a bomb vest had been found dumped in a bin. Five days after the attacks police made an early-morning raid on a flat in Saint-Denis. After three hours of siege and assault, two Paris attackers died by detonating a suicide vest, a female cousin was crushed when the third floor of the building fell on her, and a police team shot their own dog dead in the confusion.

The Islamic State assault on Paris marked the normalisation of religious terrorism in Europe. Monuments got security barriers, armed police prowled the streets, bags got searched. This was everyday life now. Politicians rejected any suggestion that more migrants equalled more terror attacks. They mopped up the blood in the Bataclan and buried the dead.

The temperature dropped and the snow fell and Christmas markets opened. A new crisis was on its way. It was a bad time to be female in Germany and Sweden.

24

A LARGELY PEACEFUL
NEW YEAR'S EVE

Sex Assaults in Germany and Sweden, 2016

Toronto was the place to go for the distilled essence of Canadian liberalism. Locals boasted that no one could beat them for tolerance on gay marriage, marijuana, immigration, and anything else they suspected right-wingers might find offensive. Two-thirds of them thought multiculturalism more important than ice hockey, a big statement from the home of the underachieving but loved Toronto Maple Leafs. Conservatives tended not to be welcome in this high-rise city on the shores of Lake Ontario.

On 1 April 2016, two right-wing heavyweights braved the liberal citadel to appear before 3,000 people at the Roy Thompson Hall. Mark Steyn and UKIP leader Nigel Farage had been invited in by the Aurea Foundation, a charity pushing a neoliberal free-market agenda. The foundation had been running debates for the last eight years on foreign aid, climate change, the rise of China. The big topic this spring was the continuing migrant crisis.

In January and February, 123,000 migrants had entered Greece. A deal with Turkey looked set to lower the numbers but migrants from Sub-Saharan Africa had already ramped up into Italy, helped by post-civil war chaos in Libya. A Pew Research Center survey in the summer found that no one was happy with the way the European Union was handling the situation. In Greece 94 per cent disapproved, 88 per cent in Sweden, 77 per cent in Italy, and 66 per cent in the Netherlands.

The Paris attacks were still in the news. Belgian police had arrested the last two jihadists in Brussels a fortnight earlier. The attackers had been part of a local Islamic State cell, although most had French citizenship. A week after the raid other cell members blew themselves up at Brussels airport and in a train carriage at Maalbeek metro station, near the European Union quartier. Thirty-two people died. In the aftermath Brussels police picked up the cell's survivors. Journalists sluiced some dark irony out of twenty-five-year-old Osama Krayem, born in Syria to Palestinian parents but raised in Sweden. At age eleven he had taken part in a Swedish documentary *Utan gränser – en film om idrott och integration* (Without Borders – A Film on Sports and Integration), about migrants successfully assimilating into European society. Ten years later he was in Syria fighting for Islamic State.

The Aurea Foundation caught the zeitgeist with its debate about immigration in Toronto. In the conservative corner: Steyn and Farage. Fighting for liberal values: British historian Simon Schama and former United Nations Human Rights commissioner Louise Arbour. The motion: 'Be it resolved, give us your tired, your poor, your huddled masses yearning to breathe free...'.

Arbour and Schama kicked off the debate with the argument that democracies had a duty to help refugees. Multiculturalism was enriching, morally and financially. Nations who had turned away Jewish refugees in the 1930s indirectly pushed them into the Nazi gas chambers. Criticising Angela Merkel's migrant policies opened the door to racism. Farage and Steyn fought back with claims that refugees were economic migrants from violent and misogynistic cultures. They brought crime, social disruption and rape. Young women in Germany and Sweden were afraid to walk the streets.

The liberals thought Steyn and Farage were overdoing the sex and misogyny angle. Arbour mocked them as 'newborn feminists' for their sudden concern with women's rights. Schama, one of those men who came out the womb dripping condescension with his amniotic fluid, preferred to go after the rape angle.

'I'm just struck by how obsessed with sex these two guys are, actually,' he said. 'It's a bit sad, really.'

The audience gave that a big laugh. Steyn lumbered to his feet for the rebuttal. Anyone watching in high definition could see the veins throbbing in his forehead.

I'm slightly amazed at our colleagues' ability to get big laughs on gang rape. Madame Arbour scoffs at the newfound feminists over here. I'm not much of a feminist but I draw the line at the three-year-old getting raped and the seven-year-old getting gang-raped in a basement. And when Simon tells us all, well funnily enough we're all obsessed with sex, maybe we don't get enough action in the Toronto singles bars ... . Madame Arbour, as she said, is a feminist of a certain generation. And those feminists were very clear, as Madame Arbour was very clear in Sudan, that rape was not about sex, whatever Simon may say, rape is about power, which is what Madame Arbour says. And we're not talking about the kind of sex that I want to have. I ain't into three-year-old girls.

Then a long list of migrant sex crimes from ten days in Germany delivered in a voice barely keeping its fury under control.

'And I congratulate you on getting big laughs with that Simon and you, Louise. Because if I'd known that, I'd be doing open-mic night on gang rape at a comedy club. It isn't funny. IT ISN'T FUNNY.'

And now the audience were applauding as hard for Steyn as they had laughed with Schama. The British historian looked uncomfortable. He'd chosen the wrong angle of attack. The end of last year in Germany had been a horror show.

*

New Year's Eve was a big deal in Cologne. The city of medieval stone and modern concrete had party boats cruising down the Rhine, a firework display that turned the sky into a garden of neon flowers, huge crowds gathered under the twin spires of Cologne Cathedral, beer everywhere and clubs open all night. *Frohes Neues Jahr*. In 2015 the party turned sour.

By the early evening of 31 December gangs of men were gathering in the square between the cathedral and the railway station. A twenty-three-year-old Syrian migrant called Basel Esa and his friends sensed trouble and kept their distance.

'There were mostly refugees,' Esa said, 'from Algeria, Morocco, Somalia, Afghanistan, Iraq or, like us, from Syria. At one point, I looked around on the square in front of the train station to see if there were any Germans. I couldn't see any.'

The men were young and drinking heavily, passing round bottles of whiskey and Martini. The alcohol hit them hard. Some danced and one man mooned the whole station while his friends hooted with laughter. The atmosphere got aggressive. German men walking through the square got fireworks blasted at them. Girls were surrounded. Esa watched as the drunks grabbed them, groped breasts, flipped up skirts and pulled down knickers until the girls cried. 'They were dumb, uneducated men,' he said. 'They think that if a German woman is wearing tight clothes, she's cheap and has no honour.'

The police didn't have enough numbers to do anything. Some of the groups were 100 strong. The attacks got more violent. Men surrounded lone women, ripped off their clothes and stole bags, shoved their fingers into exposed vaginas. An undercover policeman was attacked. Esa and his friends left. He thought he knew why it was happening.

'Many refugees from countries like Algeria know that they stand little chance of working or studying here,' he said. 'They will probably get sent back anyway. So they think that no rules apply to them, that they can do whatever they like. They talk about this very openly.'

Eighty policemen at the railway station tried to clear the gangs but could do nothing. Drunken men ripped up their identification papers in front of officers. Women asking for help were swarmed by fresh gangs of men and dragged away. It was screaming and noise and vomit across the station and square. The police tried to keep the trains running as gangs wandered across the tracks and gave up trying to arrest anyone.

'I am Syrian, you must treat me kindly!' one man shouted. 'Mrs Merkel has invited me.'

Eventually the night faded out and the sun came up. The gangs dispersed and people trudged home and the cleaning crews sanded the vomit. The next morning Cologne's official police account tweeted that New Year's Eve had been 'largely peaceful'.

*

It took a wave of outrage on social media for the press to cover the story. The first articles appeared on 5 January, but the police kept quiet for another four days. Mayor of Cologne Henriette Reker, a mop-topped fiftysomething recently elected on a sympathy vote after a right-winger stabbed her in the neck for liking foreigners too much, announced no link between refugees and the attacks.

Women marched through Cologne demanding action, angry at Reker telling them to keep strangers at arm's length. The sarcastic hashtag #einearmlaenge trended. Swiss artist Milo Moiré thought it would help if she stood naked in Cologne square holding a sign. Germans got angry at what they saw as a cover-up of migrant crime by government, press and police. Sales of pepper spray and applications for handgun licences went up.

As the stories tumbled out, reports of similar attacks came in from Düsseldorf, Dortmund, Hamburg, Frankfurt, Stuttgart. Police eventually revealed that 1,200 women had been assaulted by 2,000 men across the country on New Year's Eve. Several women had been raped. Six hundred assaults took place in Cologne and 400 in Hamburg. Only eighty-three arrests had been made. The crimes took place in dark, crowded areas with little CCTV coverage. Six men would go to jail, with the longest sentence being just under two years for theft and sexual assault.

Germany was not the only country affected. Figures emerged showing sex assaults in Sweden had been on the rise for a year. In 2015, 3 per cent of Swedish women were victims of a sex attack, double that of three years earlier. Most of these attacks took place in public places, committed by strangers against victims aged sixteen to twenty-four. Sweden wasn't keen on recording race and ethnicity but the evidence seemed to point at new migrants, often of Muslim background. The foreign media jumped all over the story but the situation was complicated. Rapes still remained at around their 2012 level while sexual molestation had gone up by about half, with the main issue being women groped on the street.

Swedish media downplayed any racial aspects to the crime figures, frightened of giving support to the far-right Sverigedemokraterna (Swedish Democrats). SD activists accused the establishment of ignoring migrant crime and circulated pictures they claimed showed newspapers whitening up pixelated photographs of foreign-born criminals. The party had got 12.9 per cent in the 2014 election. Opinion polls two years later put them on nearly double that.

Foreign news outlets took the apocalyptic route, mimicking counter-jihad blogs with claims that Sweden had become the rape capital of Europe and that its very infrastructure was collapsing.

They ran stories on swimming pools having women-only sessions, sex assaults at a music festival ignored by the government, riots by migrants in Rinkeby, women afraid to go out alone, attacks on churches.

'We don't go out on the streets here after dark,' said an anonymous woman. 'It is too dangerous. I have lived here for twenty-five years and it has gotten worse and worse. The situation now is so tense that it is impossible for me to go to, say, the supermarket to get some milk.'

No one, government or civilian, could be neutral about the alleged wave of migrant sex crimes. Everybody started with a conclusion and worked their way back to an argument. The right claimed governments and police had covered up a tsunami of rape and assault; the left called it a difficult situation distorted by racist scare stories.

'Migrant Sex Criminal: I Hate Sweden, I'm Just Here to F*** Swedish Girls,' said a Breitbart headline.

'Are Migrants Really Raping Swedish Women?' responded a sceptical *Daily Beast*.

Public opinion leant towards the first headline, even in liberal Toronto. When the Aurea Foundation opened its debate on migration the audience had voted 77 per cent in favour of welcoming refugees. The final vote at the end other evening saw that figure drop to only 55 per cent, a significant result for Steyn and Farage. The counter-jihad hoped to see that attitude translated to a broader audience.

'And now reality begins,' wrote Dymphna at the Gates of Vienna. 'What will be the reaction of German women as they attempt to avail themselves of heretofore relatively safe public spaces?'

Arson attacks against migrant hostels continued across Germany and spread to the Czech Republic. Some foreigners got beaten up in Cologne for having brown faces. Angela Merkel warned against the spectre of Nazism. In Finland a group called Soldiers of Odin, looking like Hells Angels who'd lost their motorcycles, started street patrols to protect the public. Chapters sprung up in a few other countries, including Canada. On 23 January 2016 Pegida organised a conference in the Czech Republic with its branches from other countries, including Stephen Lennon's mob, and a selection of small conservative or rightist parties like Italy's Lega Nord and Poland's Ruch Narodowy. Czech party Úsvit-Národní Koalice hosted. The attendees signed the Prague Declaration.

'The goal of the network is international understanding,' said Bachmann. 'For only by the profound solidarity among peoples will it be possible for us to cooperatively ward off the population replacement and the Islamisation of Europe that goes with it. Submission is out of the question.'

The conference trumpeted the creation of Fortress Europe, an international coalition to defend the continent. All it achieved was a global day of marches on 6 February. Pegida marched 8,000 strong in Dresden; 250 rallied in Canberra, Australia, including a woman dressed as a suffragette carrying a sign about child marriage and Islam; Stephen Lennon and Paul Weston of Pegida UK addressed 300 in Birmingham; an Amsterdam march was cancelled after a suspicious package; the leader of Pegida's Irish branch was hospitalised by protesters; 1,500 Pegida supporters marched through Prague; a small Canada march was swarmed by leftist protesters; a Pegida rally in Calais was banned and police arrested retired Foreign Legion general Christian Piquemal when he turned up anyway.

It should have been a triumph for the counter-jihad with its warnings of colony collapse in Western Europe finally vindicated, its worldview accepted, a Bat Ye'or book in every home, an English Defence League in every government. It didn't happen. Targeted opposition to Islam got swallowed by a wider nationalism that opposed immigration; Fortress Europe's most lasting contribution was the 'Rapefugees Not Welcome' graphic that would turn up on t-shirts and signs at future protests.

The public preferred to express their opposition to Muslim immigration through more respectable channels. Mainstream politics in Europe was about to get shaken up.

25

NATIONALISM BACK ON THE MENU

Outrage and Voting Patterns in Western Europe, 2016

Outside the conference centre a lot of angry anarchists with black clothes and handwritten signs were getting teargassed by police. They'd come to Cologne in April 2016 for a protest against the annual conference of an up-and-coming right-wing party. It started with chanting, graduated to shoving matches with police officers, and ended in a riot. Photojournalists dodged truncheons and flying barriers to get pictures of the chaos, then flashed their press passes to get back inside the venue, bleak and airy as a plane hanger.

It was a different world in here, cold and quiet, with a crowd of middle-class, middle-aged Germans sat in banks of uncomfortable seats and clapping politely at speeches. A lot of bifocals, white hair, and tweed jackets. Alternative für Deutschland didn't look like a threat to democracy.

The party had been around since early 2013 as a Eurosceptic presence in Hesse state, started by political, media and academic heavyweights who didn't like European Union overreach. AfD got 4.7 per cent of the vote in that year's federal election. By the next year the party had split into warring nationalist and EU reformist wings. The former wrestled its way to the top and changed the official AfD slogan from '*Mut zur Wahrheit*' (Courage for the Truth) to '*Mut zu Deutschland*' (Courage for Germany).

Alternative für Deutschland's nationalist faction took inspiration from Thilo Sarrazin, a veteran social democrat politician with an executive job at the Deutsche Bundesbank. Sarrazin had the grey hair, grey moustache and grey suit of a typical time server. His only distinctive feature was a permanent sneer caused by surgeons severing some important nerves when they dug a tumour out of the right side of his face. Even with the curled lip, he still looked like the last man to destroy his career for the sake of some inconvenient truths.

In 2010 Sarrazin surprised everyone when he wrote *Deutschland schafft sich ab* (Germany Abolishes Itself), 512 pages of closely worded argument for immigration restriction. The bulk of his objections centred on the economic consequences of low-skill foreigners undercutting the wages of the native working class, but Sarrazin veered into counter-jihad territory with the claim Muslim migrants could not assimilate into German culture.

'Integration requires effort from those being integrated,' he said. 'I have no respect for anyone who does not make that effort. I do not have to recognise anyone who lives on welfare, denies the legitimacy of the very state that provides that welfare, refuses to care for the education of his children, and constantly produces new little headscarf-girls. This is true of 70 per cent of the Turkish and 90 per cent of the Arab population in Berlin.'

Deutschland schafft sich ab sold 1.5 million copies in nine months. Sarrazin lost his Bundesbank job and had to fight to stay in the Sozialdemokratische Partei Deutschlands (Social Democratic Party of Germany). Royalties from the bestseller cushioned the blow.

With Sarrazin's book as their Bible, the AfD nationalists steered the party into seven seats at the EU parliament, fourteen seats in Saxony, eleven in Brandenburg, and more across the country. They got 9 per cent of the vote. By now, Alternative für Deutschland were presenting themselves as conservative, traditional, family-orientated, sceptical about climate change, and pro-Europe but anti-Eurozone. The media saw uptight bourgeois types living in the past whose worst nightmare was getting a neighbour black as a pint of Guinness. The left saw the cloven hoof of Nazism.

The migrant crisis pushed Alternative für Deutschland further into the nationalist right. Party members who still believed in EU reform walked out, taking five MEPs with them and accusing the leadership of having turned into the political wing of Pegida. The AfD denied the charge but its April 2016 annual conference in Cologne steered the party firmly into the counter-jihad. Outside, leftists and police chased each other around the car park in clouds of white teargas. Inside, party activists called for a ban on burqas, calls to prayer, and other public displays of Islam. The conference held tense debates on the ritual slaughter of animals and freedom of religious worship.

'Islam is foreign to Germany,' said Hans-Thomas Tillschneider, an academic and journalist with a head shaped like a lightbulb, 'and for that reason it can't invoke the principle of religious freedom in the same way as Christianity.'

Party members applauded. Party leader Björn Hoecke gave a speech about the greatness of German culture and incongruity of having a Holocaust memorial ('a memorial of shame') in the centre of Berlin. Inside, the attendee held up blue or red cards to vote on the AfD's new counter-jihadist direction. Everything passed.

'Islam is not a part of Germany,' the party announced to the press.

Local elections were due in the autumn of 2016, with the more important federal ones happening the next year. German observers wondered if they were watching the start of a nationalist and counter-jihad rise to power. Over the border in France, others were thinking the same thing. The country had experienced another jihadist terror attack, this time under the clear summer sun of Nice. Eighty-six dead, and shoes and bags and children's toys scattered along the Promenade des Anglais.

*

Tourists, playboys and well-off retirees loved Nice, a golden strip of sunshine on France's southern coast. It had clean air, blue sea, cloudless skies. Thousands flew in to enjoy the pebble beach and walk the broad slab of café au lait promenade at the sunbathers' backs with its wire postcard racks and lazy traffic.

Bastille Day was a big occasion here. On 14 July 2016 the crowds turned out during the day to see a military parade and open-air concerts. In the evening they crowded the beach and a pedestrianised strip of the Promenade des Anglais to watch fireworks turn the sky into an explosion of sea anemones and gunpowder smoke. The pyrotechnics were dying away and the crowd applauding when the truck drove right through them.

The 19-tonne white Renault Midlum was doing 56 miles an hour when it turned onto the promenade and jumped the pavement. It crushed people under its wheels, passed the Centre Universitaire

Méditerranéen, then the children's hospital, hit more people, squeezed through a police barrier and accelerated into the pedestrian zone where everyone was packed tight as matches in a box. The Midlum zig-zagged down the promenade and sent bodies bouncing off the bumpers and coming apart under the wheels. Everywhere was panic, screams and horror.

The man in the truck cab was a Tunisian jihadist with a criminal record and a residency permit who ate pork, beat his wife and drank. A few months earlier Mohamed Lahouaiej-Bouhlel had rediscovered his ancestral religion and turned radical with help from former Islamic State soldiers living in his neighbourhood. Radical Islam provided a spiritual safe space from mental problems, a troubled bisexuality and a nasty divorce.

A few hours before the attack, Lahouaiej-Bouhlel sent his brother a few selfies taken the previous day. They showed him among happy crowds on the promenade. He was smiling.

The truck drove for 1.7 kilometres and killed eighty-six people, including ten children. Over 400 more were injured. Police shot through the windscreen and a man skidded his motorcycle under the wheels but the truck only stopped when its engine gave out by the Palais de la Méditerranée hotel. Two policemen shot Lahouaiej-Bouhlel dead as he struggled out the cab holding a pistol. Four Tunisians and two Albanians would later be arrested for helping him prepare the attack. It was the thirteenth Islamic terror incident in France in just over four years. The total cost so far was 244 dead.

France had birthed some counter-jihadist groups, like Riposte Laïque (Secular Response), Vérité, Valeurs et Démocratie (Truth, Values and Democracy), L'Alliance FFL, and others. Most groups seemed led or linked to Jean-Michel Clément, a big-eared Frenchman better known as Gandalf who had wavy grey hair and a track record speaking at the annual counter-jihad conferences organised by Edward May. His groups had websites, ideologies, and the occasional march but never amounted to more than a handful of incestuously connected activists. Counter-jihad hopes in France increasingly centred on a more mainstream far-right party that was getting bigger every year.

'I am furious,' said Front National leader Marine Le Pen after the attack in Nice, 'because I hear the same words, notice the same reactions in the political class, but see no action that gives us an ounce of extra security.'

The Front National had been around since 1972 as an umbrella for small far-right parties nibbling at the flanks of French politics. It brought together everyone from old Vichy functionaries nostalgic for the collaborationist days of Maréchal Philippe Pétain to army veterans still angry over the loss of French Algeria and the kind of young radicals who had hung around with Dominique Venner in their student days.

The party needed a big personality to hold itself together, and found one in Jean-Marie Le Pen. Dark-haired and farmer-faced, Le Pen served in Indochina and Algiers with the Foreign Legion, got involved with student politics, dabbled in the music industry with compilation albums of communist and Nazi songs, and spent a few years in the National Assembly representing a populist tax protest party. He fought a duel, sometimes wore an eye patch, and had a colourful love life.

Le Pen guided the Front National along the conventional nationalist track of anti-communism, anti-immigration, anti-European integration, and the iron fist of law and order. The party remained a minority interest until the 1980s when strategic alliances with smaller but mainstream rightist parties brought it to public attention. The FN got ten seats in the European elections of 1984 and began to grow. By 2002 Le Pen shocked France when he made it to the run-offs of the presidential elections, although the resulting backlash ensured he never stood a chance of winning.

The counter-jihad had no appeal to the party under Le Pen. The fascist old guard still held enough anti-Semitism in their hearts to support the Arab world against Israel. Arguments about hijabs and radicalism were dismissed by activists who claimed immigration, not Islam, was the problem. As late as 2007 Le Pen was reaching out to French Muslims, calling them 'a branch of the French tree'.

His daughter Marine took over the party four years later and rebranded the Front as edgy patriots who overlapped the counter-jihad in the Venn diagram of politics. A Jewish boyfriend and a circle of gay advisors helped with the image change. She compared Muslims praying in the streets to Nazi occupation during the war and ended up in court for it. The judges acquitted her. In the 2014 European elections the Front National got nearly 25 per cent of the vote and more seats than any other party.

'An earthquake,' said Socialist prime minister Manuel Valls.

'A severe defeat for the [conservative] right,' said former prime minister Alain Juppé.

Then came *Charlie Hebdo* and the Paris attacks. Presidential elections were coming up in the spring of 2017. Counter-jihad activists kept their fingers crossed for a Le Pen victory in France, and an Alternative für Deutschland landslide in Germany. They had equally high hopes for another politician in the Netherlands. Geert Wilders had a blond bouffant, a winning smile, and no far-right baggage. Some thought he might end up running his country.

*

In 2016 nearly 1.2 million migrants entered Europe, only slightly less than the previous year. The demographic change injected counter-jihad policies into mainstream political discourse. In recent years Swiss voters had supported constitutional referendums to oppose mass immigration (50.3 per cent), expel foreigners who committed crimes (52.3 per cent), and ban the construction of minarets on mosques (57.5 per cent). The referendums had been pushed by the Schweizerische Volkspartei (Swiss People's Party), which was also behind a widely disseminated cartoon showing minarets poking up from a Swiss flag like intercontinental ballistic missiles. In 2015 the party got 29.4 per cent in the federal election, the largest vote for a single party in Swiss history. Observers blamed the increase in the country's Muslim population from 1 per cent in 1980 to 5 per cent in 2013.

Similar fears about the spread of Islam had almost won the Austrian presidency for the Freiheitliche Partei Österreichs (Austrian Freedom Party), which had domesticated itself into more conservative territory since its 1956 foundation by a former SS Brigadeführer. In early 2016 its gormless-looking gun enthusiast candidate almost became president. Some recounts, court cases and a re-run saw Norbert Hofer lose to a Green Party candidate by a small margin. Opponents blamed the migrant crisis for Hofer's near success. Prominent Freiheitliche Partei Österreichs MP Oskar Freysinger, who looked like an Easter Island statue with a ponytail, was on the advisory board of Stop Islamization of Nations.

Across the border in Germany, the September local elections saw the now openly counter-jihad Alternative für Deutschland beat Angela Merkel's Christlich Demokratische Union Deutschlands (German Christian Union) into third place in her home state.

'It is only a small step, a line in the sand, a minor push back,' said a commenter at Gates of Vienna, 'but at least a beginning. Still it is important to do what is possible, even if it is a small slice. I fear it is very urgent to get this in place.'

Merkel's government had taken a hammering from all sides, not helped by police releasing figures showing migrants committed 142,500 crimes in the first six months of 2016. That was around 780 a day. By the end of the year crime figures were looking even worse. Non-German suspects had committed 2,512 rapes or sexual assaults that year, an average of seven a day; most attackers were Syrians, although Afghans, Iraqis, Pakistanis, Iranians, Algerians, Moroccans, Eritreans, Nigerians and Albanians were strongly represented. The German police admitted that migrants made up less than 2 per cent of the population but accounted for 8.6 per cent of all crime suspects, with non-Germans settled in the country making up another 30.5 per cent.

'The proportion of foreign suspects, and migrants in particular,' said Thomas de Maizière, 'is higher than the average for the general population. This cannot be sugarcoated. There is an overall rise in disrespect, violence and hate. Those who commit serious offences here forfeit their right to stay here.'

Not all parties managed to capitalise on the popularity of counter-jihad thought. Vlaams Belang in Flanders had repositioned itself as a pro-Israel party, jettisoning any remaining anti-Semitism in the name of a joint front against Islam. Belgium's Jews didn't buy it but party representatives made trips to Israel and met government ministers. The softened image helped votes to a highpoint in 2007 (12 per cent and seventeen seats in the Chamber of Representatives) but couldn't stop a rapid decline. Seven years later they had only 3.67 per cent of the vote and three seats, with similar declines in the regional and European parliaments. A fresh-faced competitor in the form of the Nieuw-Vlaamse Alliantie (New Flemish Alliance) had arrived, mimicking the independent Flanders rhetoric but without any of the far-right history. It hoovered up Vlaams Belang votes and kept its rhetoric about Islam low-key.

Counter-jihad activism in Belgium continued to revolve around blogs and small parties like *The Brussels Journal*, Pierre Renversez's nonali.be, Les Résistants secular network, and Women Against Islamisation, run by Vlaams Belang MP and former Miss Belgium Anke van Dermeersch. None had much hope of winning any elections.

The Netherlands would happily have seen its own nationalist right fade away like Vlaams Belang. Geert Wilder's Partij voor de Vrijheid had won nine seats in the Tweede Kamer back in 2006 and twenty-four the following election; as the country's third-biggest party it served in a coalition government for two years and looked set for a bigger role. Not many thought it a coincidence that the end of 2016 saw Geert Wilders convicted on charges of incitement and encouraging discrimination. The charges dated back to a Wilders speech at a Partij voor de Vrijheid rally in The Hague two years earlier. Wilders had been in cheerful form as he bantered with a noisy crowd.

'Do you want more or fewer Moroccans in this city and in the Netherlands?' he asked.

'Fewer! Fewer!' chanted the crowd.

'Well, we'll arrange that then,' said Wilders.

It didn't help that an interview he'd given the previous week had the PVV leader hoping the electorate would vote for a safer city with fewer Moroccans. Wilders had dodged a similar charge back in 2011 after comparing Islam to fascism and the Quran to Hitler's *Mein Kampf*. That case dragged on for several controversial years. Judges refused to listen to an academic who supported Wilders' comments; Wilders mocked the trial by trying to call Theo van Gogh's murderer as an expert witness. Even left-wing media outlets started talking about freedom of speech. The trial collapsed in June when the court ruled his comments to be legitimate political commentary.

'His crime is maintaining that Europe's civilization is rooted in the values of Jerusalem, Athens, Rome, and the Enlightenment,' said Gisèle Littman in her Bat Ye'or persona, 'and not in Mecca, Baghdad, Andalusia, and al-Kods.'

In the 2016 trial the court found him guilty but imposed no penalty. It was an odd compromise that only boosted Wilders' profile. His views hadn't changed much since Theo van Gogh's death. He still saw Islam as a totalitarian ideology that needed to be stopped, Israel as a heroic nation that needed Western support, Muslim immigration into Europe as a disaster that had to end, and assimilation as a process to be imposed on Islamic communities if they refused to adopt Western humanist traditions. Wilders kept in contact with other counter-jihad figures, appearing with Pamela Geller and Robert Spencer at a 2010 Stop Islamization of America rally in New York and employing *Brussels Journal* founder Paul

Beliën as his personal assistant for a while. His commentary often echoed Bat Ye'or.

'Islam is the Trojan Horse in Europe,' he told the Dutch parliament. 'If we do not stop Islamification now, Eurabia and Netherabia will just be a matter of time. One century ago, there were approximately fifty Muslims in the Netherlands. Today, there are about one million Muslims in this country. Where will it end? We are heading for the end of European and Dutch civilisation as we know it.'

Wilders wrote a book called *Marked for Death: Islam's War Against the West and Me*, published in English by an American firm. It rehashed the usual arguments and revealed he and his wife lived in safehouses under twenty-four-hour guard. Polls on the national broadcaster NPO1 television channel made him Dutch politician of the year four times in six years. It was a rare day he was not in a Dutch newspaper or on television.

'Half of Holland loves me,' he said, 'and half of Holland hates me. There is no in between.'

Many people thought Wilders had a serious chance of winning in 2017, along with Marine Le Pen and Alternative für Deutschland. The world seemed to be turning in a counter-jihad direction. A divisive presidential election across the Atlantic had turned America upside down and showed widespread support for counter-jihad measures. It had been a wild ride. An unconscious Hillary Clinton slung face down into a van, email servers getting hacked, Black Lives Matter activists shouting down a Jewish socialist for being too white, and the candidacy of billionaire loudmouth Donald Trump.

Some of Trump's policies came straight from the counter-jihad playbook: ban Muslim immigration, create a registry. Geert Wilders had even spoken at a pro-Trump event in Cleveland. Chief engineer on the Trump train was Steve Bannon, founding member of Breitbart News, the right-wing site that employed veteran activists like Pamela Geller and Robert Spencer. Thanks to Breitbart, counter-jihadism rubbed shoulders with fellow Trump supporters on the alt-right, a transgressive internet movement of white nationalists, disaffected conservatives and nihilistic internet trolls.

By the time the election was over, half of America wanted to kill the other half.

26

PULSING WITH THE ALT-RIGHT IN ORLANDO

Rainbow Flag and Counter-Jihad, 2016

At fifty-eight years old Pamela Geller looked like a rich woman trying to hold onto her looks by any means necessary, up to and including witchcraft. A lot of gym work, regular trips to the salon, a few jabs of Botox, a generous layer of makeup. She'd also developed an edgy sense of humour somewhere along the line.

'A jihadi walks into a gay bar,' she said. 'What does he order? Shots for everyone.'

On 12 June a twenty-nine-year-old security guard called Omar Mateen carried his semi-automatic rifle into the neon-blue world of Pulse, a gay nightclub in Orlando popular with the Hispanic crowd. Mateen killed forty-nine people and holed up in a bathroom with hostages. For the next three hours he rang media outlets to claim responsibility for the attack on behalf of Islamic State, condemn US actions in Iraq and Syria, and describe the two Chechen brothers behind a jihadist bombing at the 2013 Boston Marathon as 'his homeboys'. Eventually a SWAT team broke through an exterior club wall and shot him eight times.

Mateen was a dull-eyed New Yorker of Afghan descent with a fringe so straight it looked drawn with a ruler. He had spent most of his short life trying to make it in law enforcement but got kicked out of the Florida police academy for threatening to shoot someone at a barbecue. His food had accidentally touched pork on the grill. Mateen went on become a security guard, break up with his wife, remarry, and take a lot of steroids.

At some point he self-radicalised into a militant Islamist and was loud enough about it to catch the FBI's attention. A 2013 investigation uncovered nothing – some thought this was because his father was a long-time FBI confidential informant – and Mateen continued his path towards spree killer.

The Pulse massacre was the biggest Islamic terror attack in America since 9/11, bringing the total killed by jihadists since 2002 to around ninety in nine attacks. In the aftermath a lot of people tried to claim that the killer was gay or bisexual or HIV-positive but police investigations disproved the allegations. Mateen was just a radical Islamist. One narrative suggested he hated homosexuals and got pushed over the edge by seeing two men kissing in public; another held that he hadn't even known Pulse was a gay club and asked a bouncer why there were no women around as he entered.

The attack took place in the run-up to the American presidential elections, with both parties on the verge of selecting their nominees. Hillary Clinton led the field for the Democrats; businessman and former reality TV star Donald Trump had destroyed his Republican competitors with a populist campaign built on anti-immigration rhetoric and civic nationalism. Trump's 'Make America Great Again' baseball caps were everywhere and the media couldn't quite believe he wanted to enforce a temporary moratorium on Islamic immigrants and build a wall down south to keep out the Mexicans.

Hillary Clinton preferred the open-borders route and was smart enough to embrace the Black Lives Matter movement, a nationwide protest about African American persecution at the hands of police. It gave her an edge over challenger Bernie Sanders, an ageing Jewish socialist with a big youth following. No one in the Clinton camp was unhappy with the optics when Sanders got his microphone hijacked by BLM activists at an event in Seattle. Black America thought the veteran campaigner had his priorities wrong in preferring class war to identity politics.

Donald Trump seemed in a stronger position, but his nomination wasn't a sure thing. In July 2016 Republican delegates packed the Quicken Loans Arena in Cleveland to select their candidate. Rumours flew that some anti-Trump types wanted to change the convention floor rules to switch around the votes and deny him the nomination.

Trump fans hit the convention in force to show their support. The LGBT contingent threw Wake Up! (The Most Fab Party at the RNC) on the second day of the conference. It had a serious counter-jihad flavour. Geller was one of the speakers up at the podium, in front of posters showing a smooth-chested young twink in a Make America Great Again hat. It was less than a month after the Pulse massacre and her joke about shots got a big laugh. It turned out gay Republicans for Trump liked edgy humour too.

'It's not funny,' she said, 'because it's true.'

The speaker before her at Wake Up! had been Geert Wilders, who saw a chance to promote his views in America and leech some energy off Trump's momentum. The audience liked his blunt assessment of Muslim migration as a suicidal policy and threat to the kind of liberal values that allowed LGBT lifestyles. There were about 3.3 million Muslims living in the USA, most first- or second-generation immigrants. This was up from somewhere close to 2 million in 2001.

'Get rid of your political correctness,' Wilders told them.

He threw in some Bat Ye'or references to Eurabia and left the podium to applause and whoops. Pamela Geller came on wearing a rainbow-sequinned top with the slogan 'Love Will Win' and a pair of tight leather trousers, dark and reflective as an oil slick. The counter-jihad was a well-funded proposition this side of the Atlantic and Geller its most recognisable public face.

Geller's marriage hadn't survived the politics, but a 2007 divorce left her comfortable. Her ex-husband only got to enjoy a year of bachelorhood before death swooped in; the life insurance paid out to Geller and made her wealthy. It didn't stop her campaigning. Geller's Stop the Islamization of America had got a planned Islamic cultural centre in New York shut down a few years back. On 3 May 2015 she organised a First Annual Muhammad Art Exhibit and Contest in Texas with a $12,500 award for best drawing. Geert Wilders turned up and gave a speech. The contest was attacked by two American Muslims with criminal records and rifles. They shot a policeman in the foot and got killed by a SWAT team. The next month Boston police shot dead an American Muslim who had planned to decapitate Geller in revenge.

'I am the number one target of the Islamic State right now,' she said. 'I am standing up to them while the political and media elites cower and kowtow.'

She gave a fiery speech at Wake Up! that linked the counter-jihad to the gay community. The Republicans were the only party standing against jihad; the Democrats would open the door to homophobic jihadists. Muslim men raped native girls; the left had embraced Islam.

'You've got to love Trump,' she said, 'because he gives them all the middle finger. His ban on Muslims from jihad nations is logical, rational and reasonable.'

Geller had got the invite to Wake Up! through a contact at Breitbart News, a right-wing site that liked antagonising liberals. She had been writing there for the last seven years and had become pals with a fellow journalist. Milo Yiannopoulos was organiser of Wake Up! and a growing star in the American media. He followed Geller onto the podium in a white tank-top with a rainbow graphic Uzi submachine gun (slogan: 'We Shoot Back') and started telling an enthusiastic audience how they could stop Islamic terror. Yiannopoulos was gay, British, fabulous, and hard-right.

*

Milo Yiannopoulos had a posh mum and a father involved in the rougher end of the nightclub business, which his son liked to claim involved body bags, protection money and violence. Yiannopoulos senior stayed out of politics but did occasionally take to Twitter to jovially threaten his son's critics: 'I wish i could meet Mr. Arthur [a *Guardian* journalist] I'd like to shake hands with his windpipe but i am not sure he would enjoy the meeting as much as i would.'

Anyone who couldn't tell if Yiannopoulos senior was being serious needed to tune into Gavin McInnes's show on Rebel Media, a right-wing outlet started by Ezra Levant. Milo came on as guest and told a story about helping out his father with the hand stamps at a London nightclub as a pre-teen.

'People used to ask me, what is your dad like? He must be like a Greek Tony Soprano or something. And I'd say yeah, I'll tell you the story. So I'm doing the stamps one night [...] and there's an altercation at the front door and there's all this rowdiness and somebody says "Get Nicky, Get Nicky", Nicky's my dad, so my dad sort of lumbers down like Tony Soprano if he was Greek and a bit less of a pussy and he says "What's going on, what's going on? What's the problem here?" And they sort of have an argument and he says "I'm sorry mate, you're not coming in, if she says you're not coming in, you're not coming in."

'And the guy looks at my dad and says "No one ever says no to you, do they Nicky?"'

'And my dad says "People say no to me all the time. They say NO, NICKY, NO!"'

'And then he knocks the guy out.'

Yiannopoulos was born Milo Hanrahan. His parents divorced when he was six and he was raised Catholic by a combination of mother, stepfather and Greek grandmother whose name he'd adopt as a journalist. He went through grammar school (expelled), University of Manchester (dropped out) and Wolfson College, Cambridge (sent down). Yiannopoulos came out of it all a disorganised ball of charisma with enough drive to push his way into the tech journalism business. He wrote for *The Daily Telegraph* and started a website that collapsed with accusations of unpaid staff before eventually bobbing up again under different ownership.

He was open about his rightist opinions and developed a camp conservative persona that came across like Freddy Mercury impersonating William F. Buckley. There were appearances on national television as a fast-talking provocateur, then a higher profile when he jumped into Gamergate, a 2014 internet controversy that was either an eruption of misogyny and racism from computer game fans against progressive voices in the industry, or gaming journalism circling the wagons after getting caught giving favourable reviews to bad games by liberal friends, depending on where you stood. Yiannopoulos went with the latter view.

In late 2015 he got a job at Breitbart News and spent time in America developing a media career, busy as an ant farm. Breitbart was fully on board the Trump train from the start and Yiannopoulos cheerfully shovelled coal into the firebox. He put his name to the 29 March 2016 story *An Establishment Conservative's Guide to the Alt-Right* that tried to domesticate a transgressive anti-establishment movement that was starting to get make its presence known on the internet. Breitbart chief Steve Bannon thought the alt-right could help get Trump elected. Yiannopoulos cleaned it up and made excuses for any excesses.

'Anything associated as closely with racism and bigotry as the alternative right will inevitably attract real racists and bigots,' said the article. 'These are the people that the alt-right's opponents *wish* constituted the entire movement. They're less concerned with the welfare of their own tribe than their fantasies of destroying others.'

Liberal journalists weren't so sure. From where they stood the racism and bigotry looked like the core of the alt-right. That summer Yiannopoulos turned up in Orlando after the Pulse terror attack for an outdoor press conference with a scrum of supporters and some people from Rebel Media. Yiannopoulos wanted to convince America's gay community that the Republican Party, never traditionally their friend, could protect them from Islamic homophobia.

'My hope after today, after the ugly and disgusting thing that happened here,' said Yiannopoulos, 'is that gay people say too, like the Jews did after the Second World War, never again and gay people too, let Islamic fundamentalist preachers and Muslims everywhere who are tempted into thinking they can treat gay people like this, they can treat women like this, they can treat Latinos like this, they can treat black people like this, they can treat anyone like this, [know] that we will shoot back.'

Behind him someone held up a rainbow version of the Gadsden flag (a coiled rattlesnake over the logo 'Don't Tread on Me') and the crowd lowered camera phones for long enough to applaud and cheer. Yiannopoulos had dressed as serious as he ever got for the occasion with a pinstriped suit in dark blue, crisp white shirt, tasteful pink tie, aviator shades. He'd even ditched the usual blond hair dye.

'The Orlando shooting isn't just the deadliest terrorist attack on U.S. shores since 9/11,' he said. 'It is also, by far, the worst act of violent homophobia in the nation's history and the deadliest mass shooting in America ever.'

At his side was Gavin McInnes, a bearded Canadian alternative media type with drug addiction, bad punk bands, and founding the Vice media empire on his conscience. He'd left all that behind to reinvent himself as an edgy right-wing commenter, married and religious, with a programme on the Rebel Media internet channel. He turned up in Orlando to support Yiannopoulos. He kept his speech short.

'Fuck Islam,' McInnes said.

Then he gave Yiannopoulos an open mouth kiss. The crowd cheered. Next month Yiannopoulos was at Wake Up!, with the Gadsden flag on the wall behind the DJ, and 'LGBT for Trump' founder Cris Barron introducing him as 'the world's most dangerous faggot'. The speech pushed the narrative that Democrats sympathised with Islam too much to be trusted by the gay community. Yiannopoulos claimed the Pulse nightclub massacre was the bleeding edge of Muslim homophobia and Trump's plan to stop Muslim migrants entering America was a gay-friendly stance. Yiannopoulos bubbled with enthusiasm for the presidential candidate he was starting to call 'daddy'.

'The most pro-gay candidate in American electoral history,' he said. 'The left's stranglehold on homosexuals is over.'

A lot of applause, some chanting, and then the music kicked in for a night of hedonism. Out in the Quicken Loans Arena, Donald John Trump was announced as the official Republican presidential candidate. The next month Hillary Clinton saw off Bernie Sanders with some help from friends counting the votes at the Democratic National Convention.

Trump's campaign manager Steve Bannon couldn't wait for the election. He was cutting deals with voting blocs all over America. One was the old-school counter-jihadists of ACT! for America. Another represented something newer and darker brewing in corners of the internet which Bannon and Yiannopoulos had tried to harness without fully understanding. The alt-right was headed for the mainstream.

27

THAT'S WHERE YOU'RE WRONG, KIDDO

Counter-Jihad Thought, the Alt-Right and the Trump Campaign, 2016

It was always a shock to realise Steve Bannon didn't drink. He looked like the kind of guy central casting sent along when the director ordered a sixtysomething Irish police detective from 1975 who liked his whisky. A slicked-back thatch of hair the colour of dirty steel, square face on a square body, watery and watchful eyes in a blotchy face. All he needed was a sports coat and a hip flask and Bannon could have been stepping out of a cop car on the mean streets of New York City back in the days people didn't go to Central Park after dark.

Appearances can deceive. Bannon was a teetotal millionaire whose life had been changed by René Guénon.

He encountered the Frenchman's work while serving in the Navy. Bannon joined up in the late 1970s after doing time in a Catholic military high school and getting a degree in Urban Planning from Virginia Tech. It was an upward career path for the son of a blue-collar Irish American family from Virginia who all voted Democrat, worshipped John F. Kennedy, and were traditional enough in their Catholicism to prefer the Latin Mass.

Bannon wasn't much of a political animal back then but spent his off-duty hours reading widely about religion and metaphysics. His spiritual quest went from Christian mysticism to Eastern religions, circled around Zen Buddhism, then returned to Catholicism. Somewhere along the road he encountered Guénon and was deeply impressed by the Traditionalist view of a cultural decline so morally corrupting that its victims saw their hell-bound descent as progress. Bannon wasn't converting to Islam any time soon but the Frenchman's call to reinstate religion and tradition struck a long, reverberating chord.

'We shouldn't be running a victory lap,' Bannon said, 'every time some sort of traditional value gets undercut.'

Watching the failed 1980 attempt to free American hostages in Iran soured him on the Democrats; serving in the Pentagon as special assistant to the Chief of Naval Operations turned him into a supporter of Ronald Reagan's Republican administration. His new-found interest in politics layered nationalism and small government onto a bedrock of Catholic-inflected Guénonian Traditionalism.

Bannon quit the service to make money as an investment banker. A post in Los Angeles provided an entry into the entertainment business and by the 1990s he was the film producer behind Sean Penn's *The Indian Runner* and a media magnate canny enough to earn himself a slice of the *Seinfeld* profits. There were other investments, three daughters from three failed marriages, some cushy CEO positions, and time in a Hong Kong video game company that used cheap Chinese gamers to farm virtual gold in *World of Warcraft* and sell it to cash-rich, time-poor players in the West. Bannon had no interest in Anders Breivik's favourite game but returned home impressed by the influence of online communities on the real world. The money rolled in.

Soon Bannon was rich enough not to care about other people's opinions. He dressed sloppily enough to make Michel Houellebecq look like a Ralph Lauren catalogue model, and pushed his politics into everybody's faces. In 2004 he wrote, produced and directed a documentary about his hero Ronald Reagan called *In the Face of Evil*, based on a bestselling biography by conservative journalist Peter Schweizer. Making the film introduced Bannon to Andrew Breitbart, a blond Jewish bear of a man who'd made a big name for himself in online conservative media.

Breitbart had helped out in the early days of the *Drudge Report* and was involved in the launch of *The Huffington Post* when it was still a Republican concern. Now he had plans to launch his own website, unapologetically pro-Israel and pro-freedom but iconoclastic enough to go after unworthy Republicans in the George W. Bush administration. His team of journalists, many of them orthodox Jews, had no problem tearing into any competing media outlets that got in the way. They worshipped their boss.

'He wasn't actually very political,' said journalist Ben Shapiro, 'that is, he had almost no interest at all in policy. Yet he lived his life at the forefront of political debate [...] What defined and motivated Andrew was his unique ability to perceive the gross double standard that the media, the political establishment, and the pop culture employ in their war on those with whom they disagree.'

Bannon liked what he heard and helped fund the 2007 Breitbart News launch. The site's politics meshed with his own, and he enjoyed its attacks on warmongering neoconservatives in the White House. Bannon's nationalism, haunted by memories of the Iran debacle, had no time for overseas adventures. The site's cheerleading for Israel fitted in well with his growing counter-jihadism.

'We are in an outright war against jihadist Islamic fascism,' Bannon told a conference at the Vatican. 'And this war is, I think, metastasizing far quicker than governments can handle it.'

Clashes between Islamic and Western values in Europe added immigration control to his political worldview. He supported movements like UKIP, the Front National, America's Tea Party, the Partij voor de Vrijheid and nationalists everywhere from Egypt to South Korea.

In the evening of 1 March 2012, Andrew Breitbart dropped dead of a heart attack while out walking in Los Angeles. When the shock wore off, rival factions waged a brief power struggle over his webpage. Bannon came out on top thanks to close contacts with the money men financing the site. The new version of Breitbart News got an even more vicious reputation than the original incarnation, going after anyone who opposed its views with bared fangs. Bannon didn't care who he offended. He was very rich, had blue-collar contempt for the establishment and possessed a rock-hard ideology that parsed politics through the metanarrative of Traditionalism.

'Honey badger don't give a shit,' he said, borrowing a line from a viral video.

He hosted Breitbart's radio show on the SiriusXM Patriot conservative channel and frequently had counter-jihadists as guests. Counter-jihadism already had a place in Breitbart, with both Pamela Geller and Robert Spencer on the payroll, but the movement ramped up in prominence under the new order. Left-wing magazine *Mother Jones* estimated Bannon invited counter-jihadists on to his radio show at least forty-one times. In the autumn of 2015 Brigitte Gabriel of ACT! for America turned up to discuss whether Europe's migrant crisis could be called an invasion. She thought it could, and referenced Bat Ye'or. 'It is not an overstatement,' Gabriel said. 'Europe will no longer be Europe by 2050. Europe has already become Eurabia. Europe is Eurabia right now.'

When the presidential elections rolled around, no one was surprised Breitbart News supported Donald Trump. On 17 August 2016 the relationship became official when Bannon was appointed chief executive of the Trump campaign. The counter-jihad was headed for the White House.

*

America knew Donald Trump as a loudmouth with a media career and a thing for Eastern bloc models. The real estate billionaire came into the world back in 1946, the fourth child of a family big in New York real estate. He learned early that boasting and a bulletproof ego could get him a lot further than honesty and sensitivity.

Trump did military school, graduated from Wharton at the University of Pennsylvania with a degree in economics, and joined the family business. He went for big projects like hotels and casinos, usually branded with his name. Gaudy flagship buildings like Manhattan's Trump Tower quickly lodged themselves in the public consciousness. He was a good negotiator and brutally efficient on-site. Contracts came in on time and under budget, and if that meant the destruction of historic art deco reliefs already promised to a museum then Trump got busy with the jackhammer and worried about the consequences later.

He became enough of a New York landmark to play himself in eight movies and ten TV programmes before breaking into the media mainstream with 2004's long-running NBC reality show *The Apprentice*. Add in a comedy haircut, no sense of shame, three supermodel wives (Czech, American, Slovenian), five entitled children, two multimillion-dollar divorces, some business bankruptcies and a lot of lawsuits, and you had a businessman more cartoon than real.

That was the public image. The real Trump was deeper and more intelligent, although never intellectual. He had political ambitions.

Trump had been a Democrat until the mid-1980s when he moved to the right and made a few tentative gestures towards a presidential run. Nothing came of it but in the late 1990s he explored his options a second time with Ross Perot's Reform Party, a maverick political movement enjoying a brief moment of challenging the political giants. Again, Trump decided not to run, but never stopped thinking it was feasible.

'I believe that if I did run for President,' he said, 'I'd win.'

He switched back to Democrat and hung out in New York with Hillary Clinton and ex-president husband Bill, admiring them enough to donate money to their Clinton Foundation. The Trump political pendulum had swung back to Republican by the time he made a speech to a conservative conference in 2011 that impressed a lot of activists. He kept up the momentum by pushing the 'birther' conspiracy theory that President Obama had been born in Kenya. The media ridiculed the idea without realising its popularity among conspiracy-friendly grassroots types. The Obama administration got its revenge at a White House Correspondents' Association dinner where speakers lined up to mock Trump's failure to prove anything. The humiliation just made him more determined to become president. A couple of years later he was spending big money researching a new effort.

An advisor connected with more radical conservative circles brought in Steve Bannon to offer advice. The Breitbart man didn't think much of Trump's chances and couldn't see a presidential run, but the billionaire impressed him with a political programme closer to nationalism than anything America had seen for a while. Trump had been listening to blue-collar workers, local activists and the crowds involved in ACT! for America. They convinced him ordinary Americans cared deeply about immigration from South and Central America, with its wage reductions and competition and cultural change, and worried over the dangers of Islamic terrorism. When Trump finally launched his campaign on 16 June 2015, Breitbart News was solidly behind him.

The official Trump platform pushed military isolationism, except for pre-emptive strikes against jihadist threats; opposition to illegal immigration that involved extending the existing Mexican border fence with a 1,000-mile-long wall; a moratorium on Muslim migration from high-risk countries; opposing climate change legislation; tax reform; and trade tariffs to protect American industry. Bannon liked the programme and admired Trump for not backing down when the Republican establishment turned on him.

The counter-jihad loved the moratorium idea. They'd been demanding it for years. Gates of Vienna, Pamela Geller, Jihadwatch, ACT! for America and many others jumped on the Trump bandwagon. Bannon made sure the counter-jihad world heard all about an early 2016 briefing Trump attended at Frank Gaffney's Center for Security Policy on the dangers of sharia law in America. Over in the UK, Melanie Phillips wrote a passionate defence of Trump for *The Times* that called his critics 'bigots and racists'.

Trump did well in the debates with other Republican candidates, wounding them with sharp and brutal putdowns. His rallies attracted huge audiences, and protests from Democrats who thought his immigration policies racist. Fights erupted outside arenas; inside, Trump insulted hecklers and had them thrown out. He was divisive and controversial but a large chunk of the population liked him. Someone put up a series of compilation videos on YouTube called *You Can't Stump the Trump*. They got more views than most primetime television programmes.

'All these millions and millions of people,' said Trump. 'It's a movement.'

Bannon was in the background the whole time, liaising with the campaign team as he weaponised Breitbart on their behalf, but never officially on the payroll. But not even his media skills could stop some painful reverses in the summer of 2016. Fox News got caught in a sex scandal that deposed its pouchy-faced and reluctantly pro-Trump CEO; campaign manager Corey Lewandowski got kicked out for briefing the press against internal enemies; and replacement Paul Manafort turned toxic when his connections with unsavoury Ukrainian politicians made the newspapers. Hillary Clinton soon had a double-digit lead in the polls. The Trump train had run out of fuel.

Trump replaced Lewandowski with Kelly Conway, a leggy blonde scarecrow who'd done polling work for Frank Gaffney's Center for Security Policy, but senior Republicans urged him to take on a new campaign chief executive willing to fight dirty enough to scrape a win.

Steve Bannon got the call. He accepted more from a sense of duty than belief in victory.

'Congrats chief,' Milo Yiannopoulos emailed.

'U mean "condolences",' Bannon replied.

The Breitbart boss upped the nationalist rhetoric and intensified attacks on Hillary Clinton. Trump began referring to 'Crooked Hillary', and raising awkward questions about financial irregularities in the Clinton Foundation and her use of a private email server while in government. Soon the Democrat candidate's health would be in the sniper sights after she collapsed in front of the cameras and had to be carried face down into a van.

Clinton remained too far ahead in the polls to be damaged. A speech she gave on 25 August in Nevada should have put a stake through the heart of any possible Trump victory. It savaged Steve Bannon's connections to the alt-right, the internet movement of white nationalists, disaffected conservatives and nihilistic internet trolls. They made the counter-jihad look like liberals.

*

The alt-right started as a fresh coat of paint for white nationalists tired of the movement's obsession with Nazi Germany. Sites like Richard Spencer's Alternative Right and Greg Johnson's Counter-Currents Publishing pushed a new kind of far-right politics that dropped the hagiographies of Nazi Übermenschen for philosophical articles on Martin Heidegger, Julius Evola, Ernst Jünger, Charles Maurras, Francis Parker Yockey (*Imperium: The Philosophy of History and Politics*), the white ethnostate and the metaphysics of power.

The old far-right had been defeatist and stuck in the past, a generation of skinheads and paramilitaries and Ku Klux Klan sheet wearers eulogising 1930s fascism and publicising hard-luck tales of white decline and minority crime. The new wave preferred optimism and predicted a white ethnostate inside a few generations. Spencer held public conferences in Washington DC and acted like the leader of a respectable political movement. Blogs talked race realism, IQ tests, crime figures and long lists of which important people were Jewish.

This new kind of white nationalism spread its tentacles and made tentative contact with other transgressive parts of the internet. The manosphere was an archipelago of blogs and sites for men avoiding women, men who hated women, men who wanted to have sex with lots of women, and men who thought evolutionary psychology explained why their girl left them for someone taller. Most readers were white and felt disenfranchised by the social justice side of American liberalism they encountered every day in workplaces, colleges and clubs. Tentacles swirled and entwined. Manosphere blogs started talking about crime and race; white nationalists borrowed the manosphere imagery of 'taking the red pill' to describe their own journeys into the heart of darkness.

Other groups bleeding into the alt-right included the neoreactionaries, hypergraphic futurists of the dark enlightenment who all seemed to work in tech and obsess over cryptocurrency; edgier libertarians; paleoconservatives; conspiracy theorists who assumed that no government ever voluntarily told the truth; and straight-up Nazis. Not everyone liked each other, not everyone agreed. But they all hated liberalism.

One alt-right tentacle probed its way on to the 4chan message board, a dank corner of the internet where everything from animals being cute to people shooting themselves in the face got homogenised by the computer screen into an emotionally remote set of images not much related to real life. The young crowd shared gifs of cute cats, fantasised that girls in anime were their waifus, mocked victims in shotgun suicide photographs as 'an hero', fapped relentlessly to porn, trolled each other with disgusting images, and freaked out the normies with memes of Nazi soldiers marching past Auschwitz. Then they mixed and matched everything in a way guaranteed to baffle and offend anyone outside their online incubator.

The /pol/ or politically incorrect board at 4chan became an alt-right clown world. The serious talk of Spencer or Johnson, of neoreaction and evolutionary psychologists, got chopped and diced into irreverent memes, often featuring Pepe, a harmless green cartoon frog who'd been around the internet for years. Putting him in a Nazi uniform for some race-baiting meme seemed hilarious to 4chan's /pol/acks; taking alt-right talking points to vicious extremes seemed even funnier.

The boards had on obsession with badly drawn cartoons of Chilean dictator Augusto Pinochet ('You can't just throw someone out of a helicopter because they're a commie'; 'That's where you're wrong, kiddo'); worshipping Trump as a God

Emperor and rebranding mainstream Republicans who opposed him as 'cuckservatives'; spreading memes that looked suspiciously counter-jihad, such as Remove Kebab, which sprang from an old video of Republika Srpska soldiers playing a politicised folk song and evolved into a call to physically kick Muslims out of Europe; pictures of charging crusaders with swords raised ('Excuse me, do you have a moment to talk about Jesus?'); and endlessly expanding the universe of Pepe the frog with Italian disco songs and the imaginary nation of Kekistan.

The alt-right never seemed sure if /pol/ was on its side or just involved in some deeply ironic trolling. Perhaps it didn't matter. Those 4chan memes disseminated the message far across the internet. The term alt-right escaped its founders to become a Rorschach inkblot that reflected whatever observers wanted to see. For some it was a reborn Nazi Germany inexplicably centred on a bunch of virginal shut-ins with a fixation on Japanese anime and synthwave; for others a deeply intellectual movement that challenged modern liberal views of equality and open borders; some just saw a lot of aggressive males who didn't like feminism much and wanted Donald Trump to win.

For Steve Bannon the movement looked like a potential alternative base for the Republican Party, with enough internet savvy to bypass media gatekeepers and take Trump's message straight to voters. He approved its mentions of René Guénon and Julius Evola, but didn't much like the anti-Semitism with its (((triple parentheses))) around Jewish names. He tasked Milo Yiannopoulos with writing an article that cleaned up the movement and turned it into a borderline respectable challenger to the political establishment.

The Yiannopoulos story went viral, mainly because it enabled liberal journalists to finally understand all the Twitter abuse they'd been getting from accounts with green frog icons. For a short moment it seemed to work. Diehard Trump supporters who'd never read Breitbart identified themselves as alt-right to reporters at rallies.

Then it went wrong. Bannon officially joining the Trump campaign gave the Democrats an opening for the knife. A week after his appointment, speechwriters cooked up a text for Hillary Clinton that boiled the alt-right back to its white nationalist roots, ignored any complexities, and blamed the whole mess on Bannon.

'The de facto merger between Breitbart and the Trump campaign represents a landmark achievement for the alt-right,' Clinton told a college crowd in Reno. 'This is not conservatism as we have known it. This is not Republicanism as we have known it. These are race-baiting ideas, anti-Muslim and anti-immigrant ideas, anti-woman – all key tenets making up an emerging racist ideology known as the Alt-Right.'

'Pepe!' shouted out a 4chan fan in the audience. No one seemed to notice.

She accused Bannon of bringing the far-right into a presidential campaign, and Trump of knowingly retweeting white nationalist memes. The media storm that followed made the alt-right calve like an iceberg as anyone vaguely respectable distanced themselves. Bullets flew close to the ground. Counter-jihadists found themselves under fire from reporters who couldn't tell the difference between Bat Ye'or and Joseph Goebbels. Jihadwatch's Robert Spencer had a hard time convincing people he wasn't Richard Spencer. No one seemed to listen to counter-jihad claims that numerous factors, notably anti-Semitism, meant they had never overlapped with the alt-right more than peripherally in the Venn diagram of politics.

Jewish journalists at Breitbart lined up to back their boss. Pamela Geller wrote a piece titled 'As a Jew, I Stand with Steve Bannon'. The Breitbart chief appreciated the support but didn't think Clinton's speech would make a difference to voter intentions. Not many agreed. A typically pugnacious Trump counter-attack had knocked Clinton's poll ratings down a few points but journalists remained convinced the toxic alt-right connection had sunk any chance of Republican victory. A tape which emerged shortly afterwards of Trump chatting about women, recorded eleven years earlier, hammered the final stake into the campaign's vampiric heart.

'I just start kissing them. It's like a magnet. Just kiss. I don't even wait. And when you're a star, they let you do it. You can do anything. Grab 'em by the pussy. You can do anything.'

Voters went to the polls on 8 November. The media, the pollsters and most of the Trump campaign staff thought Clinton would win. The counter-jihad had lost its big chance to push its views into the White House.

AFTERMATH

MAKING AMERICA GREAT
AGAIN IN NEW YORK

They elected him. The orange face, the wispy haircut, the tough-guy New York talk. On 9 November 2016 Donald John Trump became the forty-fifth president elect of the United States of America.

He got 63 million votes in all the right places and was swept into the White House on a wave of populism, nationalism and red baseball caps with the slogan 'Make America Great Again'. The Democrats couldn't believe it. The media had told them voters wanted a progressive future of transsexual bathroom rights and open borders. Now they had Islamophobic rhetoric and giant walls.

Celebrities tweeted out shocked disbelief ('I am in tears' – Ariana Grande; 'Anyone else want to puke?' – Kristen Bell; 'How do we explain this to future generations of women?' – Will Arnett; 'Retweet if you want a recount' – Lindsay Lohan) and the Democrat campaign headquarters filled up with crying volunteers. Calls to suicide hotlines hit a record high. Media outlets deleted carefully prepared stories of a Clinton win. Foreign leaders who'd been too open about their preferences prepped themselves for a humiliating congratulatory call to the new president.

Trump saw in the victory at Trump Tower in Manhattan, spending most of the evening isolated in the same penthouse apartment from which he'd watched the burning towers of the World Trade Center on 9/11. He and Melania emerged when voting figures began suggesting a possible win. The couple came down to the fourteenth-floor war room with its wall of big-screen televisions and watched disbelieving news anchors call state after state for the Republicans. Advisors and speechwriters and aides milled around high-fiving each other. Soon everyone was up in the penthouse where Bannon and advisor Stephen Miller helped Trump write his victory speech at the kitchen table. Then it was off to the Hilton for champagne and partying until dawn.

The inauguration took place two and half months later in front of half a million people outside the Capitol Building in Washington DC. A few thousand protesters turned up to make their feelings known. Anarchists in black masks set fire to a limousine and let off fireworks; five Black Lives Matter activists chained themselves together at a security checkpoint. The #notmypresident hashtag trended on Twitter.

'Today, we are not merely transferring power from one administration to another, or one party to another,' said Trump, 'but we are transferring power from Washington DC, and giving it back to you, the people.'

The counter-jihad rejoiced. Brigitte Gabriel of ACT! for America was invited to visit the White House, and ACT! board member Michael Flynn, a retired lieutenant-colonel, served briefly as Trump's National Security advisor. Steve Bannon got a post as chief strategist. Breitbart editor Sebastian Gorka, author of 2016's *Defeating Jihad: The Winnable War*, became Trump's deputy assistant; Gorka's wife Katharine got a post as adviser to the secretary of Homeland Security. Within ten days of taking office Trump signed executive order 13769, which barred citizens from seven Muslim nations entering America.

'Our man is delivering the goods,' said Pamela Geller. 'It's what freedom is supposed to look like. We have been living under the boot of leftist autocrats for so long, we forgot it could be this good. We have been set free. Every day is Christmas.'

The new administration made a mess of implementing the order. Airport security detained hundreds of travellers deplaning from journeys that had been legal when they started. Visas were revoked, granted, revoked again. Thousands of protesters gathered at airports with signs and flags. Legal challenges hit the courts. A Hawaiian judge issued a temporary restraining order against 13769 in March. The White House redrafted the measure as executive order 13780, morphed it into a Presidential Proclamation, and spent the rest of the year fighting all comers in court to get it accepted. The proclamation finally came into effect at the end of the year to find a crowd of further legal challenges already queuing up to take another swing.

Steve Bannon wasn't around to watch 13769 take effect. In the aftermath of Trump's victory, the Democrats and their friends in the media decided the new administration was a reborn Third Reich and went hunting for leverage. The attacks had little effect on Trump, who had a Jewish daughter, a Jewish son-in-law and a lot of support in Tel Aviv, but Bannon's alt-right flirtation made him a target. A barrage of subtext, innuendo and open attack came raining down. Bannon recognised the strategy. He'd toyed with it himself in the election campaign when he thought his boss might not win.

'Our back-up strategy,' Bannon said, 'is to fuck [Clinton] up so bad that she can't govern. If she gets 43 per cent of the vote, she can't claim a mandate.'

Trump had won the election on only 46.1 per cent of the vote. Now the media were describing the immigration executive order and the Mexican wall as fascism, doing everything they could to undermine the legitimacy of the administration. A BBC article linked Bannon to long-dead neo-Nazi sorceress Savitri Devi because of a supposed similarity in worldview. A casual mention of Julius Evola was used as evidence Bannon worshipped the baron as a guru.

The former Breitbart chief hung on until an alt-right rally in Charlottesville, Virginia spiralled into violence that left one protester dead after a car ploughed through a crowd. The alt-right had already splintered into a hardcore of white nationalists and a more conservative-friendly 'alt-lite' faction; the hardcore hoped the rally would show their ascendancy, but didn't count on tough opposition and some dubious policing choices. The last vestiges of love between the alt-right and anything vaguely mainstream died that day. Richard Spencer's public speaking opportunities dried up, doxed activists lost their jobs, and the alt-right reverted to an internet movement fighting to get its message past social media censorship. Soon it had shrunk to the same small world of white nationalists who started the whole thing, sharing *Mürdoch Mürdoch* videos and parsing Evola quotes, wondering if they had made the most of their moment in the media spotlight.

The White House appeased public anger over Charlottesville by sacking Bannon. He returned to Breitbart News but remained in contact with the president. That link snapped with the January 2018 publication of Michael Wolff's *Fire and Fury*, an unsympathetic account of the Trump administration's first year that had some uncomplimentary quotes from Bannon. The Breitbart board dropped him and Trump savaged his former chief executive.

'When he was fired, he not only lost his job, he lost his mind,' said Trump. 'Steve was a staffer who worked for me after I had already won the nomination by defeating seventeen candidates, often described as the most talented field ever assembled in the Republican party.'

Bannon was rich and well connected enough not to care much. He remained a political operator, pulling strings and planting stories, reading René Guénon in his mansion. Comments in early 2018 that Islam had a place in the West may have owed more to a renewed interest in Traditionalism than a sudden conversion to liberalism. Perhaps it fitted in somewhere with Bannon's increasingly evangelical promotion of populism in America, Europe and elsewhere. On the wall of his office hung a kitsch painting: Bannon as Jacques-Louis David's Napoleon. It had been a gift from UKIP chief Nigel Farage, who credited the Breitbart chief with helping to bring about a political earthquake on the other side of the Atlantic.

*

Euroscepticism runs deep in British bones. Any island that has been invaded by Italians, Scandinavians and French over the centuries and still can't cook has a self-evidently deep resistance to neighbouring cultures. The British don't like being told what to do by foreigners, which has made its membership of the European Union a shaky proposition from the start.

'[Britain] is separated from the continent,' wrote military strategist Humphrey Slater when people first started talking about common markets 'by an invaluable stretch of cold water.'

The idea of a unified Europe had been around since the nineteenth century. Victor Hugo preached '*Les États-Unis d'Europe*' at the 1849 International Peace Congress. It took a hundred more years and two world wars for the seeds of the European Union to sprout, and then another thirty years for Britain to join. Initial Anglophone doubt turned to enthusiasm, then back to doubt again. By the next century opposition to the EU was strong enough to birth UKIP.

On 23 June 2016 the Conservative government caved in to pressure from Eurosceptics in its own ranks and held a referendum on leaving the European Union, hoping for a mandate to stay in. They made sure voters understood that leaving would involve huge financial penalties and political chaos. Polls indicated most people accepted the logic of remaining with the EU. The counter-jihad wanted the opposite.

'I hope so much for Brexit,' said Pegida's Lutz Bachmann. 'The European Union is a bunch of alcoholics in Brussels who rule with no knowledge of the ideology of each country.'

The result came in on 24 June and shocked a lot of people. A sliver above half the electorate voted to leave. UKIP cracked open the champagne. Nigel Farage had achieved his life mission and was grateful enough to Breitbart News for pushing the Eurosceptic message that he gave Steve Bannon the mock Jacques-Louis David painting.

Voters decided to leave the EU for many reasons, but one important factor was the migrant crisis. Not long before the vote, Angela Merkel had announced plans to ease the burden on Germany by resettling migrants across Europe. The governments of Eastern Europe protested loudest but the British were equally emphatic about not adding to their existing immigration issues. Campaigners talked about how the country now received more migrants each year than it had done for the entirety of the period between 1066 to 1950, an impressive-sounding statistic that didn't take into account population growth. A crowded island nation will never be comfortable with open borders. It was enough to tip the vote towards leaving the European Union.

Liberals had barely recovered when Trump's election flipped the world upside down. Nerves were still twanging when Europe's far-right nationalist parties began their march towards the ballot box in the 2017 elections.

The Netherlands held a general election that March. Journalists speculated with quiet horror about Geert Wilders' Partij voor de Vrijheid coming out on top and forming a counter-jihadist government. Some openly called Wilders a neo-Nazi; others muttered darkly that any rising right-wing movement attracts extremists like rats to a damp cellar. Wilders' supporters thought the establishment was terrified of losing its cushy jobs and cheered on their hero's promised Trump-style moratorium on Muslim immigration. Other parties decided not to work with the PVV, leading Wilders to warn of a 'revolution' in the Netherlands if he was locked out of government.

Hirsi Ali looked on from America. She had citizenship and was married to Conservative-leaning British academic Niall Ferguson. There had been two autobiographies, more campaigning against Islam, a cancelled tour of Australia, and the label of 'anti-Muslim extremist' from the Southern Poverty Law Center. Hirsi Ali hoped Wilders would win but knew first-hand the resistance of the Dutch to counter-jihadism. She wasn't surprised when the PVV failed to live up to expectations and came second with 13 per cent of the votes, an increase of only five seats.

'I would still like to co-govern as the PVV, if possible,' said an optimistic Wilders. 'But if that doesn't work ... we'll support the cabinet, where needed, on the issues that are important to us.'

The call to government never came. In May, France held its presidential election. The establishment had been compromised by corruption, failure and the migrant crisis. Voters preferred to make a choice between Marine Le Pen of the Front National and little-known career politician Emmanuel Macron of En Marche!, a newly formed centrist party. Macron got 66.1 per cent of the vote, although the Front National's 10.6 million votes gave it hope for the June legislative elections. That hope died when Macron's party won a huge majority the next month with 310 seats. Le Pen and the Front National were near the rear of the pack with only eight.

Europe faced more nationalist disappointment when Germany held its federal elections in September. Alternative für Deutschland came in third with ninety-four seats in the Bundestag, compared to 200 for Angela Merkel's Christlich Demokratische Union Deutschlands. Merkel did some deals and remained chancellor; the usual alliances meant AfD had no hope of getting its hands on any levers of power.

Populism had not broken through in the way many hoped or feared in 2017 but it was clear that previously marginal nationalist, counter-jihadist and anti-immigration views had become part of mainstream political discourse. It was already illegal to wear a face veil in parts of Switzerland; Slovakia passed a law effectively preventing Islam ever gaining official status as a religion; the Freiheitliche Partei Österreichs in Austria had promised to build a border fence to keep out Muslim migrants. The days of the counter-jihad as atomised individuals hunched behind computer screens had gone. Defence Leagues, Stop Islamisation groups, and Pegida offshoots had dropped away like booster rockets tumbling and flaming towards the ocean. What remained melded with the new nationalism and shot towards the stars as something new and bigger.

Street activism wasn't completely dead. In the autumn of 2017 a group called the Football Lads Alliance managed to get 40,000 people marching against Islamic extremism in London. Alan Ayling was rumoured to be involved somehow; if true, the businessman kept quiet about it. The FLA turnout had been boosted by three Islamic terror attacks in Britain that year. A March vehicle attack in London killed five people, in May a suicide bomber killed twenty-two at the Manchester Arena during an Ariana Grande concert, and in June another vehicle attack in London killed eight. Other terror attacks in Europe included a vehicle attack in Barcelona that killed sixteen, a lorry driven through a Berlin Christmas market killing eleven, and a series of attacks on soldiers and police in Paris.

The counter-jihad old guard searched for a new role, or faded out, or doggedly trudged down the same paths. Edward May and the Gates of Vienna crowd continued to report terror attacks, migrant crimes, and political updates, but the feeling of being modern-day Paul Reveres warning the populace of coming danger had gone. The last of May's Counterjihad conferences had been a 2013 event in Warsaw. The English Defence League and its offshoots had wound down like broken watches, as had the various Stop Islamisation movements in Europe. Bachmann's Freiheitlich Direktdemokratische Volkspartei achieved little and Pegida was fading out.

Gisèle Littman continued to publish under the name Bat Ye'or, with *Europe, Globalization, and the Coming of the Universal Caliphate* coming out in 2011 and *Understanding Dhimmitude* hitting bookshelves two years later. She gave occasional talks but was now in her eighties and unwilling to leave Switzerland. The appearance of flag-waving nationalism in Europe cannot have been comforting.

Over in Britain, Melanie Phillips continued her journalist career with *The Times* and a regular gig on BBC Radio 4's *The Moral Maze*. She wrote a few more books, including an autobiography, but nothing as explicitly counter-jihadist as *Londonistan*. Her connection with the movement had never been strong, thanks to Vlaams Belang's role in organising the first conference in Brussels, and the hooligan nationalism of the English Defence League. Phillips wanted to believe the Front National and the Sverigedemokraterna were being honest when they claimed to have dropped the anti-Semitism, but had seen too much of life to be completely convinced.

'Much of the rest may be opportunistic repositioning by nationalist parties,' she said, 'realizing they can now make common cause against Muslim aggression with terrified and abandoned European Jews.'

Bruce Bawer stayed in Norway and in 2017 self-published an explicitly counter-jihadist novel. *The Alhambra* followed the adventures of a gay American filmmaker living in a pre-9/11 Amsterdam who discovers an Islamic bomb plot against a right-wing politician. It got good reviews on counter-jihad sites like *Frontpage*. In Belgium, Paul Beliën parted company with Geert Wilders and carried on his crusade against Islam and the European Union through *The Brussels Journal*.

Stephen Lennon remained important in the European counter-jihad world. Tommy Robinson had long ceased to be a mask and had become an identity. He made some speeches at Pegida rallies in Dresden and the Czech Republic, but the UK version died on its feet with poor attendance and low funds. Lennon wrote an autobiography called *Enemy of the State*, a self-published job that sold well, although reviews were thin on the ground. He had the kind of minor celebrity status that involved panic buttons, police cars parked outside the house, and parts of town he could never visit and come out alive.

He became a reporter for the Canadian channel Rebel Media, owned by Ezra Levant, whose friend Mark Steyn was still going strong as a conservative media pundit alongside Ann Coulter. Lennon quit in February 2018 and went independent, juggling his new lifestyle with legal action against Cambridgeshire police for harassment. He got some satisfaction when Nick Lowles of non-profit Hope Not Hate privately apologised for all the attacks over the years, explaining the left had underestimated the threat of radical Islam. The veteran left-wing activist Lowles might have been motivated by the National Union of Students accusing him of Islamophobia for criticising radical Islam and paedophile grooming in Rochdale. In late May 2018 Lennon went back to prison after getting arrested for contempt of court while reporting on a Muslim-related child rape case. He got thirteen months.

The entry of the counter-jihad into the mainstream attracted a few of the more daring celebrities. Christopher Hitchens had died of oesophageal cancer at the end of 2011 but his friend Martin Amis picked up the torch. 'What I am,' said the British author, 'is an Islamophobe.'

Others went the other way. On 17 February 2018 the second Modest Fashion Week for Muslim designers was held in London. American actress Lindsay Lohan turned up in a hijab.

*

From some angles the counter-jihad was full of New Yorkers traumatised by 9/11, from others a vehicle for conservative Jews to fight an ancient Middle Eastern war on a new battleground. Others saw a mob of working-class football fans, or the far-right trying to hide behind a more respectable facade. A battle against homophobia and misogyny; racist invective against an alien other that threatened white privilege; a shield to protect European cultures and values from extinction; a new crusade, with all that entails.

The counter-jihad was most successful in America, where its better-connected elements were able to plug into a pre-existing network of well-financed conservative, Christian and Jewish organisations. This gave them ideological leverage when Donald Trump came along and built a presidential campaign around Republican grassroots concerns. Executive order 13769 wouldn't have happened without ACT! for America and Frank Gaffney, Pamela Geller and Steve Bannon.

The European arm of the counter-jihad was more diverse in membership but less well monied. The marches and rallies put its ideology on the map but only the migrant crisis and a wave of Islamic State terror attacks could get the political establishment to take them seriously. Even then, their beliefs had to creep in through the back door via established nationalist parties, who struggled to transform popular feeling into votes.

Both wings of the counter-jihad have succeeded in injecting previously marginal beliefs into the mainstream, at the cost of coarsening them and losing control of how they are interpreted. The future of the counter-jihad is uncertain but it will likely end up a patch on a nationalist quilt, not a whole cloth. The future for the West in its relations with Islam is equally uncertain. The collapse of Islamic State in 2018 has slowed terror attacks and disillusioned many radicalised Muslims around the world.

At a best guess, in 2016 the Muslim population of the European Union, and associated countries Norway and Switzerland, was 25.7 million, about 4.9 per cent of the total. Back in 2006, the EU had 15 million Muslims, making 3.2 per cent of the population total. Accurate figures further back are harder to find.

Over in America, the Muslim population in 2016 was around 3.3 million, about 1 per cent of the total. Back in 2001 the figure was closer to 2 million, about 0.7 per cent.

At least 661 people in the European Union have been killed in terror attacks that occurred after 11 September 2001. Expand the field to include Russia, Turkey, Macedonia, Bulgaria and Georgia, and the figure is over 2,000. About ninety-eight have been killed in the USA over the same period, rising of course to more than 3,000 if the original al-Qaeda attacks are counted. Numerous other attacks wounded or maimed victims. Some never got further than plots stillborn the moment police kicked in the door.

Those are the figures. The counter-jihad would urge us to add in crime and cultural change, rapes and burqas, coalition soldiers in dusty villages and Islamic Staters stalking the Bataclan. Liberals prefer to push vibrancy and diversity, fairness and equality, bigots dripping pig blood on mosque doors and refugee doctors saving lives in overextended hospital wards. The left think the West will get stronger when white supremacy is dismantled by an expanded colour palette of skin tones and diversity of places to worship. Geopolitical types with long memories suggest Eastern Europe will become Byzantium to the West's Rome, one side of the continent thriving while the former seat of power declines and dies. Cultural commentators warn of a coming new generation in the West so conservative it will make the alt-right look like Saul Alinsky; of third-, fourth-generation Muslim migrants with no loyalty to ancestral homelands or the nation they inhabit but a firm identity in the horizontal reality of international Islam. Readers of Oswald Spengler believe the migrant crises, enthusiasm for equality, and hierarchies turned upside down are proof the West is on the far side of history's bell curve and going down fast. Some even think Spengler's second religiosity, when the inhabitants of a dying civilisation turn back to God, will see its flowering in Islam. European Christianity, they remind us, began as a Jewish desert religion adopted by the pagans in Rome.

'How 100,000 Britons Have Chosen to Become Muslim,' ran a *Daily Mail* headline as far back as 2011, 'and Average Convert is 27-Year-Old White Woman.'

Fans of German soldier and writer Ernst Jünger, who had died in 1998 after a long and eventful life, point out that he expressed sympathy for Islam before his death, lauding it as a religion for warriors and travellers. He also liked the idea of having four wives.

Something everyone seems to agree on, left or right, is that mass migration has made Europe an authoritarian place and will make it more so in the future. Some like this, some don't. Impeccably liberal policies of providing havens for refugees, welcoming cheap labour, and opening borders have made Western nations into a new generation of cleft states, full of mutually antagonistic groups. The melting pot needs an increasingly thicker, heavier lid to stop it boiling over. Fans of Samuel Huntington see modern Germany or Sweden as new Ukraines, frontlines of mutually incompatible worldviews ready to explode. Holding such cleft states together will require a ruthless disregard for human rights and the destruction of the liberal values that birthed the situation in the first place. If authoritarianism fails, then violent conflict between incompatible ethnic, cultural, and religious interests is inevitable.

A multicultural state is an empire in miniature. And no empire in human history has ever ruled itself through liberalism and tolerance.

We have to weigh all this up and keep our thumbs off the scale in a way the counter-jihad and its enemies can never manage. Decide whether Islam is an existential threat to Western liberal democracy or a slandered religion of peace that just wants to co-exist. Even Houellebecq the mage on the cover of *Charlie Hebdo* might find that kind of prediction beyond his powers.

NOTES

Introduction

'We must consider the ...' http://www.euro-islam.info/country-profiles/italy/

'Four months after 9/11 ...' http://abcnews.go.com/images/pdf/931a4Islam.pdf

'It is my hypothesis ...' The Clash of Civilizations?, Huntington (*Foreign Affairs*, Vol. 72, No. 3, Summer 1993)

'A conflict between liberal ...' The Clash of Civilizations?, Huntington (*Foreign Affairs*, Vol. 72, No. 3, Summer 1993)

'I'd be taking a ...' What Trump and Clinton did on 9/11, Kruse, *Politico Magazine*, 10 September 2016 (http://www.politico.com/magazine/story/2016/09/trump-hillary-clinton-september-11-911-attacks-nyc-214236)

'Every nation has to ...' What Trump and Clinton did on 9/11, Kruse, *Politico Magazine*, 10 September 2016 (http://www.politico.com/magazine/story/2016/09/trump-hillary-clinton-september-11-911-attacks-nyc-214236)

'I think our motto ...' https://en.wikiquote.org/wiki/Ann_Coulter

'Faith is the surrender ...' https://en.wikiquote.org/wiki/Christopher_Hitchens

1 Gay, Libertarian, and Populist in Hilversum

'I don't hate Islam ...' Pim Fortuyn op herhaling: 'De islam is een achterlijke cultuur', *de Volkskrant*, 9 February 2002 (https://www.volkskrant.nl/binnenland/pim-fortuyn-op-herhaling-de-islam-is-een-achterlijke-cultuur~a611698/)

'Dangerous. A polder Mussolini ...' Holland's Own Kennedy Affair: Conspiracy Theories on the Murder of Pim Fortuyn, Van Buuren (*Historical Social Research/Historische Sozialforschung*, Vol. 38, No. 1 (143), 2013)

'If anything were to ...' Holland's Own Kennedy Affair: Conspiracy Theories on the Murder of Pim Fortuyn, Van Buuren (*Historical Social Research/Historische Sozialforschung*, Vol. 38, No. 1 (143), 2013)

'Soon most big towns had ...' Europe Deals with Immigration, Starr, *Slate*, 14 October 2008 (http://www.slate.com/articles/news_and_politics/how_they_do_it/features/2008/europe_deals_with_immigration/failure_to_integrate_in_the_netherlands.html)

'When you need to ...' The Search for an Extinct Volcano in the Dutch Polder: Pilgrimage to Memorial Sites of Pim Fortuyn, Colombijn (*Anthropos*, Bd. 102, H. 1. (2007))

'New Dutchmen have to ...' Fortuyn, Van Gogh, Hirsi Ali: Why the Unholy Trinity was Driven Out of the Netherlands, Beunders (*Contagion: Journal of Violence, Mimesis, and Culture*, Vol. 15/16, 2008-2009)

'As you may know ...' Vlak voor de val, Haveman, *de Volkskrant*, 16 February 2002 (https://www.volkskrant.nl/archief/vlak-voor-de-val~a626223/)

'In my eyes this ...' Trial Opens in Amsterdam in Slaying of Popular Dutch Politician, Simons, *New York Times*, 28 March 2003 (https://www.nytimes.com/2003/03/28/world/trial-opens-in-amsterdam-in-slaying-of-popular-dutch-politician.html)

2 *Am I Beating My Wife Hard Enough?*

'I know not everyone ...' Holland's Own Kennedy Affair. Conspiracy Theories on the Murder of Pim Fortuyn, Van Buuren (*Historical Social Research/Historische Sozialforschung*, Vol. 38, No. 1 (143), 2013)

'A gay critic was ...' http://www.sociosite.org/jihad_nl_en.php#daderprofiel

'That is a habit ...' Holland's Own Kennedy Affair. Conspiracy Theories on the Murder of Pim Fortuyn, Van Buuren (*Historical Social Research/Historische Sozialforschung*, Vol. 38, No. 1 (143), 2013)

'I'm Theo van Gogh ...' *Infidel*, Hirsi Ali (Atria Books, 2007) p311

'I picked up the ...' *Infidel*, p271

'The true doctrine of ...' 'Huntington' in Holland. The Public Debate on Muslim Immigrants in The Netherlands, Vellenga (*Nordic Journal of Religion and Society* 21 (1) (2008))

'The oppression of women ...' Absolute Infidel: The Evolution of Ayaan Hirsi Ali, Schafer & Koth, *The Humanist*, 22 December 2007 (https://thehumanist.com/magazine/january-february-2008/features/absolute-infidel-the-evolution-of-ayaan-hirsi-ali)

'A Muslim woman has ...' https://nl.wikipedia.org/wiki/De_zoontjesfabriek

3 No Sympathy for Unbelievers

'Have mercy, have mercy ..." Amsterdam-Oost, een jaar geleden, *Trouw*, 2 November 2005 (http://www.trouw.nl/tr/nl/4324/Nieuws/article/detail/1713577/2005/11/02/Amsterdam-Oost-een-jaar-geleden.dhtml)

'We will defeat them ...' Massacre in Madrid, Tremlett, *The Guardian*, 12 May 2004 (https://www.theguardian.com/world/2004/mar/12/alqaida.spain1)

'All those umbrellas in ...' *America Alone: The End of the World as We Know It*, Steyn (Regnery Publishing, 2006) p37

'I don't hate Muslims ...' I don't hate Muslims. I hate Islam, says Holland's rising political star, Traynor, *The Guardian*, 17 February 2008 (https://www.theguardian.com/world/2008/feb/17/netherlands.islam)

'It has been shown ...' 'Huntington' in Holland. The Public Debate on Muslim Immigrants in The Netherlands, Vellenga (*Nordic Journal of Religion and Society* 21 (1) (2008))

'To the enemy I ...' https://theblisterneverends.wordpress.com/2010/04/10/inbloedgedoopt/

I don't feel your ...'. Muslim Radical Confesses to Van Gogh Killing in Court Tirade, Browne (*The Times*, 12 July 2005)

'The streets saw marches ...' Lions of Tawhid in the Polder, Aarts & Hirzalla (*Middle East Report*, No. 235, Summer 2005)

'He was outspoken ...' Neoliberal Xenophobia: The Dutch Case, Demmers & Mehendale (*Alternatives: Global, Local, Political*, Vol. 35, No. 1, January–March 2010)

'He was an asshole ...' Neoliberal Xenophobia: The Dutch Case, Demmers & Mehendale (*Alternatives: Global, Local, Political*, Vol. 35, No. 1, January–March 2010)

4 Dhimmitude in Londonistan

'Twenty-four-year-old ...' *My Treasured Possessions*, Manoli (Xulon Press, 2012) p36

'Dhimmitude is a complex ...' An Egyptian Jew in Exile, Gordon, *New English Review*, 6 October 2011 (https://myislam.dk/articles/en/yeor%20an-egyptian-jew-in-exile.php)

'*Eurabia* was dismissed as ...' Tales from Eurabia, *The Economist*, 22 June 2006 (http://www.economist.com/node/7086222)

'I just saw a ...' Voices of 7/7: The Survivors' Testimonies Form a Searing but Inspiring Memorial to the 52 Victims, *The Independent*, 4 March 2011 (http://www.independent.co.uk/news/uk/home-news/

voices-of-77-the-survivors-testimonies-form-a-searing-but-inspiring-memorial-to-the-52-victims-2231571.html)

'Until we feel security ...' London Bomber Video Aired on TV, *BBC News*, 2 September 2005 (http://news.bbc.co.uk/2/hi/uk/4206708.stm)

'Mental dhimmitude has been ...' https://www.jihadwatch.org/2005/07/bat-yeors-theory-of-the-british-collapse

"A revolt,' said Orebi ...' Eurabia Scholars Gather in The Hague, Belen, *The Brussels Journal*, 20 February 2006 (https://www.Brusselsjournal.com/node/840)

5 Self-Censorship during the Cartoon War

'Two days of meetings ...' An Extraordinary Meeting, Whitaker, *The Guardian*, 12 December 2005 (https://www.theguardian.com/world/2005/dec/12/saudiarabia.islam)

'A few were straight ...' Cartoon Violence and Freedom of Expression, Keane (*Human Rights Quarterly*, Vol. 30, No. 4, Nov. 2008)

'Modern, secular society is ...' Muhammeds Ansigt, *Jyllands Posten*, 30 September 2005 (http://jyllands-posten.dk/indland/ECE4769352/Muhammeds-ansigt/)

'We have been addressing...' How a Meeting of Leaders in Mecca Set Off the Cartoon Wars Around the World, Howden, Hardaker, & Castle, *The Independent*, 10 February 2006 (http://www.independent.co.uk/news/world/middle-east/how-a-meeting-of-leaders-in-mecca-set-off-the-cartoon-wars-around-the-world-6109473.html)

'What is happening in ...' Blasphemy and Violence, Hassner (*International Studies Quarterly*, Vol. 55, No. 1, March 2011)

'Europe You Will Pay ...' Cartoon Protest Slogans Condemned, *BBC News*, 5 February 2006 (http://news.bbc.co.uk/2/hi/4682262.stm)

'The 450 demonstrators came ...' 'Magnificent 19' Praised by Muslim Extremists, O'Neill, *Daily Telegraph*, 12 September 2003 (http://www.telegraph.co.uk/news/uknews/1441270/Magnificent-19-praised-by-Muslim-extremists.html)

'Self-censorship over Islam ...' http://www.realclearpolitics.com/Commentary/com-2_5_06_MP.html

'Bat Ye'or's scholarship is ...' http://www.dhimmitude.org/books/Eurabia.html

'They are fuelled by ...' *Londonistan: How Britain is Creating a Terror State Within*, Phillips (Encounter Books, 2006) p169

'The book got positive reviews ...' Why We Now Grow Our Own Terrorists, Burleigh, *The Daily Telegraph*, 16 July 2006 (http://www.telegraph.co.uk/culture/books/3653861/Why-we-now-grow-our-own-terrorists.html)

6 Medieval Rags and Christian Atheists in Florence

'*Brutto stronzo* [arsehole] … *vaffanculo* …' Oriana Fallaci and the Art of the Interview, Hitchens, *Vanity Fair*, December 2006 (http://www.vanityfair.com/news/2006/12/hitchens200612)

'The most disastrous conversation …' Oriana Fallaci, Incisive Italian Journalist, is Dead at 77, Fisher, *New York Times*, 16 September 2006 (http://www.nytimes.com/2006/09/16/books/16fallaci.html)

'To speak of oneself …' Oriana Fallaci, Incisive Italian Journalist, is Dead at 77, Fisher, *New York Times*, 16 September 2006 (http://www.nytimes.com/2006/09/16/books/16fallaci.html)

'I sat at the …' http://www.giselle.com/oriana.html

'By the 1970s she …' http://www.danielpipes.org/3967/appreciating-orianafallaci

'Has anyone ever told …' Oriana Fallaci and the Art of the Interview, Hitchens, *Vanity Fair*, December 2006 (http://www.vanityfair.com/news/2006/12/hitchens200612)

'You ask me about …' Oriana Fallaci, McGregor & Hooper, *The Guardian*, 16 September 2006 (https://www.theguardian.com/news/2006/sep/16/guardianobituaries.italy)

'And I'm very, very …' La Rabbia e l'Orgoglio, Fallaci, *Corriere della Sera* (29 September, 2001)

'Because when the destiny …' La Rabbia e l'Orgoglio, Fallaci, *Corriere della Sera* (29 September, 2001)

'Some reviewers loved it …' She Said What She Thought, Steyn (https://www.steynonline.com/4478/she-said-what-she-thought)

'Written in the hot …' Holy Writ, Hitchens, *The Atlantic*, April 2003 (http://www.theatlantic.com/magazine/archive/2003/04/holy-writ/302701/)

'While Westerners will never …' A Spit in the Face, Turner (*The Occidental Quarterly*, Spring 2005)

'From the Strait of …' *The Force of Reason*, Fallaci (Rizzoli International, 2006) p35

'The sons of Allah …' Oriana Fallaci and the Art of the Interview, Hitchens, *Vanity Fair*, December 2006 (http://www.vanityfair.com/news/2006/12/hitchens200612)

7 Riding the Islamic Tiger

'The pair had met …' http://www.euro-islam.info/country-profiles/italy/

'A recent poll among …' http://www.euro-islam.info/country-profiles/italy/

'Neither group had much…' Muslim Wins Italian Court Ban on Crucifixes in

Classroom, Arie, *The Guardian*, 27 October 2003 (https://www.theguardian.com/world/2003/oct/27/italy.sophiearie)

'When I heard, I ...' Prophet of Decline, Varadarajan, *The Wall Street Journal*, 23 June 2005 (https://www.wsj.com/articles/SB111948571453267105)

'The fact remains that ...' La disintegrazione del sistema, Freda (https://romagnaidentitaria.files.wordpress.com/2014/02/docslide-it_franco-giorgio-freda-la-disintegrazione-del-sistema-1.pdf)

'Europe is no longer ...' Prophet of Decline, Varadarajan, *The Wall Street Journal*, 23 June 2005 (https://www.wsj.com/articles/SB111948571453267105)

'He is adorable! He ...' Oriana Fallaci and the Art of the Interview, Hitchens, *Vanity Fair*, December 2006 (http://www.vanityfair.com/news/2006/12/hitchens200612)

'Show me just what ...' http://w2.vatican.va/content/benedict-xvi/en/speeches/2006/september/documents/hf_ben-xvi_spe_20060912_university-regensburg.html

'And of course now ...' Papal Bull, Hitchens, *Slate*, 18 September 2006 (http://www.slate.com/articles/news_and_politics/fighting_words/2006/09/papal_bull.html)

8 The Warblogger Who Fell from Grace in Brussels

'I grew up in ...' Right-Wing Flame War!, Dee, *New York Times*, 21 January 2010 (http://www.nytimes.com/2010/01/24/magazine/24Footballs-t.html)

'A victory for European ...' Right-Wing Flame War!, Dee, *New York Times*, 21 January 2010 (http://www.nytimes.com/2010/01/24/magazine/24Footballs-t.html)

'The polls showed 22 per cent ...' *The Islamophobia Industry*, Lean (Pluto Press, 2012) pxi

'Charles Johnson is one ...' https://thediaryofdaedalus.com/2012/09/30/the-ruse-and-fail-of-little-green-footballs-part-vi-current-events-the-future-of-lgf/

'The Quran's commandments to ...' https://www.jihadwatch.org/islam-101

'The jihadists will not ...' https://www.splcenter.org/fighting-hate/extremist-files/individual/robert-spencer

'Her golden skin is ...' Pamela Geller's War, Howard, *Village Voice*, 28 November 2012 (https://www.villagevoice.com/2012/11/28/pamela-gellers-war/)

'Beheadings in Egypt, clerics ...' Pamela Geller's War, Howard, *Village Voice*, 28 November 2012 (https://www.villagevoice.com/2012/11/28/pamela-gellers-war/)

'Let him come ...' The 1683 Battle of Vienna: Islam at Vienna's Gates, Dyck (http://warfarehistorynetwork.com/daily/military-history/the-1683-battle-of-vienna-islam-at-viennas-gates/)

'At the siege of ...' http://gatesofvienna.blogspot.com

'The Baron and Dymphna ...' https://pjmedia.com/rogerlsimon/2005/10/22/
gates-of-vienna-ahoy

'We agree with Fjordman ...' http://gatesofvienna.blogspot.com/2006/09/
emperor-is-naked.html

'Islamophobic songs with catchy ...' http://gatesofvienna.blogspot.com/2006/09/
emperor-is-naked.html

9 A Gathering of Crusaders

'All they wanted was ...' https://wikispooks.com/wiki/Anders_Gravers

'During an online meeting ...' http://gatesofvienna.blogspot.com/2007/04/
uk-and-scandinavia-counterjihad-summit.html

'We really are at ...' http://gatesofvienna.blogspot.com/2006/09/emperor-is-
naked.html

'It is not our ...' http://gatesofvienna.blogspot.com/2007/09/arrests-in-Brussels.
html

'The EC correlated a ...' http://gatesofvienna.blogspot.com/2007/10/more-on-
bat-yeor-at-counterjihad-summit.html

'He's a self-taught ...' https://thediaryofdaedalus.com/2017/11/17/
analog-computing-magazine-july-1986-ramcopy/

'One thing is clear ...' https://pamelageller.com/2008/11/vlaams-belang-t.html/

'Some of the topics ...' http://gatesofvienna.blogspot.com/2008/05/slouching-
towards-vienna.htm

10 Middle Eastern Soccer Moms in Fort Hood

'The Muslims bombed us ...' Drawing U.S. Crowds with Anti-Islam Message,
New York Times, 7 March 2011 (http://www.nytimes.com/2011/03/08/
us/08gabriel.html?pagewanted=all)

'I was struck by ...' Brigitte Gabriel Wants You to Fight Islam, *Buzzfeed*, 27
September 2016 (https://www.buzzfeed.com/davidnoriega/meet-the-charming-
terrifying-face-of-the-anti-islam-lobby?utm_term=.nm21Z33kv#.swBmnMMEk)

'They train us how ...' Rancho Councilman Heads to Afghanistan,
The OCR, 30 April 2012 (http://www.ocregister.com/2012/04/30/
rancho-councilman-heads-to-afghanistan/)

'America has been infiltrated ...' Drawing U.S. Crowds with Anti-Islam
Message, *New York Times*, 7 March 2011 (http://www.nytimes.
com/2011/03/08/us/08gabriel.html?pagewanted=all)

"Allahu Akbar,' he said ...' Fort Hood shootings: the meaning of 'Allahu Akbar' (*The Daily Telegraph*, 6 November 2009)

'I can't wait to ...' http://abcnews.go.com/Blotter/major-hasans-mail-wait-join-afterlife/story?id=9130339

'They still don't know ...' http://pamelageller.com/2010/01/head-scratchers-at-pentagon-review-of-the-shooting-rampage-at-fort-hoods-soldier-readiness-center-th.html/

'How could you build ...' *The Islamophobia Industry*, p78

'The evangelical Family Research ...' *The Islamophobia Industry*, p95

'Elisabeth Sabaditsch-Wolff was ...' http://gatesofvienna.blogspot.com/2010/07/acting-for-america.html

11 *Crushed by the Wheels of History*

'Don't disappoint my decline-hungry ...' Fantasies of Friendship: Ernst Jünger and the German Right's Search for Community in Modernity, Bures (University of California PhD History thesis, 2014) p50

'When the first volume ...' Books: Patterns in Chaos, *Time*, 10 December 1928

"It fell,' said Voltaire ...' Who Will Eclipse America?, Johnson, *Project Syndicate*, 19 September 2011 (https://www.project-syndicate.org/commentary/who-will-eclipse-america)

'In many things Spengler ...' Fantasies of Friendship: Ernst Jünger and the German Right's Search for Community in Modernity, p41

'Counter-jihad maven Robert ...' https://www.jihadwatch.org/2008/12/spencer-lapsing-into-spengler

'Even mainstream magazine The ...' Hitch on Steyn, *The Atlantic*, 22 January 2007 (https://www.theatlantic.com/daily-dish/archive/2007/01/hitch-on-steyn/231334/)

'He called himself a ...' http://www.robertfulford.com/2005-11-19-steyn.html

'[Bob Dylan] was at ...' http://www.steynonline.com/7561/how-does-it-feel

'Most people reading this ...' It's the Demography, Stupid, *The Wall Street Journal*, 4 January 2006 (https://www.wsj.com/articles/SB122531242161281449)

'Critics would claim that ...' http://gatesofvienna.blogspot.com/2006/11/why-future-may-not-belong-to-islam.html

'Islam is in decline ...' https://www.Brusselsjournal.com/node/1360

'The global Muslim population ...' http://www.pewforum.org/2011/01/27/the-future-of-the-global-muslim-population/

'Pajamas Media called his ...' https://pjmedia.com/eddriscoll/2011/08/02/mort-sahl-meets-oswald-spengler/

'This is the pitiful ...' Mark Steyn: Ann Coulter is also asking for it, Steyn, *National Post*, 22 March 2010 (http://nationalpost.com/opinion/mark-steyn-ann-coulter-is-also-asking-for-it)

'If the President's penis ...' http://www.steynonline.com/7616/dont-say-im-violent-or-ill-kill-you

'It is preposterous to ...' https://townhall.com/columnists/anncoulter/2001/09/14/this-is-war-n865496

'Take a camel ...' Students Divided Over Coulter's Cancelled Speech, *CTV News*, 24 March 2010 (https://ottawa.ctvnews.ca/students-divided-over-coulter-s-cancelled-speech-1.495283)

'Lots of Americans loathe ...' Mark Steyn: Ann Coulter is also asking for, Steyn, *National Post*, 22 March 2010 (http://nationalpost.com/opinion/mark-steyn-ann-coulter-is-also-asking-for-it)

12 Breasts, Bears, Bibles

'Many women who do ...' Iran: Fashion that Moves the Earth, *The New York Times*, 20 April 2010 (http://www.nytimes.com/2010/04/20/world/middleeast/20briefs-Iran.html)

'In the name of ...' http://freethoughtblogs.com/blaghag/2010/04/in-the-name-of-science-i-offer-my-boobs/

'On 26 April over ...' https://en.wikipedia.org/wiki/Boobquake

'A toothy brunette with ...' http://thejenome.com/

'I was initially intrigued ...' http://feministing.com/2010/04/27/where-were-all-of-the-feminists-oh-right-busy-planning-a-boobquake/comment-page-1/

'Islam is the greatest ...' Richard Dawkins Hits Back at Allegations He is Islamophobic after Berkeley Event is Cancelled, Mortimer, *The Independent*, 26 July 2017 (https://www.independent.co.uk/news/people/richard-dawkins-islamophobic-berkeley-event-cancelled-islam-muslim-uc-university-california-a7860281.html)

'Liberal dudes are the ...' http://blog.iblamethepatriarchy.com/2010/04/23/spinster-aunt-reads-boobquake-emails/

'I'm the last of...' http://www.billmaher.com/

'What's facetious about that ...' A history of the Bill Maher's 'Not Bigoted' Remarks on Islam, Jalabi, *The Guardian*, 7 October 2014

(https://www.theguardian.com/tv-and-radio/tvandradioblog/2014/oct/06/
bill-maher-islam-ben-affleck)

'We have to warn …' Muslim Group Says It Is Warning, Not
Threatening, *South Park* Creators, Itzkoff, *The New York Times*,
21 April 2010 (https://artsbeat.blogs.nytimes.com/2010/04/21/
muslim-group-says-it-is-warning-not-threatening-south-park-creators/)

'A survey found 71 per cent …' Majority of Americans Oppose
South Park's 'Muhammad' Censor, Riley, *The Christian
Post*, 30 April 2010 (http://www.christianpost.com/news/
surveymajority-of-americans-oppose-south-park-censor-44966/)

'We, the undersigned, condemn …' Cartoonists Condemn Threat that
Led to *South Park* Censorship, Parker, *St. Louis Post-Dispatch*, 29
April 2010 (http://www.stltoday.com/news/local/columns/editors-desk/
cartoonists-condemn-threat-that-led-to-south-park-censorship/article_oe8c88bd-
c65f-5767-b555-8f5e2964d6f2.html)

'She claimed the event …' https://en.wikipedia.org/wiki/
Everybody_Draw_Mohammed_Day

'It is precisely the …' https://thinkprogress.org/
petraeus-quran-burning-could-endanger-troops-6150c7780353/

13 Surfing with the Casuals in Luton

'God didn't all of …' *Step Into Liquid*, dir. Brown (2003)

'Surfing and religion are …' Hang ten for Ha-Shem, Perman (http://www.
guiltandpleasure.com/index.php?site=rebootgp&page=gp_article&id=26)

'He called himself Nachum …' Hang ten for Ha-Shem, Perman (http://www.
guiltandpleasure.com/index.php?site=rebootgp&page=gp_article&id=26)

'My politics are not …' The Surfing Rabbi, Dowling, *Salon*, 3 August 1999
(http://www.salon.com/1999/08/03/rabbi/)

'The Muslim onslaught is …' https://www.newswithviews.com/Shifren/
nachum108.htm

'Police cleared a square …' Two arrested after protest at soldiers' homecoming
parade in Luton, Percival, *The Guardian*, 11 March 2009 (https://www.
theguardian.com/uk/2009/mar/10/two-arrested-army-protest-luton)

'If you go pick …' *Enemy of the State*, Robinson (CreateSpace Independent
Publishing Platform, 2015) Kindle edition

'By 2001 there were …' https://en.wikipedia.org/wiki/
Islam_in_the_United_Kingdom

'Muslims made up about …' https://en.wikipedia.org/wiki/
Demography_of_Luton

'Chaotic alliance stirs up ...' English Defence League: Chaotic Alliance Stirs up Trouble on Streets, Booth, Taylor, & Lewis, *The Guardian*, 12 September 2009 (https://www.theguardian.com/world/2009/sep/11/english-defence-league-chaotic-alliance)

'You've got to have ...' http://uaf.org.uk/2012/01/edl-strategist-alan-lake-suspended-from-manager-job-at-city-bank/

"Early on,' he said ...' *Enemy of the State*, Kindle edition

'No more than sixty ...' *Enemy of the State*, Kindle edition

14 *Cannibal Dogs and Conquering Signs*

'I'm still waiting for ...' https://www.youtube.com/watch?v=pTBF-CRLFgk

'They think the League ...' What are Israeli Flags and Jewish Activists Doing at Demonstrations Sponsored by the English Defence League?, Adar, *Haaretz*, 13 August 2010 (https://www.haaretz.com/1.5099679

'Our members are not ...' The English Defence League and the Surfing Rabbi, Dysch, *The Jewish Chronicle*, 14 October 2010 (https://www.thejc.com/news/uk-news/the-english-defence-league-and-the-surfing-rabbi-1.18829)

'Working with our street ...' What are Israeli Flags and Jewish Activists Doing at Demonstrations Sponsored by the English Defence League?, Adar, *Haaretz*, 13 August 2010 (https://www.haaretz.com/1.5099679

'It was chaos ...' 'Patriot' league plots more clashes with anti-fascist activists, Booth & Travers, *The Guardian*, 9 August 2009 (https://www.theguardian.com/uk/2009/aug/09/defence-league-casuals-birmingham-islam)

'League marches were human ...' 'No Surrender to the Taliban': Football Hooliganism, Islamophobia and the Rise of the English Defence League, Garland & Treadwell (*Papers from the British Criminology Conference* Vol. 10, 2010)

'Lennon turned it down ...' *Enemy of the State*, Kindle edition

'You have to understand ...' *Enemy of the State*, Kindle edition

'When I was introduced ...' http://barthsnotes.com/2010/10/25/english-defence-league-rally-at-israeli-embassy/

'Cameron was no fan ...' David Cameron Makes Dash to West Midlands, Authi (*Birmingham Mail*, 6 May 2010)

'They can't live like ...' 'No Surrender to the Taliban': Football Hooliganism, Islamophobia and the Rise of the English Defence League, Garland & Treadwell (*Papers from the British Criminology Conference*, Vol. 10, 2010)

'I sincerely hope that ...' EDL Jewish Division Leader Moore Quits, Lipman, *Jewish Chronicle*, 29 June 2011 (https://www.thejc.com/news/uk-news/edl-jewish-division-leader-roberta-moore-quits-1.24427)

'Paul Ray is a ...' *Enemy of the State*, Robinson (CreateSpace Independent Publishing Platform, 2015) Kindle edition

'A 2004 poll found ...' *New British Fascism: Rise of the British National Party*, Goodwin (Routledge, 2011) p117

'Marshy, as it quickly ...' *Enemy of the State*, Kindle edition

'The EDL had invited ...' *Casuals United*, Marsh & Cardiff (The Mashed Swede Project, 2012) no page numbering

'Its main Facebook page ...' Pulling Back the Curtain: An Examination of the English Defence League and Their Use of Facebook, Reynolds (University of St Andrews PhD Thesis, 2015) p151

'The League got another ...' http://www.pewresearch.org/fact-tank/2017/08/09/muslims-and-islam-key-findings-in-the-u-s-and-around-the-world/

15 The Greatest Monster in Oslo

'You are going to ...' Anders Behring Breivik's Norway Shooting Spree Relived in Chilling Detail, Blair, *The Daily Telegraph*, 20 April 2012 (http://www.telegraph.co.uk/news/worldnews/europe/norway/9217315/Anders-Behring-Breiviks-Norway-shooting-spree-relived-in-chilling-detail.html)

'He belonged to the ...' *One of Us: The Story of Anders Breivik and the Massacre in Norway*, Seierstad (Farrar, Straus and Giroux, 2015) Kindle edition

'In 1980 Norway had ...' https://en.wikipedia.org/wiki/Islam_in_Norway

'Get dressed ...' *One of Us: The Story of Anders Breivik and the Massacre in Norway*, Kindle edition

'It's important to make ...' *One of Us: The Story of Anders Breivik and the Massacre in Norway*, Kindle edition

16 A Very Positively Minded Individual

'If a pipe is ...' *One of Us: The Story of Anders Breivik and the Massacre in Norway*, Kindle edition

'When I wake up ...' *2083: A European Declaration of Independence*, Berwick [Breivik] (PDF Document, 2011)

'Our most important task ...' https://en.wikipedia.org/wiki/Fjordman

'I'm an extremely patient ...' *2083: A European Declaration of Independence*, Berwick [Breivik] (PDF Document, 2011)

'I'm the greatest monster ...' Jeg er det største monsteret siden Quisling, Brenna, Hopperstad, Vikås, Nygaard & Ravndal, *Verdens Gang*, 2 January 2012 (http://www.vg.no/nyheter/innenriks/terrorangrepet-22-juli-anders-behring-breivik/jeg-er-det-stoerste-monsteret-siden-quisling/a/10042693/)

17 *Perfection of Writing by Means of an Assault Rifle*

'I had to kill ...' Richard Millet. Soldat Perdu, Launet, *Libération*, 5 September 2012 (http://next.liberation.fr/livres/2012/09/05/richard-millet-soldat-perdu_844210)

'He is heterosexual ...' Ragnarök on the Seine, Smith, *The American Reader*, 4 December 2013 (http://theamericanreader.com/ragnarok-on-the-seine/)

'Then Millet praised the ...' Reflections on the Richard Millet Case, Lévy, *Huffington Post*, 24 September 2012 (http://www.huffingtonpost.com/bernardhenri-levy/a-falangist-at-the-nrf-re_b_1866898.html)

'... and talked about the...' Ragnarök on the Seine, Smith, *The American Reader*, 4 December 2013 (http://theamericanreader.com/ragnarok-on-the-seine/)

'Breivik is without a ...' Ragnarök on the Seine, Smith, *The American Reader*, 4 December 2013 (http://theamericanreader.com/ragnarok-on-the-seine/)

'I'm one of the ...' French Essayist Blames Multiculturalism for Breivik's Killing Spree, Crumley, *Time*, 28 August 2012 (http://world.time.com/2012/08/28/french-essayist-blames-multi-culturalism-for-breiviks-norwegian-massacre/?xid=rss-topstories)

'The state charged Anders ...' Norway Massacre Suspect Appears to Be Insane, His Lawyer Says, Reuters, *Haaretz*, 26 July 2011 (https://www.haaretz.com/1.5035103)

'The real reason for ...' Mocking Justice in Norway: The Breivik Trial Targets Contrarian Intellectuals, Kirchick (*World Affairs*, September/October 2012)

'In Norway, to speak ...' Inside the Mind of the Oslo Murderer, Bawer, *Wall Street Journal*, 25 July 2011 (http://www.wsj.com/articles/SB10001424053111903999904576465801154130960)

'I have read Breivik's so-called ...' http://gatesofvienna.net/2017/09/interview-with-fjordman/

'I refuse to be ...' Mocking Justice in Norway: The Breivik Trial Targets Contrarian Intellectuals, Kirchick (*World Affairs*, September/October 2012)

'I'm no more responsible ...' Icelandic Leftist Poisons Robert Spencer, Spencer, *Frontpage*, 16 May 2017 (http://www.frontpagemag.com/fpm/266719/icelandic-leftist-poisons-robert-spencer-robert-spencer)

'We can categorically state ...' Pulling Back the Curtain: An Examination of the English Defence League and Their Use of Facebook, p166

'He suggested Alan Ayling ...' Right-Winger Defamed as 'Breivik Mentor', Awarded €5,000 in Damages, Mangion, *Malta Today*, 28 January 2014 (http://www.maltatoday.com.mt/news/court_and_police/36038/right-winger-defamed-as-breivik-mentor-gets-5-000-20140128)

'LOL bare pussyhole edl ...' Pulling Back the Curtain: An Examination of the English Defence League and Their Use of Facebook, p170

'But I was still ...' *Enemy of the State*, Kindle edition

'There's only so many ...' *Casuals United*, no page numbering

'Too many people involved ...' Anti-Jihad Critics Spared a Show Trial in Norway, Bawer, *Frontpage*, 18 June 2012 (https://www.frontpagemag.com/fpm/134667/anti-jihad-critics-spared-show-trial-norway-bruce-bawer)

'No one dwelt on ...' http://www.dominiquevenner.fr/?s=breivik&x=0&y=0

18 It Isn't Easy Being Loved by Idiots in Paris

'We will pray ...' Far-Right French Historian, 78-Year-Old Dominique Venner, Commits Suicide In Notre Dame In Protest Against Gay Marriage, Lichfield, *The Independent*, 21 May 2013 (http://www.independent.co.uk/news/world/europe/far-right-french-historian-78-year-old-dominique-venner-commits-suicide-in-notre-dame-in-protest-8625877.html)

'Suicide d'un anti-mariage ...' Suicide D'un Anti-Mariage Gay Dans Notre-Dame, *Europe 1*, 21 May 2013 (http://www.europe1.fr/faits-divers/suicide-d-un-anti-mariage-gay-dans-notre-dame-1524647)

'Do you believe that ...' Colombey-les-deux-Mosquées, Shatz, *London Review of Books*, 9 April 2015 (http://www.lrb.co.uk/v37/n07/adam-shatz/colombey-les-deux-mosquees)

'It is by deciding ...' The Fascist History Behind Dominique Venner's Suicide at Notre Dame, Sessions, *The Daily Beast*, 23 May 2015 (http://www.thedailybeast.com/articles/2013/05/23/the-fascist-history-behind-dominique-venner-s-suicide-at-notre-dame.html)

'I did not choose ...' Muslim Terrorism in Paris, Michel Houellebecq's Cowardice, and the Islamization of France: An Interview with Russian writer Elena Choudinova, Author of The Notre Dame de Paris Mosque, Girin, *Chronicles*, 12 January 2015 (https://www.chroniclesmagazine.org/muslim-terrorism-in-paris/)

'Cautious estimates put Muslim ...' Muslim Population in Europe: 1950-2020, Kettani (*International Journal of Environmental Science and Development*, Vol. 1, No. 2, June 2010)

'My novel does not ...' http://pedestrianinfidel.blogspot.com/2005/10/elena-chudinova-russias-orianna.html

'I am not very ...' https://www.brainyquote.com/quotes/quotes/h/hplovecr745848.html

'If religion were true ...' https://www.brainyquote.com/quotes/authors/h/h_p_lovecraft.html

'Anti-Islamic activism does ...' Muslim Terrorism in Paris, Michel Houellebecq's Cowardice, and the Islamization of France: An Interview with Russian writer Elena Choudinova, Author of The Notre Dame de Paris Mosque, Girin, *Chronicles*, 12 January 2015 (https://www.chroniclesmagazine.org/muslim-terrorism-in-paris/)

'I was carried by ...' The double life of Catherine M, Berens, *The Guardian*, 19 May 2002 (https://www.theguardian.com/books/2002/may/19/biography.features)

'He told interviewers he ...' The American Menace in the Houellebecq Affair, Armus (*French Politics and Society*, Vol. 17, No. 2, Spring 1999)

'I didn't think Muslims...' Michel Houellebecq, the Art of Fiction No. 206, Hunnewell, *The Paris Review*, Issue 194, Fall 2010 (http://www.theparisreview.org/interviews/6040/the-art-of-fiction-no-206-michel-houellebecq)

19 A Drawing Never Killed Anyone

'When people ask me ...' https://www.youtube.com/watch?v=t97G3gRH_Rg

'My book describes the ...' Scare Tactics: Michel Houellebecq Defends His Controversial New Book, Bourmeau, *The Paris Review*, 2 January 2015 (http://www.theparisreview.org/blog/2015/01/02/scare-tactics-michel-houellebecq-on-his-new-book/)

'Charlie Hebdo was sixteen ...' Charlie Hebdo Sales are Coming Back to Earth, One Year After the Deadly Attack on its Paris Office, James, *International Business Times*, 1 June 2016 (http://www.ibtimes.com/charlie-hebdo-sales-are-coming-back-earth-one-year-after-deadly-attack-its-paris-2252333)

'The publication started with ...' https://charliehebdo.fr/en/history/

'Other covers featured Muslim ...' http://www.understandingcharliehebdo.com/

'Yes, I am anti-Semitic ...' 'Anti-Semitic' Satire Divides Liberal Paris, Burke, *The Guardian*, 3 August 2008 (https://www.theguardian.com/world/2008/aug/03/france.pressandpublishing)

'A drawing has never ...' A Drawing Has Never Killed Anyone, Simons, *Spiegel Online*, 20 September 2012 (http://www.spiegel.de/international/europe/charlie-hebdo-editor-in-chief-on-muhammad-cartoons-a-856891.html)

"Wait!' says the jihadist ...' Charlie Hebdo: l'incroyable Prémonition du Dessinateur Charb, *La Libre*, 7 January 2015 (http://www.lalibre.be/actu/international/charlie-hebdo-l-incroyable-premonition-du-dessinateur-charb-54ad24183570d587e328c30e)

20 Je Suis Charlie

'Two hooded and armed ...' Charlie Hebdo: Le Témoignage de la Dessinatrice Coco, Mauriaucourt, *L'Humanité*, 7 January 2015 (http://www.humanite.fr/charlie-hebdo-le-temoignage-de-la-dessinatrice-coco-562041)

'Alluha Akbar ...' The Globe in Paris: Police Identify Three Suspects, Mackinnon, *The Globe and Mail*, 7 January 2015 (http://www.theglobeandmail. com/news/world/deadly-shooting-at-french-satirical-newspaper-report/ article22329480/)

'Do you want to ...' Charlie Hebdo Attack: Paris Cop Shot Dead in Street Was Muslim, *NBC News*, 8 January 2015 (http://www.nbcnews.com/storyline/paris-magazine-attack/ charlie-hebdo-attack-paris-cop-shot-dead-street-was-muslim-n282121)

'We have avenged the ...' Charlie Hebdo: Gun Attack on French Magazine Kills 12, *BBC News*, 7 January 2015 (http://www.bbc.com/news/ world-europe-30710883)

'What we saw today ...' Thousands Rally in Paris after Charlie Hebdo Shooting: 'No Words Can Express Our Anger', Overton, *The Star* [Toronto], 7 January 2015 (https://www.thestar.com/news/world/2015/01/07/thousands_ rally_in_paris_after_charlie_hebdo_shooting_no_words_can_express_our_anger. html)

'This is like groundhog ...' https://www.realclearpolitics.com/video/2015/01/08/ bill_maher_on_paris_terror_attack_groundhog_day_head_cut_off.html

'France is not Michel ...' Slouching Toward Mecca, Lilla, *New York Review of Books*, 2 April 2015 (http://www.nybooks.com/articles/2015/04/02/ slouching-toward-mecca/)

'If ethnic fighting spreads ...' *Submission*, Houellebecq (Macmillan, 2015) p48

'Traditionally, satire has comforted ...' The Abuse of Satire, Trudeau, *The Atlantic*, 11 April 2015 (http://www.theatlantic.com/international/ archive/2015/04/the-abuse-of-satire/390312/)

'If you want to ...' Junaid Thorne Backs Charlie Hebdo Killing, *The West Australian*, 8 January 2015 (https://thewest.com.au/news/australia/ junaid-thorne-backs-charlie-hebdo-killing-ng-ya-232344)

21 Opening the Gates in Dresden

'People were shouting at ...' Meet the German Activist Leading the Movement against 'Islamization', Shuster (*Time*, 15 January 2015)

'Mostly white men over ...' Patriotic Europeans Against the Islamisation of the West Quickly Gathering Support in Germany, Kirschbaum (*Sydney Morning Herald*, 16 December 2014)

'A December 2014 poll ...' Jeder Zweite Sympathisiert mit Pegida, *Zeit Online*, 15 December 2014 (http://www.zeit.de/politik/deutschland/2014-12/ islam-pegida-fluechtlinge-deutschland-umfrage)

'In Idaho this would ...' Meet the German Activist Leading the Movement Against 'Islamization', Shuster (*Time*, 15 January 2015)

'Well, there was already ...' Meet the German Activist Leading the Movement against 'Islamization', Shuster (*Time*, 15 January 2015)

'Pamela Geller and Robert ...' Anti-Muslim Subway Posters Prompt NYPD to Increase Security in Stations, *Huffington Post*, 25 September 2012 (http://www.huffingtonpost.com/2012/09/25/anti-muslim-subway-posters-nypd-increase-security_n_1912239.html)

'A poll just after ...' EXCLUSIVE: 'I Will Gag the Hate Clerics': Cameron to Launch New Terror Task Force to Bring an End to Religious Extremism, Walters, *Daily Mail*, 25 May 2013 (http://www.dailymail.co.uk/news/article-2330945/David-Cameron-launch-new-terror-task-force-stamp-religious-extremism.html)

'I couldn't believe that ...' *Enemy of the State*, Kindle edition

'I read more about ...' *Quitting the English Defence League: When Tommy Met Mo* (BBC Documentary, 28 October 2013)

'Obey Allah or burn ...' *Enemy of the State*, Kindle edition

'He joined the British ...' https://en.wikipedia.org/wiki/Liberty_GB

'I am, and have ... UK Lawyers, Human Rights Activists Launch 'Sharia Watch' Org to Monitor UK Islamism, Kassam, *Breitbart*, 24 April 2014 (http://www.breitbart.com/london/2014/04/24/lawyers-launch-anti-shariah-initiative/)

'The Charlie Hebdo march ...' Record Turnout at Dresden PEGIDA Rally Sees More Than 25,000 March, Brady, *Deutsche Welle*, 12 January 2015 (http://www.dw.com/en/record-turnout-at-dresden-pegida-rally-sees-more-than-25000-march/a-18186820)

22 The Brilliant Blue of the Aegean Sea

'It was "Jihad 2.0" ...' https://www.alexandredelvalle.com/single-post/2015/10/28/Il-caos-siriano-%E2%80%93-Il-Jihadismo-20

'Most minors were male ...' Two-thirds of Child Refugees Screened by Officials Found to Be Adults, Home Office Figures Show, Dominiczak & Swinford, *Daily Telegraph*, 18 October 2016 (https://www.telegraph.co.uk/news/2016/10/18/two-thirds-of-child-refugees-entering-uk-found-to-be-adults-figu/)

'Commonly referred to as ...' http://gatesofvienna.net/2015/08/the-european-migration-crisis/

'She made a big ...' https://pamelageller.com/2015/05/isis-in-rome.html/

'The concept of immigration ...' https://pamelageller.com/2015/08/islam-in-europe-police-warn-of-no-go-zones-in-germany.html/

'Today we see an ...' Germany's Anti-Islam PEGIDA Rallies Surge Amid Migrant Crisis, Eckardt, *NBC News*, 19 October

2015 (http://www.nbcnews.com/storyline/europes-border-crisis/germanys-anti-islam-pegida-rallies-surge-amid-migrant-crisis-n447026)

'Over 2015 there were ...' Trial in Firebombing of Refugees Exposes Far-Right Grip in Germany, Smale, *New York Times*, 27 February 2016 (https://www.nytimes.com/2016/02/27/world/europe/germany-migrant-arson-trial.html)

'He was twenty-five years old ...' Police in Serbia Arrest Migrant Carrying the SAME Passport as that Found Close to Stade De France Suicide Bomber... Fuelling Speculation ISIS are Using Forgeries to Fool Investigators, Stevens & Robinson, *Daily Mail*, 17 November 2015 (http://www.dailymail.co.uk/news/article-3321632/Police-arrest-migrant-carrying-passport-Paris-suicide-bomber-sneaked-Europe-posing-migrant.html)

23 *Wheat Fields in the Bataclan*

'First of all I ...' What Happened at the Bataclan?, *BBC News*, 9 December 2015 (http://www.bbc.com/news/world-europe-34827497)

'Like a gust of ...' What Happened at the Bataclan?, *BBC News*, 9 December 2015 (http://www.bbc.com/news/world-europe-34827497)

'He was left-handed ...' Paris attacks: Diners killed in Le Carillon and Le Petit Cambodge Restaurants, Masanauskas, *Herald Sun*, 14 November 2015 (http://www.heraldsun.com.au/news/paris-attacks-diners-killed-in-le-carillon-and-le-petit-cambodge-restaurants/news-story/78b5db3d89a75ed791f9d3d3839f49fc?nk=2144b6cb68dd6ee104867119c93529a9-1503656435)

'You can thank President ...' Paris Attacks: Bataclan Hostage Reveals Traumatic Minute-By-Minute Account of ISIS Slaughter Inside Concert, Dubuis, *Daily Mirror*, 19 October 2015 (http://www.mirror.co.uk/news/world-news/paris-attacks-bataclan-hostage-reveals-6858608)

'In the wake of ...' http://gatesofvienna.net/2015/11/petition-for-a-moratorium-on-all-middle-eastern-refugee-resettlement-in-the-usa/

'We have a terrible ...' http://gatesofvienna.net/2015/11/france-going-from-dreadful-to-nightmarish-under-a-veneer-of-everyday-routine/

'So many of the ...' https://www.alexandredelvalle.com/single-post/2015/12/03/Aleteia-Le-grand-entretien-avec-Alexandre-Del-Valle-%C2%AB-Daesh-veut-provoquer-un-syndrome-de-Stockolm-g%C3%A9n%C3%A9ralis%C3%A9-en-Occident-%C2%BB

'The old definition of ...' It's the Demography, Stupid, Steyn, *Wall Street Journal*, 4 January 2006 (https://www.wsj.com/articles/SB122531242161281449)

'A Pew Research Centre ...' http://www.pewresearch.org/fact-tank/2017/08/09/muslims-and-islam-key-findings-in-the-u-s-and-around-the-world/

'A separate survey of ...' https://www.brookings.edu/blog/markaz/2015/12/09/
what-americans-really-think-about-muslims-and-islam/

24 *A Largely Peaceful New Year's Eve*

'Two thirds thought multiculturalism ...' http://knowledge.wharton.upenn.edu/
article/what-the-u-s-can-learn-from-canadas-immigration-policy/

'I'm just struck by ...' https://www.youtube.com/watch?v=-zHoDANH-R8

'I'm slightly amazed at ...' https://www.youtube.com/watch?v=-zHoDANH-R8

'And I congratulate you ...' https://www.youtube.com/watch?v=-zHoDANH-R8

'A Pew Research Center ...' http://www.pewglobal.org/2016/06/07/
euroskepticism-beyond-brexit/pm_2016-06-07_brexit-03/

'There were mostly refugees ...' It Was Sickening, Koschnitzke, *Zelt Online*,
13 January 2016 (http://www.zeit.de/gesellschaft/zeitgeschehen/2016-01/
new-years-eve-cologne-refugee-syria-report)

'They were dumb, uneducated ...' It Was Sickening, Koschnitzke, *Zelt Online*,
13 January 2016 (http://www.zeit.de/gesellschaft/zeitgeschehen/2016-01/
new-years-eve-cologne-refugee-syria-report)

'Many refugees from countries ...' It Was Sickening, Koschnitzke, *Zelt Online*,
13 January 2016 (http://www.zeit.de/gesellschaft/zeitgeschehen/2016-01/
new-years-eve-cologne-refugee-syria-report)

'I am Syrian, you ...' Das Protokoll zur Kölner Chaos-Nacht zum
Nachlesen, *Welt*, 7 January 2016 (https://www.welt.de/politik/deutschland/
article150729450/Das-Protokoll-zur-Koelner-Chaos-Nacht-zum-Nachlesen.html)

'Mayor of Cologne Henriette ...' Twitter storm as Cologne Mayor Suggests
Women Stay at 'Arm's Length' from Strangers, *Deutsche Welle*, 5 January 2016
(http://www.dw.com/en/twitter-storm-as-cologne-mayor-suggests-women-stay-at-
arms-length-from-strangers/a-18962430)

'In 2015, 3 per cent of ...' https://www.bra.se/bra-in-english/home/crime-and-
statistics/rape-and-sex-offences.html

'The party had got ...' https://yougov.se/news/2015/08/20/
sd-ar-sveriges-storsta-parti/

'Migrant Sex Criminal: I ...' Migrant Sex Criminal: I Hate Sweden, I'm Just
Here to F*** Swedish Girls, Hale, *Breitbart News*, 28 July 2016 (http://www.
breitbart.com/london/2016/07/28/migrant-sex-attacker-hate-sweden/)

'Are Migrants Really Raping ...' Are Migrants Really Raping Swedish Women?,
Zaleski, *Daily Beast*, 7 November 2016 (http://www.thedailybeast.com/
are-migrants-really-raping-swedish-women)

'We don't go out ...' Where Females Fear to Tread: KATIE HOPKINS
Reports from Sweden, The Scandi-Lib Paradise Where Terrified Women Have

Vanished from the Streets and a Conspiracy of Silence and Self-Censorship on Immigration Buries the Truth, Hopkins, *Daily Mail*, 1 March 2017 (http://www.dailymail.co.uk/news/article-4269576/KATIE-HOPKINS-reports-Scandi-lib-paradise-Sweden.html)

'And now reality begins …' http://gatesofvienna.net/2016/01/groped-and-molested-in-the-hauptbahnhof/

'The goal of the …' Anti-Islam Groups Launch Europe-Wide Coalition Pledging to Defend 'Western Civilisation, Gutteridge, *Daily Express*, 28 January 2016 (http://www.express.co.uk/news/politics/638910/anti-islam-groups-launch-Europe-coalition-defending-western-civilization-EDL-march-UK)

'Pegida marched 8,000 strong …' PEGIDA in Europe: Irish leader hospitalised; French General Arrested, Edmunds, *Breitbart News*, 7 February 2016 (http://www.breitbart.com/london/2016/02/07/2964843/)

25 Nationalism Back on the Menu

'Integration requires effort from …' Sarrazin Muss Sich Entschuldigen, *Zeit Online*, 1 October 2009 (http://www.zeit.de/politik/deutschland/2009-10/sarrazin-aeusserung-integration/komplettansicht)

'Islam is foreign to …' https://counterjihad.com/islam-not-part-germany

'Party leader Bjoern Hoecke …' German Fury at AfD Hoecke's Holocaust Memorial Remark, *BBC News*, 18 January 2017 (http://www.bbc.com/news/world-europe-38661621)

'Islam is not a …' https://counterjihad.com/islam-not-part-germany

'I am furious …' La Droite à l'offensive contre l'exécutif, Jaigu, *Le Figaro*, 17 July 2016 (http://www.lefigaro.fr/politique/2016/07/15/01002-20160715ARTFIG00263-la-droite-a-l-offensive-contre-l-executif.php)

'As late as 2007 …' The 'Counter-Jihad' Movement: The Global Trend Feeding Anti-Muslim Hatred, Williams & Lowles (Hope Not Hate, 2012)

'An earthquake …' France in Shock, Charlemagne, *The Economist*, 26 May 2014 (https://www.economist.com/blogs/charlemagne/2014/05/national-fronts-victory)

Merkel had taken a …' Angela Merkel Under More Pressure Over Refugee Policy as It Is Revealed Migrants Committed 142,500 Crimes In Germany During The First Six Months Of 2016, Robinson, *Daily Mail*, 1 November 2016 (http://www.dailymail.co.uk/news/article-3893436/Angela-Merkel-pressure-refugee-policy-revealed-migrants-committed-142-500-crimes-Germany-six-months-2016.html)

'It is only a …' http://gatesofvienna.net/2016/04/who-are-the-real-nazis-in-21st-century-germany/

'The German police admitted that ...' https://www.gatestoneinstitute.org/10304/germany-migrants-crime

'The proportion of foreign ...' https://www.gatestoneinstitute.org/10304/germany-migrants-crime

'Do you want more ...' Geert Wilders, Dutch Politician, Distracts From Hate-Speech Trial With More Vitriol, Siegal, *New York Times*, 31 October 2016 (https://www.nytimes.com/2016/11/01/world/europe/geert-wilders-netherlands-hate-trial.html?mcubz=0)

'His crime is maintaining ...' Geert Wilders and the Fight for Europe, Bat Ye'or, *National Review*, 16 February 2009 (https://www.nationalreview.com/2009/02/geert-wilders-and-fight-europe-bat-yeor/)

'Islam is the Trojan ...' https://web.archive.org/web/20080614074737/http://www.groepwilders.com/website/details.aspx?ID=44

'Half of Holland loves ...' *Why the Dutch are Different: A Journey into the Hidden Heart of the Netherlands*, Coates (Nicholas Brealey Publishing, 2015) p230

26 *Pulsing with the Alt-Right in Florida*, 2016

'A jihadi walks into ...' Inside Milo's 'Gays For Trump,' Virulently Anti-Islam Party at the RNC, Norton, *Salon*, 20 July 2016 (https://www.salon.com/2016/07/20/inside_milos_gays_for_trump_virulently_anti_islam_party_at_the_rnc/)

'A three-hour hostage ...' FBI Boston Chief: In Call, Mateen Referred To Tsarnaevs As His 'Homeboys', *WBUR News*, 13 June 2016 (http://www.wbur.org/news/2016/06/13/mateen-orlando-tsarnaevs-monday)

'The Pulse massacre was ...' https://en.wikipedia.org/wiki/Terrorism_in_the_United_States#Islamist_extremism

'There were about 3.3 ...' http://www.pewresearch.org/fact-tank/2016/01/06/a-new-estimate-of-the-u-s-muslim-population/

'This was up from ...' http://www.danielpipes.org/blog/2003/04/how-many-muslims-in-the-united-states

'Get rid of your ...' Inside Milo's 'Gays For Trump,' Virulently Anti-Islam Party at the RNC, Norton, *Salon*, 20 July 2016 (https://www.salon.com/2016/07/20/inside_milos_gays_for_trump_virulently_anti_islam_party_at_the_rnc/)

'It's not funny ...' Inside Milo's 'Gays For Trump,' Virulently Anti-Islam Party at the RNC, Norton, *Salon*, 20 July 2016 (https://www.salon.com/2016/07/20/inside_milos_gays_for_trump_virulently_anti_islam_party_at_the_rnc/)

'I am the number ...' Who is anti-Islamic activist Pamela Geller?, McMahon, *Boston News*, 4 June 2015 (https://www.boston.com/news/local-news/2015/06/04/who-is-anti-islamic-activist-pamela-geller)

'You've got to love ...' Inside Milo's 'Gays For Trump,'
Virulently Anti-Islam Party at the RNC, Norton, *Salon*,
20 July 2016 (https://www.salon.com/2016/07/20/
inside_milos_gays_for_trump_virulently_anti_islam_party_at_the_rnc/)

'I wish i could ...' Tweet, 15 January 2013 (https://twitter.com/NicHanrahan)

'People used to ask ...' The Gavin McInnes Show (https://www.youtube.com/
watch?v=TTv2q8zmbTw)

'Anything associated as closely ...' An Establishment Conservative's
Guide to the Alt-Right, Bokhari & Yiannopoulos, *Breitbart News*,
29 March 2016 (http://www.breitbart.com/tech/2016/03/29/
an-establishment-conservatives-guide-to-the-alt-right/)

'My hope after today ...' Milo in Orlando: Gays, Like Jews, Should Say 'Never
Again!', Nolan, *Breitbart News*, 15 June 2016 (http://www.breitbart.com/
milo/2016/06/15/milo-orlando-gays-say-never/)

'The Orlando shooting isn't ...' The Left Chose Islam Over Gays. Now
100 People Are Dead Or Maimed In Orlando, Yiannopoulos, *Breitbart
News*, 12 June 2016 (http://www.breitbart.com/milo/2016/06/12/
left-chose-islam-gays-now-100-people-killed-maimed-orlando/)

'Fuck Islam ...' Gavin and Milo lock lips in Orlando! 'We risked our lives to
promote YOUR hedonistic lifestyle, you ingrates!', McInnes, *The Rebel*, 19
June 2016 (https://www.therebel.media/gavin_and_milo_lock_lips_in_orlando)

'Next month Yiannopoulos was ...' Inside Milo's 'Gays For
Trump,' Virulently Anti-Islam Party at the RNC, Norton,
Salon, 20 July 2016 (https://www.salon.com/2016/07/20/
inside_milos_gays_for_trump_virulently_anti_islam_party_at_the_rnc/)

'The most pro-gay ...' Inside Milo's 'Gays For Trump,'
Virulently Anti-Islam Party at the RNC, Norton, *Salon*,
20 July 2016 (https://www.salon.com/2016/07/20/
inside_milos_gays_for_trump_virulently_anti_islam_party_at_the_rnc/)

27 *That's Where You're Wrong, Kiddo*

'We shouldn't be running ...' Inside the Secret, Strange Origins
of Steve Bannon's Nationalist Fantasia, Green, *Vanity Fair*,
12 July 2017 (https://www.vanityfair.com/news/2017/07/
the-strange-origins-of-steve-bannons-nationalist-fantasia)

'He wasn't actually very ...' Andrew's Politics: He Hated Bullies,
Shapiro, *Breitbart News*, 1 March 2013 (http://www.breitbart.com/
big-journalism/2013/03/01/andrew-hated-bullies/)

'We are in an ...' Inside the Secret, Strange Origins of Steve Bannon's

Nationalist Fantasia, Green, *Vanity Fair*, 12 July 2017 (https://www.vanityfair.com/news/2017/07/the-strange-origins-of-steve-bannons-nationalist-fantasia)

'Honey badger don't give …' *Devil's Bargain: Steve Bannon, Donald Trump, and the Storming of the Presidency*, Green (Penguin Press, 2017) Kindle edition

'It is not an …' Brigitte Gabriel: 'Europe is Eurabia Right Now', Wilde, *Breitbart News*, 26 September 2015 (http://www.breitbart.com/big-government/2015/09/26/brigitte-gabriel-europe-is-eurabia-right-now/)

'Left-wing magazine *Mother* …' Trump's Counter-Jihad, Beauchamp, *Vox*, 13 February 2017 (https://www.vox.com/world/2017/2/13/14559822/trump-islam-muslims-islamophobia-sharia)

'I believe that if …' Trump Urged to Head Gala of Democrats, Butterfield, *New York Times*, 18 November 1987 (https://www.nytimes.com/1987/11/18/us/trump-urged-to-head-gala-of-democrats.html)

'Melanie Phillips wrote a …' Trump's Opponents are the Bigots and Racists, Phillips, *The Times*, 14 November 2016 (https://www.thetimes.co.uk/edition/comment/trumps-opponents-are-the-bigots-and-racists-8zsrsp52r)

'All these millions and …' *Devil's Bargain: Steve Bannon, Donald Trump, and the Storming of the Presidency*, Kindle edition

'Congrats chief,' Milo Yiannopoulos …' Here's How Breitbart and Milo Smuggled Nazi and White Nationalist Ideas into the Mainstream, Bernstein, *Buzzfeed*, 5 October 2017 (https://www.buzzfeed.com/josephbernstein/heres-how-breitbart-and-milo-smuggled-white-nationalism?utm_term=.ui88Moo5z#.djKZk116w)

'The de facto merger between …' Hillary Clinton Says 'Radical Fringe' is Taking Over G.O.P. Under Donald Trump, Flegenheimer, *New York Times*, 26 August 2016 (https://www.nytimes.com/2016/08/26/us/politics/hillary-clinton-speech.html)

'Trump counter-attacked, gaining …' Hillary Clinton's "Basket of Deplorables" Gaffe wasn't a Gaffe, Shephard, *New Republic*, 2016 (https://newrepublic.com/minutes/137079/hillary-clintons-basket-deplorables-gaffe-wasnt-gaffe-voters-seem-agree)

'I just start kissing …' Trump Recorded Having Extremely Lewd Conversation about Women in 2005, Fahrenthold, *Washington Post*, 8 October 2016 (https://www.washingtonpost.com/politics/trump-recorded-having-extremely-lewd-conversation-about-women-in-2005/2016/10/07/3b9ce776-8cb4-11e6-bf8a-3d26847eeed4_story.html?utm_term=.a794d2522700)

Aftermath

'Celebrities tweeted out their …' Celebrities React to Donald Trump's Presidential Victory with Shock and Horror, Lynch, *Business Insider UK*, 9 November 2016 (http://uk.businessinsider.com/celebrities-react-to

-donald-trump-presidential-election-win-2016-11?r=US&IR=T/# sarah-paulson-16)

'…'Retweet if you want …' Lindsay Lohan Defends President Trump: 'Stop Bullying Him', Kelley, *Variety*, 5 July 2017 (http://variety.com/2017/digital/ news/donald-trump-lindsay-lohan-twitter-1202487482/)

'Today, we are not …' Donald Trump Delivers Short, Populist Inaugural Address, Bierman, *Los Angeles Times*, 20 January 2017 (http://www.latimes. com/nation/politics/trailguide/la-na-trailguide-updates-donald-trump-delivers- short-populist-1484934128-htmlstory.html)

'Our man is delivering …' Geller: President Trump – True to His Word, Geller, *Breitbart News*, 26 January 2017 (http://www.breitbart.com/ big-government/2017/01/26/geller-president-trump-true-word/)

'Our back-up strategy …' *Devil's Bargain: Steve Bannon, Donald Trump, and the Storming of the Presidency*, Kindle edition

'When he was fired …' Trump Hits Back at Steve Bannon: 'When He Was Fired, He Lost His Mind', Gambino & Smith & Jacobs, *The Guardian*, 3 January 2018 (https://www.theguardian.com/us-news/2018/jan/03/ donald-trump-steve-bannon-lost-his-mind)

'Comments in early 2018 …' 'I'm fascinated by Mussolini', Farrell, *American Spectator*, March 2018 (https://usa.spectator.co.uk/2018/03/im-fascinated-by- mussolini-steve-bannon-on-fascism-populism-and-everything-in-between/)

'[Britain] is separated from …' *Jew Made in England*, Blond (Timewell Press, 2004) p119

'I hope so much …' Exclusive – PEGIDA Founder Lutz Bachmann Gives Rare Interview To Breitbart London's Raheem Kassam, Kassam, *Breitbart News*, 5 April 2016 (http://www.breitbart.com/london/2016/04/05/ exclusive-pegida-founder-lutz-bachmann-rare-interview-breitbart-london/)

'There had been two …' Branding Moderates as 'Anti-Muslim', *Wall Street Journal*, 30 October 2016 (https://www.wsj.com/articles/ branding-moderates-as-anti-muslim-1477866475)

'I would still like …' Who Won the Dutch Election and What Does It Mean for Geert Wilders and the Far-Right in the Netherlands and Europe?, Graham, *Daily Telegraph*, 16 March 2017 (https://www.telegraph.co.uk/news/2017/03/16/ won-dutch-election-does-mean-geert-wilders-far-right-netherlands/)

'Much of the rest …' http://www.melaniephillips.com/antisemitism-glass-darkly/

'What I am …' Martin Amis, Style Supremacist, Mallon, *New Yorker*, 5 February 2018 (https://www.newyorker.com/magazine/2018/02/05/ martin-amis-style-supremacist)

'He got some satisfaction …' *Enemy of the State*, Kindle edition

'At best guess, the ...' http://www.pewforum.org/2017/11/29/europes-growing-muslim-population/

'In 2006, there were ...' https://research.vu.nl/ws/files/628575/299252.pdf

'...making 3.2% of the ...' http://ec.europa.eu/eurostat/documents/3217494/5685052/KS-EH-06-001-EN.PDF/1e141477-9235-44bb-a24b-a55454c2bc42?version=1.0

'Over in America, the ...' https://en.wikipedia.org/wiki/Islam_in_the_United_States

'Back in 2001 the ...' http://www.pewforum.org/2011/01/27/table-muslim-population-by-country/

'At least 661 people ...' https://en.wikipedia.org/wiki/Islamic_terrorism_in_Europe_(2014%E2%80%93present)

'If Russia, Turkey, Macedonia, Bulgaria ...' https://www.thereligionofpeace.com/attacks/europe-attacks.aspx

'About 98 have been ...' https://en.wikipedia.org/wiki/Terrorism_in_the_United_States#Islamist_extremism

"How 100,000 Britons Have ..." How 100,000 Britons Have Chosen to Become Muslim ... and Average Convert is 27-Year-Old White Woman, Doyle, *Daily Mail*, 5 January 2011 (http://www.dailymail.co.uk/news/article-1343954/100-000-Islam-converts-living-UK-White-women-keen-embrace-Muslim-faith.html)

SELECT BIBLIOGRAPHY

Bat Ye'or, *Islam and Dhimmitude: Where Civilizations Collide* (Fairleigh Dickinson University, 2001)

Bat Ye'or, *Eurabia: The Euro-Arab Axis* (Fairleigh Dickinson University Press, 2005)

Borchgrevink, Aage, *A Norwegian Tragedy: Anders Behring Breivik and the Massacre on Utoya* (Polity Press, 2013)

Bures, Eliah, 'Fantasies of Friendship: Ernst Jünger and the German Right's Search for Community in Modernity' (University of California PhD thesis, 2014)

Buruma, Ian, *Murder in Amsterdam: The Death of Theo Van Gogh and the Limits of Tolerance* (Atlantic Books, 2007)

Chudinova, Elena, *Мечеть Парижской Богоматери* (Лепта-Пресс, 2005)

Fallaci, Oriana, *The Force of Reason* (Rizzoli International, 2004)

Fallaci, Oriana, *The Rage and the Pride* (Rizzoli, 2002)

Goodwin, Matthew J., *New British Fascism: Rise of the British National Party* (Routledge, 2011)

Green, Joshua, *Devil's Bargain: Steve Bannon, Donald Trump, and the Storming of the Presidency* (Penguin Press, 2017)

Green, Todd, *The Fear of Islam: An Introduction to Islamophobia in the West* (Fortress Press, 2015)

Houellebecq, Michel, *Submission* (Macmillan, 2015)

Lean, Nathan, *The Islamophobia Industry* (Pluto Press, 2012)

Marsh, Suzy & Cardiff, Joe, *Casuals United* (The Mashed Swede Project, 2012)

Murray, Douglas, *The Strange Death of Europe: Immigration, Identity, Islam* (Bloomsbury Publishing, 2017)

Pai, Hsiao-Hung, *Angry White People: Coming Face-to-Face with the British Far Right* (Zed Books, 2016)

Phillips, Melanie, *Londonistan: How Britain is Creating a Terror State Within* (Encounter Books, 2006)

Pilkington, Hillary, *Loud and Proud: Passion and Politics in the English Defence League* (Manchester University Press, 2016)

Reynolds, Teddy, 'Pulling Back the Curtain: An Examination of the English Defence League and Their Use of Facebook' (University of St Andrews PhD thesis, 2015)

Robinson, Tommy, *Enemy of the State* (CreateSpace Independent Publishing Platform, 2015)

Sedgwick, Martin, *Against the Modern World: Traditionalism and the Secret Intellectual History of the Twentieth Century* (Oxford University Press, 2004)

Seierstad, Åsne, *One of Us: The Story of Anders Breivik and the Massacre in Norway* (Farrar, Straus and Giroux, 2015)

Steyn, Mark, *America Alone: The End of the World as We Know It* (Regnery Publishing, 2006)

Williams, David & Lowles, Nick, *The 'Counter-Jihad' Movement: The Global Trend Feeding Anti-Muslim Hatred* (Hope Not Hate, 2012)

INDEX

Index

Index